Existential Thought and
Fictional Technique

Existential Thought and Fictional Technique

KIERKEGAARD
SARTRE
BECKETT

by Edith Kern

New Haven and London, Yale University Press, 1970

Library of Congress catalog card number: 79–81422
Standard book number: clothbound 300–01203–9;
paperbound 300–01247–0

Designed by Marvin Howard Simmons,
set in Garamond type,
and printed in the United States of America by
The Carl Purington Rollins Printing-Office of the
Yale University Press, New Haven, Connecticut.
Distributed in Great Britain, Europe, Asia, and
Africa by Yale University Press Ltd., London; in Canada
by McGill-Queen's University Press, Montreal; and
in Mexico by Centro Interamericano de Libros
Académicos, Mexico City.

Contents

A fictional technique always relates back to the novelist's metaphysics. The critic's task is to define the latter before evaluating the former.

Sartre

Proemio

From its inception, existential thought has felt itself at home in fiction. Because of its intense "inwardness" and the "commitment" of its proponents, it has expressed itself more strikingly in imaginative writing than in theoretical treatises. Entranced by the beauty of speech "when it resounds with the pregnancy of thought," Kierkegaard listened to his own sentences many times until "thought could find itself . . . completely at ease in the form."[1] According to modern existentialist thinkers, the paradox and absurdity of life can be more readily deduced from fundamental human situations portrayed in fiction than described in the logical language of philosophy which is our heritage. Existentialism's abhorrence of rigid thought systems as being alien to life and existence has equally pointed toward a preference for poetry and fiction. Indeed, Unamuno considered true philosophy, a philosophy concerned with the concrete man of flesh and blood, to be closer to poetry than to any kind of scientific thought, and he boldly proclaimed that he counted

1. Hans Peter Kahn, "Either/Or or Both/And: A Modern Interpretation of the Aesthetic Education Described by Kierkegaard and Schiller" (M.A. thesis, New York University, 1951–52), p. 49.

"among the great novels—or epic poems, it is all the same—
with the *Iliad* and the *Odyssey* and the *Divine Comedy* and the
Quijote and *Paradise Lost* and the *Faust,* also the *Ethics* of
Spinoza, and the *Critique of Pure Reason* of Kant, and the *Logic*
of Hegel."[2]

But the affinity the existential writer has felt with fiction has
confronted him with a dilemma inherent in his conception of
the individual. While Kierkegaard, Heidegger, or Sartre hardly
can be said to agree on what they consider the nature of the existent individual and his Self, they have this in common that
they think of him as a being enclosed within the horizon of his
consciousness and incapable of identifying himself with the Self
of an Other. The Other can be grasped only imperfectly and only
in terms of conjecture. Such views cannot but affect the human
relationships within the fictional world the author creates as
well as his own relationship to his fictional heroes. Is the writer
of existential fiction limited to the presentation of his own Self?
Is he to be identified fully with his fictional hero? Whereas
theoretical writing has tacitly assumed full identity between the
author and the ideas he expresses, fiction has tended rather to
discourage this assumption, even where it might impose itself.
Moreover, the worlds of fiction have been traditionally peopled
by a variety of characters, while their author, omniscient and
ubiquitous, has played the part of their god. Is the existential
author, forgetful of subjective limitations, to enter their minds?
Are his fictional heroes—incapable of understanding Others—to
live in totally solipsistic worlds? How, in fact, does the existential writer see his universe and in what manner can he reveal it?
Disregarding such questions, most critics have been concerned
exclusively with the ideas expounded in existential writing

2. José Huertas-Jourda, *The Existentialism of Miguel de Unamuno,*
University of Florida Monographs (Humanities), No. 13 (1963), p. 31.

and have shown little concern for the fictional techniques they required of novelists. In doing so they have ignored problems which have been uppermost in the minds of these writers: Kierkegaard's striving for a complete harmony between thought and form; Sartre's assumption of a direct relationship between a novelist's fictional technique and his metaphysics;[3] Beckett's praise of Joyce for having made form content, content form,[4] and of Proust for having made one "a concretion of the other, the revelation of a world."[5]

It is my intent in this study to scrutinize such form and techniques in some of the works of these authors where they are most strikingly expressive of their metaphysics. I have chosen Kierkegaard because he is usually referred to as the father of existentialism; Sartre because he is considered its modern exponent par excellence; and Beckett because he has inherited salient existential concerns from both. My study will lead, I hope, to new insights into Kierkegaard's polynomous "pseudonymity," the monolithic quality of Sartrean characters, the "unnamableness" of the Beckettian world, and the tendency of existential writers to present their heroes as authors who disclose themselves as they disclose Being, of which they are a part, in language, which is a part of it.

3. Jean-Paul Sartre, "On *The Sound and the Fury:* Time in the Work of Faulkner," *Literary and Philosophical Essays,* trans. A. Michelson (New York, Collier Books, 1962), p. 84. (The original appeared in 1939.)

4. Samuel Beckett, "Dante . . . Bruno. Vico . . . Joyce," in Beckett et al., *Our Exagmination Round His Factification for Incamination of Work in Progress* (London, Faber & Faber, 1961), p. 14. (The work was first published in 1929.)

5. Samuel Beckett, *Proust* (New York, Grove Press, 1931), p. 67.

KIERKEGAARD

Any attempt to define existentialism within strictly philosophical lines inevitably leads to frustration. Coined and promulgated by Gabriel Marcel and other French journalists during and after World War II, the term came to smack of sensationalism and was popularly employed to designate a philosophy of despair— even if much existentialist writing would belie this assumption. For these reasons and others more specifically philosophical, most writers and philosophers labeled existentialist have declined to accept the epithet. When, in 1946, a distinguished group of philosophers met at the Club Maintenant in Paris to hear Jean Wahl present a brief history of existentialism, they agreed that only Sartre, Simone de Beauvoir, and Merleau-Ponty—the philosophers sometimes referred to as the Paris School—could be called existentialists, because they alone had willingly accepted the term which had been thrust upon them.[1] Yet we may recall that even their acceptance of it had been of rather recent date. Sartre did not use the term in his first basic philosophical work, *Being and Nothingness* (originally *L'Etre et le Néant*, 1943), and

1. Jean Wahl, *A Short History of Existentialism*, trans. F. Williams and S. Maron (New York, Philosophical Library, 1949), p. 2.

Simone de Beauvoir had, during the year of its publication, confided to her diary the amazement she felt at being asked whether she was an "existentialist."[2] Though her studies of Kierkegaard and Heidegger had brought her in contact with the word "existential," the term "existentialist" had not been familiar to her. It is fortunate for the literary critic, however, that the philosophers gathered around Jean Wahl agreed on a nucleus of thought common to all existential thinking. For this makes it possible to study its impact on fictional forms and techniques.

Though the philosophers meeting with Wahl doubted whether Kierkegaard himself should be called an existentialist or even a philosopher of existence (he had no desire to be a philosopher, much less one with a fixed doctrine), they agreed that "the word *existence* in the philosophic connotation it has today was first used by Kierkegaard" Wahl realized that such thinking might be traced back to the philosophies of Schelling, Kant, and even St. Augustine. But he felt also that "we are able to recognize and understand these early prefigurations of the philosophy of existence only because a Kierkegaard existed." What he and his colleagues considered most significant was the fact that Kierkegaardian thought had sprung mainly from opposition to Hegel's passion for a logical system. As Wahl summarized it, "opposing the pursuit of objectivity and the passion for totality which he found in Hegel, Kierkegaard proposed the notion that truth lies in subjectivity"[3] To Kierkegaard man was an existent, a "moment of individuality"; he refused to consider him a mere paragraph in a system. This emphasis on individuality and subjectivity has had, as we shall see, far-reaching implications not only in philosophical but also in formal literary terms.

If we turn to Kierkegaard himself, as he takes issue with the

2. Edith Kern, *Sartre: A Collection of Critical Essays,* Twentieth Century Views (Englewood Cliffs, N.J., Prentice-Hall, 1962), pp. 2–3.
3. Wahl, *Short History,* pp. 1, 9, 3–4.

philosophers of his time and with Hegel in particular, we find him objecting to all systematization of thought. "An existential system cannot be formulated," he maintained in his *Concluding Unscientific Postscript* (1846),[4] "Existence itself is a system— for God; but it cannot be a system for any existing spirit." For "system and finality correspond to one another, but existence is precisely the opposite of finality." Indeed, he continued, "Existence separates and holds the various moments of existence discretely apart; systematic thought consists of the finality which brings them together" *(CUP,* 107). While speculative philosophy insisted that subjectivity is untruth, or rather that truth lies only in objectivity, Kierkegaard went so far to to state that to seek objectivity is to be in error, that truth can be found only by each individual existent, and that it can never represent a finality but must remain a persistent striving and becoming. Truth is never realized, he believed, as along as the subject is in existence *(CUP,* pp. 109–11). This means also that "life can only be explained after it has been lived, just as Christ only began to interpret the Scriptures and show how they applied to him—after his resurrection."[5] Moreover, since any search for a system—be it the most perfect—necessarily had to be made by an existent individual, this search could not be objective, unless in a rather comical, world-historical absent-mindedness man forgot what it is to be an existent individual *(CUP,* 108–09). It was, then, the subjective experience of each human individual that was stressed as opposed to the "objective tendency, which proposes to make everyone an observer, and in its maximum to

4. Søren Kierkegaard, *Concluding Unscientific Postscript,* trans. David F. Swenson and Walter Lowrie (Princeton, N.J., Princeton University Press, 1941); henceforth cited in the text as *CUP.*

5. *The Journals of Søren Kierkegaard: A Selection,* ed. and trans. Alexander Dru (London, Oxford University Press, 1938), p. 57, entry of April 14, 1838.

transform him into so objective an observer that he becomes almost a ghost, scarcely to be distinguished from the tremendous spirit of the historical past" *(CUP,* 118). Kierkegaard granted objectivity only to mathematical propositions, but he also concluded that in such propositions the truth is an indifferent truth *(CUP,* 182). Otherwise he could think of the "knower" only as a unique "existing individual" who over and over again had to find *his* truth in the either/or of decision.

As the choice of *Either/Or* as title for one of his works clearly implies, Kierkegaard thought of his philosophy—if such it may be called—above all in ethico-religious terms. What he deplored more than anything in the Hegelian system was the absence of an Ethics. "While the Hegelian philosophy goes on and becomes an existential system in sheer distraction of mind, and what is more, is finished—without having an Ethics (where existence properly belongs)—" he wrote "the more simple philosophy which is expounded by an existing individual for existing individuals, will more especially emphasize the ethical" *(CUP,* 110). He exhorted philosophers to remember "what it means to be a human being. Not, indeed, what it means to be a human being in general; for this is the sort of thing one might even induce a speculative philosopher to agree to; but what it means that you and I are human beings, each one for himself." It is well known and therefore does not have to be discussed here that in Kierkegaard's case such thinking was based on profound religiosity. His formula denoting a definition of faith was that the self "by relating itself to its own self and by willing to be itself . . . is grounded transparently in the Power which constituted it."[6] Thus he believed in an eternal essential truth of which the individual in his most passionate inwardness was able to partake, a truth which was totally subjective and yet tran-

6. Søren Kierkegaard, *The Sickness Unto Death* together with *Fear and Trembling,* trans. Walter Lowrie (Garden City, N.Y., Doubleday, Anchor Books, 1954), p. 262; henceforth cited in the text as *SD.*

scended subjectivity. Here, in fact, Kierkegaard saw the paradox of existence: that in man—and in Christ in the most exalted way —eternal essential truth had come into being in time (CUP, 181–88).

The impact of such thinking on literary form is manifold. Kierkegaard's "more simple philosophy" expounded by an "existing individual" for "existing individuals" could not find its mold in coldly speculative treatises but clamored for more appropriate ones. A writer so conscious, moreover, of the union of content and form that he could sit for hours "in love with the sound of speech—when it resounds, that is, with the pregnancy of thought"; who would many times repeat to himself the sentences he was finally to write down; who profoundly lived through and enjoyed the genesis of his thoughts and their struggle to fall into a form wherein they could be completely at ease—such a writer had to be aware of the need for a perpetual renewal of forms and the inadequacy of those tradition had handed down to him. Kierkegaard's entire work is indicative of his search for new, more adequate forms to express his thought— for forms as expressive of his thought as thought itself: forms stressing subjectivity in its process of becoming and on its road toward inwardness, toward the eternal, essential truth, and thereby toward its Self.

One obvious literary form expressive of subjectivity is, of course, that of the first person. Kierkegaard employs this form not only in narratives but also in essays and even on occasions when he discusses philosophical questions. In his Concluding Unscientific Postscript, for instance, the pseudonymous author Johannes Climacus writes not in the manner of an impersonal, objective observer but presents himself to the reader as an existent, an individual speaking as an "I" to a "thou": "Let us then proceed, but let us not try to deceive one another. I, Johannes Climacus, am a human being, neither more nor less; and I assume that anyone I may have the honor to talk with is

5

also a human being. If he presumes to be speculative philosophy in the abstract, pure speculative thought, I must renounce the effort to speak with him; for in that case he instantly vanishes from my sight, and from the feeble sight of every mortal" *(CUP, 99)*.

Within the framework of his aesthetic existence, the pseudonymous author acquires even stronger subjective actuality as he engages in a comically dramatic and seemingly quite personal quarrel with the Hegelian System:

> Here first an assurance respecting my own humble person. I shall be as willing as the next man to fall down in worship before the System, if only I can manage to set eyes on it. Hitherto I have had no success; and though I have young legs, I am almost weary from running back and forth between Herod and Pilate. Once or twice I have been on the verge of bending the knee. But at the last moment, when I already had my handkerchief spread on the ground, to avoid soiling my trousers, and I made a trusting appeal to one of the initiated who stood by: "Tell me now sincerely, is it entirely finished; for if so I will kneel down before it, even at the risk of ruining a pair of trousers (for on account of the heavy traffic to and from the System, the road had become quite muddy)"—I always received the same answer: "No, it is not yet finished!" And so there was another postponement—of the System, and of my homage. System and finality are pretty much one and the same, so much so that if the system is not finished, there is no system. [*CUP*, 97–98]

In Kierkegaard's *Either/Or*[7] the first-person approach is used throughout, although the book consists of various literary genres,

7. Søren Kierkegaard, *Either/Or,* trans. D. F. and L. M. Swenson (2 vols.), (Garden City, N.Y., Doubleday, Anchor Books, 1959); henceforth cited in the text as *EO.*

only some of which are customarily associated with this form. It begins with a part designated as "Diapsalmata," lyrical out-pourings which the poet addresses *ad se ipsum* (to himself) and which establish an "I"–"I" relationship. An essay which follows the "Diapsalmata" is entitled "The Immediate Stages of the Erotic or the Musical Erotic" and, in spite of its scholarly title, is written in the first person and registers its author's very personal and subjective reaction to Mozart's *Don Giovanni. Either/Or* subsequently presents us with three essays: "The Ancient Tragical Motif as Reflected in the Modern," "Shadowgraphs," and "The Unhappiest Man"—all in the form of lectures to an imaginary society which bears the strange name of Symparanekromenoi (according to experts, an impossible word formation and freely translated by Eduard Geismar of Copenhagen as "the fellowship of buried lives," that is, a society composed of people who are, if not physically, spiritually dead and entombed) *(EO, 1,* 450 n.l.). Lectures can only be pronounced by an individual and estab-lish of necessity an "I"–"thou" relationship, but usually the speaker stresses his objectivity while here subjectivity is em-phasized. Following these lectures, we find in *Either/Or* a review of the French playwright Scribe's *The First Love,* and again Kierkegaard has the critic present himself to the reader as an imaginary "I." Indeed, the pseudonymous author A avails him-self of the opportunity here to make brief reference to an event "in his own life": "Concerning the special occasion for the present little critique, it has a certain relation to my own insig-nificant personality, and dares to recommend itself to the reader with the normal quality of being trivial. Scribe's play, *The First Love,* has in numerous ways affected my personal life and this contact has occasioned the present review, which thus, in the strictest sense, is the child of the *occasion" (EO, 1,* 238). This brilliant review, based on so subjective and even personal an ap-proach, is followed by an essay entitled "The Rotation Method," whose very first sentence confronts us with author A in the first person. "Starting from a principle," he writes, "is affirmed by people of experience to be a very reasonable procedure; I am willing to humor them, and so begin with the principle that all men are bores" *(EO, 1, 281)*. "The Diary of the Seducer," which forms the last section of *Either/Or*'s first part, does not even have to be investigated with regard to its subjectivity. Diaries are obviously first-person accounts, and so are personal letters which, in this case, both precede the Seducer's diary and are inserted into it. *Either/Or*'s entire second part, which also consists of letters, falls into the same category.

To the reader aware of the most crucial episode in Kierkegaard's own life, namely, the breaking of his engagement to Regina Olsen, the sense of subjectivity, conveyed through this persistent use of the first person in the diverse parts of *Either/Or*, is further heightened by the fact that almost each part in its own way bears a relationship to this episode. Kierkegaard not only seems to hide behind the masks of the "authors," A and B, as well as that of the editor, Victor Eremita, but also seems to play ever new variations on this important theme of his life. It is not in the least accidental, therefore, that the Seducer is given the name Johannes and that he shares this name with Mozart's Don Giovanni, with Johannes Climacus, the pseudonymous author of *Postscript,* and with Johannes de Silentio, the pseudonymous author of *Fear and Trembling.* "The teller and the told" are fundamentally equated by virtue of the author's existential subjectivity, and it is not surprising that Kierkegaard greatly admired Goethe for his ability to establish not merely an external relationship to his work but to make each of his poetic productions a moment in his own development.[8] Kierkegaard considered Goethe's achievement to be a result of

8. See Søren Kierkegaard, *The Concept of Irony,* trans. Lee M. Capel (New York, Harper & Row, 1965), p. 337; henceforth cited in the text as *CI.*

"mastered irony," and he himself liked to be called "Master of Irony."[9]

While this epithet was a punning reference to the fact that Kierkegaard had written his universtiy thesis on *The Concept of Irony,* thereby gaining a master's degree, it also had a more profound significance. For irony was to him not merely a form of rhetoric but an essential element of his thought and one closely linked with his existential concept of subjectivity. In his thesis he speaks of irony as a "determination of subjectivity" and as having—not accidentally but by necessity—made its appearance in world history together with subjectivity in the person of Socrates *(CI,* 281). If one considers truth as existing only in subjectivity, one should consider the individual bound to such truth. The individual's speech—which Kierkegaard called the "phenomenon"—should then be identical with his meaning—which he called the "essence." But irony permits the speaker to separate the phenomenon from its essence, that is, to tell an untruth without betraying his subjective authenticity. In fiction this would mean merely that the speaker becomes what Wayne Booth has more recently called an "unreliable narrator." But this unreliable narrator may yet convey his truth because, as Kierkegaard tells us, "the ironic figure of speech cancels itself . . . for the speaker presupposes his listeners to understand him, hence through a negation of the immediate phenomenon, the essence remains identical with the phenomenon" *(CI,* 265).

As the German Romantics had done before him, Kierkegaard equated in that sense poetry and irony. For the ironist can speak subjectively and yet, as the poet, can hide behind the mask of a pseudonym or a fictional character. He can resort to the realm

9. "S. K. liked to be called 'Master of Irony' in view of the big book on *The Concept of Irony* by which he won his degree of Master of Arts" (Fear and Trembling, p. 266, n. 39; henceforth cited in the text as *FT*).

of the possible, the aesthetic, and, while inhabiting it in many guises, can remain authentic as long as he masters irony and avoids living "completely hypothetically and subjunctively." Kierkegaard thought of irony not only as a device of stating seriously something which is not seriously intended, or stating as a jest something which is meant seriously, but also, in metaphysical terms, as a liberation of the individual—if only in a negative sense. In conformity with Hegel, he defined irony as infinite absolute negativity, and considered "subjective freedom" to be its most outstanding feature *(CI,* 297, 270, 271). Freedom in this sense permitted man to negate the actual, putting himself above it, and to distance himself from himself, thereby reflecting upon himself as if he were a third person. Irony understood in this manner became to Kierkegaard "subjectivity of subjectivity" and thereby an intrinsic element of poetry and fiction *(CI,* 260). For in the freedom of such subjectivity raised to the second power, Kierkegaard the author could attain that "indirect form" which, in his view, alone was capable of rendering the "elusiveness," the paradox, and the dialectic of existence. Kierkegaard's conception of irony is almost identical here with that of the German critic Friedrich Schlegel, although it was that writer's novel *Lucinde* which he had singled out for criticism. Long before Kierkegaard, Friedrich Schlegel had expressed the thought that the paradoxality of existence could best be recaptured in the contradictoriness and ambivalence of irony.[10] What the Danish thinker criticized in Schlegel's novel was merely an element of "subjunctivity" due to an excess of irony. Schlegel, he felt, fell short of that mastery of irony for which he praised Goethe and which he claimed for himself.

When mastered, irony could evoke life in its immediacy and paradox without the interference of abstract analysis and

10. René Wellek, *The Romantic Age, A History of Modern Criticism,* 2 (New Haven, Yale University Press, 1955), p. 14.

thought. Already the titles chosen by Kierkegaard for some of his works show his preference for it in evoking the dialectics of existence. We have only to think of *Either/Or* or *Right Hand and Left Hand*. The drama such titles express would seem to belong to the theater, and while Kierkegaard did not write for the stage, he incorporated into other genres such dialectic juxtaposition and admired Scribe for his ability to make "dialogue . . . audible in the transparency of the situation" (*EO, 1,* 245–48, 258). If human existence was seen as a paradox because it was truth come into being in time (Heidegger later was to think in a somewhat similar way of *Dasein* as Being-in-the-world), then this truth had to be met with in the here and now —*en situation,* as Sartre came to call it. Although Kierkegaard's use of the term is not fully identical with that of Sartre, who wanted to replace a "theatre of character" by a "theatre of situation,"[11] both writers seem to agree on the importance of presenting man in the immediacy of existence. Simone de Beauvoir was therefore eminently in accord with Kierkegaardian thought when she maintained—shortly after the Paris School of Existentialism had emerged—that existentialism could not find expression in theoretical treatises alone but had to have recourse to fiction. She made reference, indeed, to Kierkegaard's "Diary of the Seducer" and his story of Abraham in *Fear and Trembling* as successful illustrations of existential thought expressed in fictional form. The novel seemed to her particularly suited to the expression of existential insights which would seem contradictory if they were to be presented categorically and systematically.[12] Only in fiction, it seemed to her, could the effort of existential thinkers to reconcile the subjective and the objective,

11. Jean-Paul Sartre, "Forgers of Myths, the Young Playwrights of France," *Theatre Arts, 30* (1946), 326.

12. "Littérature et Métaphysique," *Les Temps Modernes, 1* (1946), 1160.

the absolute and the relative, the timeless and the historical, be realized. (We must not fail to notice here the fundamental affinity between Simone de Beauvoir's existential thinking and previously discussed concepts of irony.) Because of its immediacy—and I might add in Kierkegaardian terms, because it can avail itself of the dialectics of irony—fiction can attain to the meaning which is at the heart of existence.

If, at the time of her writing, Simone de Beauvoir had been familiar with certain entries Kierkegaard had made in his journals, she would have realized that his "Diary of the Seducer" and *Fear and Trembling* are by no means isolated examples of his preference for fictional form. Those entries indicate that he was perpetually in search of fictional correlatives which would give existential and aesthetic actuality to his thought in all its dialectic complexity and paradoxality. Walter Lowrie, in his "Translator's Introduction" to *Fear and Trembling*, writes that at the time of its composition, Kierkegaard's mind was "teeming with thoughts which were to be developed in later works and with as many more which were stillborn." Six of those recorded in his journals adumbrate, as Lowrie explains, "striking themes which the following year appeared in *The Stages*. The figure of the Fashion Tailor who spoke at the Banquet is here sketched in five entries. Of the remarkable stories told in 'Quidam's Diary' . . . four are suggested here: 'A Leper's Soliloquy'; 'Solomon's Dream'; 'The Mad Accountant' (Possibility); and 'Nebuchadnezzar.'" Kierkegaard's journals contain, moreover, an "adaptation of his case to the story of Abelard and Heloise" [this is again a variation on his theme of the broken engagement], a plan for "Antigone," and outlines for a book which he planned to entitle "Conic Sections" and which was to be a study of life in Copenhagen at various hours of the day during which various classes of the population came to the fore *(FT,* 13). In addition to the novelistic "Diary of the Seducer" of *Either/Or,* Kierkegaard also projected in his journals a "Diary of the Seducer No. 2" as well as the study of a female seducer to be entitled "The Diary of a Hetaera." What is remarkable is not only the fictional and dramatic aspect of these projected works, but especially their character of subjectivity, as evidenced by the preponderance of diaries, letters, dramas, and soliloquies, as well as the dialectic attitude which is revealed in their choice.

On the surface, *Fear and Trembling,* of whose fictional character Simone de Beauvoir was so well aware, might appear objective in comparison. The story of Abraham sacrificing his son Isaac serves as the vehicle for Kierkegaard's philosophico-religious conception of the "Knight of Faith" who is obliged to rely upon himself alone, who feels the dread of his decisions and the pain of being unable to make himself intelligible to others and yet has "no vain desire to guide others" (*FT,* 90). In what seems a brilliant appraisal of the volume, the Kierkegaard scholar David F. Swenson described *Fear and Trembling* as "concerned with some of the distinctive traits of the religious concept of faith, taken in the more specific sense in which it is fundamental to the Christian consciousness. It is here depicted as a major human passion, affecting daily life at every point, its content being the entire essential reality of the individual's existence" (*FT,* 15, quoted by Walter Lowrie).

The book rightly bears the subtitle "A Dialectic Lyric." It seems to convey at first a mood of objectivity, but this mood soon changes into one of high lyricism and passion. The book's pseudonymous author addresses the reader in a brief Preface and signs his name as Johannes de Silentio, referring to himself all along in the first person. A Proem which follows the Preface, bears the Swedish title "Stemning," which Walter Lowrie considered it best to translate as "Prelude"—a term again evoking a lyric and musical quality. The actual text starts like a fairy tale ("Once upon a time") and is based on the Old Testament passage which reads "And God tempted Abraham and said unto him, Take Isaac, thine only son, whom thou lovest, and get thee into the land of Moriah, and offer him there for a burnt offering upon the mountain which I will show thee" (*FT*, 27).

In an entry in his journal (early May 1843) Kierkegaard, making reference to this text, envisioned a poet who might translate this myth into existential terms.

> Let us assume (as neither the Old Testament nor the Koran reports) that Isaac knew that the object of the journey he had to make with his father to Mount Moriah was that he should be offered as a sacrifice. If there were living now a poet in our generation, he would be able to relate what these two men talked about on the way. One might also suppose that Abraham's previous life was not blameless, and might let him now mumble under his breath that it was God's punishment, one might even perhaps let him get the melancholy idea that he must assist God in making the punishment as heavy as possible. I suppose that at first Abraham looked upon Isaac with all his fatherly love; his venerable countenance, his broken heart, has made his speech the more impressive, he exhorts him to bear his fate with patience, he has let him darkly understand that he the father suffered from it still more. However, that was of no avail.—Then I think that Abraham has for an instant turned away from him, and when again he turned toward him he was unrecognizable to Isaac, his eyes were wild, his venerable locks had risen like the locks of furies above his head. He seized Isaac by the throat, he drew the knife, he said: "Thou didst believe it was for God's sake I would do this, thou art mistaken, I am an idolater, this desire has again awakened in my soul, I want to murder thee, this is my desire, I am worse than any cannibal; despair thou foolish boy who didst imagine that I was thy father, I am

thy murderer, and this is my desire." And Isaac fell upon his knees and cried to heaven, "Merciful God, have mercy upon me!" But then said Abraham softly to himself, "Thus I must be, for it is better after all that he believes that I am a monster, that he curses me for being his father, rather than he should know it was God who imposed the temptation, for then he would lose his reason and perhaps curse God. [*FT*, 11].

But where indeed, Kierkegaard ended his musings by asking, "is there a poet in our age who has a presentiment of such collisions! And yet Abraham's conduct was genuinely poetic, magnanimous, more magnanimous than anything I have read of in tragedies." And as if unable to contain himself, Kierkegaard burst into poetry: "When the child has to be weaned the mother blackens her breast, but her eyes rest just as lovingly upon the child. The child believes it is the breast that has changed, but that the mother is unchanged. And why does she blacken her breast? Because, she says, it would be a shame that it should seem delicious when the child must not get it.—" He reasons that "this collision is easily resolved, for the breast is only a part of the mother herself. Happy is he who has not experienced more dreadful collisions, who did not need to blacken *himself*, who did not need to go to hell in order to see what the devil looks like, so that he might paint himself accordingly and in that way if possible save another person in that person's God-relationship at least. This would be Abraham's collision" (*FT*, 11–12).

In *Fear and Trembling*, Kierkegaard, or rather the pseudonymous author Johannes de Silentio, assumes the function of the poet whom the journal entry envisioned and conveys to the reader the poetic actuality of Abraham's experience. He makes us feel the dread of the father who stands ready to sacrifice his son. He makes us realize that Abraham is willing to kill what he loves most in this world, not for ethical reasons, not in the manner of the tragic hero whose sacrifice all understand and admire, but as a murderer—were it not for his faith. Yet because of his faith—and faith by its very nature is absurd according to Kierkegaard—what he was willing to sacrifice was given back to him. What might have been the subject for a religious tract is turned by Kierkegaard into high poetry and passionate drama. One must sample its language to know its beauty:

Once upon a time there was a man who as a child had heard the beautiful story about how God tempted Abraham, and how he endured temptation, kept the faith, and a second time received again a son contrary to expectation. When the child became older he read the same story with even greater admiration, for life had separated what was united in the pious simplicity of the child. The older he became, the more frequently his mind reverted to that story, his enthusiasm became greater and greater, and yet he was less and less able to understand the story. At last in his interest for that he forgot everything else; his soul had only one wish to see Abraham, one longing to have been witness to that event. His desire was not to behold the beautiful countries of the Orient, or the earthly glory of the Promised Land, or that godfearing couple whose old age God had blessed, or the venerable figure of the aged patriarch, or the vigorous young manhood of Isaac whom God had bestowed upon Abraham—he saw no reason why the same thing might not have taken place on the barren heath in Denmark. His yearning was to accompany them on the three day's journey when Abraham rode with sorrow before him and with Isaac by his side. His only wish was to be present at the time when Abraham lifted up his eyes and saw Mount Moriah afar off, at the time when he left the asses behind and went alone with Isaac up unto the mountain; for what his mind was intent upon was not the ingenious web of imagination but the shudder of thought. [*FT*, 26].

As Kierkegaard's story progresses, it is precisely this shudder of thought which we feel with Abraham at the dread of his lonely decision that made him guilty before all—except God—and that rested solely on a faith both inexplicable and absurd.

Thought and form are in such perfect harmony in *Fear and Trembling* that we are forcibly reminded again of Kierkegaard's own picture of himself as the poet as enamoured of his sounds as the flute player—when these sounds are pregnant with thought; speaking aloud perhaps a dozen times what he is finally to write down; the poet living through, enjoying, and experiencing the genesis of his thoughts and their search "until they found their form." For he considered the book one of his most perfect achievements from the aesthetic point of view and noted in his journal that, upon his death, it alone would be enough to give him the name of an immortal author. He envisioned rightly that it would be translated into foreign tongues and that readers would almost shudder at its frightful pathos—while his contemporaries, deceived by the apparent flippancy of the man they regarded to be its author, could not possibly suspect its high seriousness (*FT*, 18, 15).

If further proof were needed of the extent to which Kierke-gaard's entire being was engaged in the composition of this work, it might well be found in a letter which he addressed to his friend Boesen while engaged in writing it:

> I have finished one work which I regard important [this was probably *Either/Or*] and am in full swing with a new one. At the beginning I was ill, now I am comparatively well, that is to say, my spirit expands and presumably is killing my body. I never have worked so hard as now. I go out a little while in the morning. Then I come home and sit

> in my room uninterruptedly until about three o'clock. I am hardly able to see out of my eyes. Then I shuffle with my cane to the restaurant, but am so weak that I believe if one were to call my name aloud I would fall over and die. Then I go home and begin again ... the ideas stream down upon me—healthy, joyful, striving, merry, blessed children easily brought to birth, and yet all of them bearing the birthmarks of my personality. [*FT,* 14, quoted by Walter Lowrie].

This, then, is the subjectivity with which Kierkegaard wanted to permeate his works. He strove not in any romantic sense for a subjectivity expressing the "accidental, the angular, the selfish, the excentric, and so forth" (*CUP,* 117), but rather for that "infinite passion which constitutes ... inwardness" (*CUP,* 182–83). This passionate inwardness has made him, in the eyes of twentieth-century philosophers, seem closer to Nietzsche than either Heidegger or Sartre—though the latter are usually designated as existentialists.[13] But while Kierkegaard mainly sought his objective correlatives in the myths of the Bible and the Western world, Nietzsche turned to Greece and Persia in order to find his. Kierkegaard speaks of Abraham, Don Juan, and old folktales; Nietzsche identified himself with Dionysus, the Greek god of tragedy, with Prometheus, whom he saw in accordance with Goethe as the symbol of poetic creativity, and with Zarathustra, the Persian prophet. If both philosophers wrote the language of poetry, it is because they experienced existence like poets. "I am living through within myself," Kierkegaard wrote, "more poetry than there is in all novels put together" (*FT,* 14, quoted by Walter Lowrie).

As Kierkegaard considered Abraham's conduct poetic, so he must have thought of his own. For to the outline of Abraham's

---

13. Wahl, *Short History,* p. 37.

story, which we cited above as it is recorded in the journal, he added the words "He who has explained this riddle has explained my life. Yet who was there among my contemporaries that understood this?" (*FT*, 12, quoted by Walter Lowrie). And elsewhere in the *Journals:* "In me there is a predominant poetic tendency, and yet the mystification was essentially this, that *Fear and Trembling* reproduced my own life" (*FT*, 19, quoted by Walter Lowrie). Walter Lowrie explains in his "Translator's Introduction" to *Fear and Trembling,* that even the reader who has such acquaintance with S.K.'s story as his contemporaries did not have may need to be told that Abraham's sacrifice of Isaac is a symbol of S.K.'s sacrifice of the dearest thing he had on earth. And the reader who is not acquainted with the story must be told that in order to liberate Regina from her attachment and to 'set her afloat' S.K. felt obliged to be cruel enough to make her believe he was a scoundrel who had merely been trifling with her affections" *(FT*, 10). Regina, the girl whom he had loved, to whom he had been betrothed, and the engagement to whom he had broken, was given the part of Isaac in the story, while his own part was that of Abraham. Their relationship finds a second objective correlative in the legend of "Agnes and the Merman," which Kierkegaard tells in the same work. In this story the Merman seduces Agnes, but Kierkegaard changed the original in such a manner that the Merman's evil designs are foiled because of Agnes' complete and innocent faith in his love (*FT*, 103). *Fear and Trembling* contains still another story which must be considered an objective correlative to the Kierkegaard-Regina relationship, that of Tobias and Sarah related in the Book of Tobit. Due to demoniacal interference, all of Sarah's bridegrooms were doomed to die. But Tobias' profound love for her and her own humble willingness to let herself be saved by him break the spell and make it possible for them two to live together in happiness (*FT*, 111). A fourth variation on the Kierkegaard-Regina theme finally finds poetic expression in *Fear and Trembling* in the mysterious and perpetually altered refrain of the mother who blackens her breast when she must wean her child.

Kierkegaard's authorial efforts are comparable here to those of T. S. Eliot, whom Patrick Cruttwell has considered a master in the "mythologizing" of his life.[14] At least with regard to his own contemporaries, these Kierkegaardian efforts seem to have been completely successful. Lowrie ascribes the author's striving for such success to his adherence to an unwritten law of delicacy decreeing that the author was "never to utter verity . . . but . . . to keep verity for himself and only let it be refracted in various ways" (*FT*, 10). Yet we must not forget that such delicacy was made necessary in the first place because existential notions of subjectivity implied an identity between the teller and the told, the author and his hero. Kierkegaard's use of objective correlatives, the mythologization of his life, and its ironic refraction all served to dissolve this identity by means of poetry. But poetry, while opening to the existential author the immense realm of the possible, permitting him at one and the same time to be passionately inward and distant, merely compounded the problem of Kierkegaard the factual existent. He did not want to be a poet but rather become a "Knight of Faith." It is true that to some extent he could reconcile these two states of human existence. Both meant to him—as did irony—the negation of the finite in favor of a higher infinite: "It is through a negation of the imperfect actuality," he stated, "that poetry opens up a higher actuality, expands and transfigures the imperfect into the perfect, and thereby softens and mitigates that deep pain which would darken and obscure all things." To that extent, he thought of poetry as reconciling man to actuality. But man's true recon-

14. "Makers and Persons," *Hudson Review, 12* (Winter 1959–60), 493.

ciliation, that which would render actuality itself infinite for him, such reconciliation he saw possible in faith alone (*CI*, 312; see also *FT*, 62).

As he writes in "The Point of View of My Work as an Author," the problem of his entire authorship was "how to become a Christian." His own inward truth was thus a striving and a quest for that faith which was to ground his Self transparently in the Power which constituted it. It was a disquieting paradox of his life that in actuality he not only was a poet but also lived "a poet's existence." Moreover, as the existential individual he felt that existential truth could best and most "essentially" be expressed in "indirect form," that is, aesthetically. Hence his whole being seemed to opt for the aesthetic, while at the same time he had to reject it as something to be overcome, something inferior to ethics and even more so to religion. In the "Diapsalmata," for instance, which is the work of a poet and which, as the pseudonymous editor carefully points out, begins and ends with an aphorism concerning the poet, Kierkegaard deplores the difficulty of transcending such weakness: "Vainly I strive against it. My foot slips. My life is still a poet's existence. What could be more unhappy? I am predestined; fate laughs at me when suddenly it shows me how everything I do to resist becomes a moment in such an existence. I can describe hope so vividly that every hoping individual will acknowledge my description; and yet it is a deception, for while I picture hope, I think of memory *(EO, 1,* 35). One way in which Kierkegaard faced this paradox in his own nature was that of presenting it as one side of a dialectic from which he distanced himself by attributing it to pseudonymous authors, while he signed only his religious works with his own name. The only exception he made to this rule is the use of the pseudonym Anti-Climacus for *Sickness Unto Death*. And Lowrie is probably right in presuming that he did this in order "to relieve his fine feeling of propriety" (*SD*, 138). (Obviously the thesis on irony must be considered in a special category, since it was officially submitted to the university.)

With regard to his aesthetic writings, Kierkegaard went so far as to declare them "deceits." "Regarded integrally in its relation to the work as a whole," he wrote, "the aesthetic production is a deceit, and herein lies the deeper significance of the 'pseudonyms.' A deceit, however, is rather an ugly thing. To this I will respond: Be not deceived by the word 'deceit'! One can deceive a person about the truth, and one can (remembering old Socrates) deceive a person into the truth. Indeed, when a person is under an illusion, it is only by deceiving him that he can be brought into the truth."[15] As clearly, therefore, as he distances himself from his aesthetic works by pronouncing them a deceit in relationship to his work as a whole, just as clearly does he want them accepted on their own terms as truth. For how else could they have the power to "deceive a person into the truth"? Once more, then, the paradox is made acceptable through irony which is like the shadow of subjectivity—both having appeared in history simultaneously in the figure of Socrates. With irony abetting subjectivity, Kierkegaard could admit to himself and others that "in connection with the aesthetic and the intellectual" somewhat different laws prevail so that "to ask whether this or that is real, whether it really has happened, is a misunderstanding. So to ask betrays a failure to conceive the aesthetic and the intellectual ideality as a possibility, and forget that, to determine a scale of values for the aesthetic and the intellectual in this manner is like ranking sensation higher than thought. Ethically it is correct to put the question: 'Is it real? But only if the individual subject asks the question of himself" (*CUP*, 285–88). The aesthetic is thus granted a right of existence as long as

15. Walter Lowrie, *Kierkegaard, 1813–1855* (London, Oxford University Press, 1938), p. 248, henceforth cited in the text as *K*.

we realize that it belongs to the realm of possibility and the possible rather than of truth.

But even within the realm of the aesthetic and of a truth considered subservient to religious and ethical truth, Kierkegaard was confronted with a dilemma which grew out of his conception of the existing individual in his relationship to other existents, that is, to the Other. Kierkegaard's view of the individual precludes his knowing the Other. In his *Concluding Unscientific Postscript,* he states:

> With respect to every reality external to myself, I can get hold of it only through thinking it. In order to get hold of it really, I should have to be able to make myself into the other, the acting individual, and make the foreign reality my own reality, which is impossible. For if I make the foreign reality my own, this does not mean that I become the other through knowing his reality, but it means that I acquire a new reality, which belongs to me as opposed to him . . . When I think about something that another has done, and so conceive a reality, I lift this given reality out of the real and set it over into the possible; for a *conceived reality* is a possibility, and is higher than reality from the standpoint of thought, but not from the standpoint of reality. This also implies that there is no immediate relationship, ethically, between subject and subject. When I understand another person, his reality is for me a possibility.

The Other's reality is relegated by Kierkegaard to the realm of the thoughts we give to something we might do but have not yet done, that is, to the realm of mere possibility, or even conjecture *(CUP,* 285). This view of the Other seriously restricts the horizon of the Kierkegaardian individual—whether in real life or in a fictional world and regardless of whether fiction is considered as expressing truth or mere possibility. Such a view of the Other limits, in fact, the world of each existent individual to the horizon of his own "I," making all else conjecture.

Kierkegaard's view of the aesthetic as belonging to the realm of possibility and the possible—though these were not considered as actual truth—permitted him to create fictional characters within that realm. He could not, however, place such characters in meaningful relationship to each other without contradicting his own conception of subjectivity. This perhaps explains the use of such genres as letters, diaries, lyrical aphorisms, soliloquies, dreams, etc., which all show the individual in isolation and present the reader with only one individual consciousness expressing itself in the first person. (It also seems to explain Kierkegaard's use of myths—whose fascination consists precisely in the fact that characters are placed in situations where objects and people encountered appear impenetrable and mysterious.) But a world consisting of only one consciousness to whom all else is conjecture is a very monotonous world—especially if this consciousness is suspected of being that of the author. Kierkegaard's entire work gives evidence of his struggle with this aesthetic dilemma. His intricate pseudonymity and polynymity, which have so greatly puzzled philosophers, would, to the literary critic, seem largely the result of this dilemma.

A closer look at the "Diary of the Seducer" may illustrate Kierkegaard's efforts to reconcile literary form with his philosophical concepts of subjectivity. As the title indicates, the story is told in form of a diary. Through it we learn that, on the street one day, Johannes, the Seducer, catches sight of a lovely young girl by the name of Cordelia; that he finds out where she lives; that he insinuates himself into the friendship of an unsuspecting young man who is in love with Cordelia and knows her family; that, by abusing this friendship, he gains access to her house, where he entertains her guardian, an old aunt, while generously giving the young lover a chance to speak with Cordelia; and that he finally outwits the trusting and grateful young man. We learn of the Seducer's patient but ruthless scheming to become engaged to the girl, to arouse her passions, and to induce her subsequently —by both attracting and rejecting her—to break the engagement in utter bewilderment. We finally learn that, having shaken the very foundations of her existence, Johannes returns to her merely to seduce and abandon her.

The "Diary" has both the advantages and the disadvantages of the genre. Its staccato entries hold—in Kierkegaard's existential terms—the "moments of existence discretely apart." Because it is written by the protagonist himself, the "Diary" permits us an insight into his observations, his scheming, and his emotions in a way which foreshadows the twentieth-century interior monologue. At the same time, it limits us to his point of view. Yet it is he himself who expresses his appreciation of the genre in existential terms as he quotes with approval an ancient philosopher who had maintained that "if man were to record accurately all of his experiences, then he would be without knowing a word of the subject, a philosopher" *(EO, 1, 411)*. A, who claims to be the editor of the "Diary," informs us in the Preface that it had originally been given the fitting title of "Commentarium perpetuum No. 4" by the Seducer, who apparently had not intended it for publication but had merely kept it for his own satisfaction *(EO, 1, 300)*. Being himself a keen aesthetic observer, A also dwells upon the outstanding literary qualities of the Diary. Though some of these may be typical for any diary, they are of importance in existential terms because they give expression above all to the immediacy of existence. Thus he finds it worthy of mention that "although the experience is recorded, naturally, after it has happened—sometimes, perhaps, a long time after—yet it is often described with the dramatic vividness of an action taking place before one's very eyes" *(EO, 1, 300–01)*.

Johannes regales us, as a matter of fact, with moments of

highly dramatic quality. Sometimes drama emanates from the mere description of a scene and its setting. We see, for instance, tea time at the house of Cordelia's aunt:

> she goes over to the tea table in front of the sofa. Edward follows her, I follow the aunt. Edward tries to be secretive, he talks in a whisper; usualy he does it so well that he becomes entirely mute. I am not at all secretive in my outpourings to the aunt—market prices, a calculation of the quantity of milk needed to produce a pound of butter; through the medium of cream and the dialectic of buttermaking, there comes a reality which any young girl can listen to without embarrassment, but, what is far rarer, it is a solid, reasonable, and edifying conversation, equally improving for mind and heart. I generally sit with my back to the tea table and to the ravings of Edward and Cordelia. Meanwhile, I rave with the aunt. And is not Nature great and wise in her productivity, is not butter a precious gift, the glorious result of Nature and art! [*EO, 1,* 345]

Such a scene is, of course, more than mere drama. It is, with its tone of irony, high comedy, a satire of society. At the same time, it reveals the Seducer as the cold schemer and the brilliant ironist. No further analysis is necessary to convey to us his character. He is shown *en situation.*

Sometimes the "Diary" contains descriptions not directly relevant to the progress of the story but apt to broaden the stage which the genre might otherwise keep too small. We are permitted to share in the aesthetic delight Johannes takes in the world around him and particularly in any woman who accidentally appears on the scene.

> And now away to life and joy, to youth and beauty; show me what I have often seen, and what I never weary of seeing, show me a beautiful young woman, unfold her

beauty for me in such away that she becomes herself more beautiful; subject her to an examination of such a kind that she derives happiness from that examination! . . . I choose Broad Street, but, as you know, I can only dispose of my time until half-past one.

There comes a young woman, all stiff and starched; of course, it is Sunday today . . . Fan her a little, waft over her the cool air, glide in a gentle stream about her, embrace her with your innocent contact! How I sense the heightened color of the cheek, the reddening of the lips, the bosom's lifting . . . Is it not so, my dear, it is indescribable, it is a blessed delight to breathe this refreshing air? The little collar quivers like a leaf. How full and sound her breathing! Her pace slackens, she is almost carried along by the gentle breeze, like a cloud, like a dream . . . Blow a little stronger, with a longer sweep! . . . She draws herself together, she folds her arms a little closer to her bosom, which she covers more carefully, lest a gust of wind should prove too forward, and insinuate itself softly and coolingly under the light covering . . . Her color is heightened, her cheeks become fuller, her eye clearer, her step firmer. A little opposition tends to make a person more beautiful. Every young woman ought to fall in love with the zephyrs; for no man can rival them in enhancing her beauty, as they struggle against her . . . She turns her side to the breeze . . . Now quick! a powerful gust, so that I can guess the beauty of her form! [*EO*, *1*, 351]

By addressing the wind here the Seducer can give expression to all his sensuality. As he recollects the scene, he renders it vividly present and even projects it into the future, while his poetic delight is so contagious that we cannot help but be affected by it. Yet this very aesthetic delight is something which Kierkegaard had condemned in his thesis, *The Concept of Irony,* as the ironist poet's attainment of mere external infinity and totally lacking in inwardness *(CI,* 313).

The mood of the Seducer's diary, which editor A describes as "neither historically exact nor simply fiction, not indicative but subjunctive" *(EO, 1,* 300), corresponds in amazing detail to that which prevails in a novel which Kierkegaard, in his thesis, had criticized as that of an ironist who had not mastered irony. The work in question is *Lucinde* by Friedrich Schlegel, the theoretician and propagator of German Romanticism. Kierkegaard referred to its author as an ironist who "poetically produces himself as well as his environment with the greatest possible poetic license" and who therefore "lives completely hypothetically and subjunctively" so that "his life finally loses all continuity," until "he wholly lapses under the sway of his moods and feelings" *(CI,* 300–01). The life of the Seducer is an analogue to that of the ironist poet—in Kierkegaard's view, "a drama." What engrosses the ironist poet also enchants Johannes, namely "the ingenious unfolding of this drama" of which "he is himself a spectator, even when performing some act" *(CI,* 300). Thus, forever reflecting upon himself, the Seducer, like the ironist poet, "poetizes everything, especially his feelings. To be truly free he must have control over feeling, one must instantly displace another. When it sometimes happens that his feelings displace one another so preposterously that even he notices all is not right, he poetizes further. He poetizes that it is he who evokes the feeling and he keeps on poetizing" *(CI,* 300). In his self-reflection (Kierkegaard also referred to him as Narcissus), Johannes bears a certain resemblance to Lisette, the character in Schlegel's *Lucinde,* whose portrait Kierkegaard had thought the work's most accomplished. This hetaera was shown as seated in the midst of her artistic belongings with mirrors reflecting her image from every angle, thereby resolving her wretched life, he said, in "indefinite contours" for her "to stare at as though it were something indifferent to her" *(CI,* 311).

To some extent, Johannes also resembles Julius, the Romantic ironist hero of *Lucinde*. Like him he is—in contrast to Mozart's Don Giovanni—the reflective seducer who wants to live his own life as if it were a work of art.[16] "What others may enjoy," he writes, "I do not know with certainty. Mere possession is not worth much, and the means which such lovers employ are generally wretched enough. They do not disdain the use of money, power, influence, soporifics, and so on. But what enjoyment can there be in love if there is not the most absolute self-surrender, at least on one side?" *(EO, 1, 331)*. He feels compelled, therefore, in the manner of an artist, to elicit such complete surrender. And it seems to him that

> he who does not know how to poetize himself in a girl's feelings so that it is from her that everything issues as he wishes it, he is and remains a bungler; I do not begrudge him his enjoyment. A bungler he is and remains, a seducer, something one can by no means call me. I am an aesthete, an eroticist, one who has understood the nature and meaning of love and knows it from the ground up, and only makes the private reservation that no love affair should last more than six months at the most, and that every erotic relationship should cease as soon as one has had the ultimate enjoyment . . . To poetize oneself into a young girl is an art, to poetize oneself out of her is a masterpiece. [*EO, 1,* 363–64]

What he wants is not the mere external possession of the girl but "to enjoy her in an artistic sense." His approach, he realizes, must therefore be "as artistic as possible." She must not look

16. Friedrich Schlegel, *Lucinde,* in *Deutsche Litteratur,* Ser. 17, Vol. 4, ed. Paul Kluckhohn (Leipzig, Philipp Reclam, 1931), p. 205: "Wie seine Kunst sich vollendete und ihm von selbst in ihr gelang, was er zuvor durch kein Streben und Arbeiten erringen konnte: so ward ihm auch sein Leben zum Kunstwerk."

upon him as a deceiver, for he is not a deceiver in the ordinary sense. Nor should she think of him as a faithful lover. "The infinite possibility is precisely the interesting. If she is able to predict anything, then I have failed very badly, and the whole relationship loses its meaning" (EO, 1, 368). The Seducer's attitude is so much that of the creative artist that he speaks in the accents of Pygmalion: "I am creating for myself a heart in the likeness of her own. An artist paints his beloved; that gives him pleasure; a sculptor fashions his. I do this, too, but in a spiritual sense. She does not know that I possess this picture, and therein lies my real deception" (EO, 1, 384). The only pact to which he considers himself bound in his relation to Cordelia is his pact with the aesthetic (EO, 1, 432).

As a result of such ironic poetizing and self-reflection on the part of Johannes, we are also made witness to a situation that becomes increasingly threatening to Cordelia. As he confides to his diary the progress of his conquest in detail, we see it assume the form of a sinister military attack, bristling with imagery appropriate to warfare. In her first innocence, the girl doesn't even seem to know that he exists, he realizes; "even less what goes on in my inner consciousness, still less the certainty with which I peer into her future; for my soul demands more and more reality" (EO, 1, 330). Because of her unsuspecting innocence, he can easily plan his first attack. "It is necessary for me to gain entrance to her home," he jots down, "and in military parlance, I am ready. It promises to be, however, a rather complicated and difficult problem" (EO, 1, 334). Not yet knowing how to understand her, he decides "to wait very quietly, very inconspicuously —aye, like a soldier on vidette duty who throws himself on the ground and listens for the faintest sound of an approaching enemy" (EO, 1, 339). For, "one should always make preliminary studies, everything must be properly planned," he reminds himself (EO, 1, 338), while finally coming to the conclusion that "the strategic principle, the law governing every move in this campaign, is always to work her into an interesting situation. The interesting is the field on which the battle must be waged" *(EO, 1, 341)*. There comes a moment when he decides that he must now "go over to more direct action" and "indicate this change on the military map" *(EO, 1, 356)*. This coldly detached military strategy results in his decision that "Edward must go . . . he has reached the very end. At any moment I may expect him to go to her, and make a declaration of love . . . My relation to Cordelia is beginning to run dramatically. Something must happen, whatever it may be . . . She must be taken by surprise" *(EO, 1, 361)*. Cordelia begins to show signs of weakening: "Cordelia is not so assured in her manner toward me as she has been . . . she vacillates a little . . . Only one more investigation, and then the engagement. There can be no difficulties about this" *(EO, 1, 365)*. And somewhat later he notes confidently: "Today I harvested the fruit of a rumor I had caused to circulate, that I was in love with a young girl. By the aid of Edward it had also reached Cordelia's ears" *(EO, 1, 365)*.

Thus the moment of crisis approaches, and again it is viewed in military terms and described with military imagery. But now warfare takes on a totally untraditional character because it serves an aesthetic rather than a practical purpose.

> So now the first war with Cordelia begins, in which I flee, and thereby teach her to triumph in pursuing me. I constantly retreat before her, and in this retreat I teach her through myself to know all the power of love, its unquiet thoughts, its passion, what longing is, and hope, and impatient expectation . . . It is a triumphal procession in which I lead her, and I myself am just as much the one who dithyrambically sings praises for her victory as the one who shows the way. She will gain courage to believe in love, to

> believe that it is an eternal power, when he sees its mastery
> over me, sees my emotions. She will believe me, partly be-
> cause I have confidence in my art, and partly because funda-
> mentally there is truth in what I am doing . . . Hitherto I
> have not set her free in the ordinary meaning of the word.
> I do it now, I set her free, for only thus will I love her.
> She must never suspect that she owes this freedom to me . . .
> That the engagement should bind her is foolishness; I will
> have her only in her freedom . . . The more abundant
> strength she has, the more interesting for me. The first war
> was a war of liberation, it was only a game; the second is a
> war of conquest, it is for life and death. [*EO, 1,* 379–380]

And finally there is recorded the victory of the strategist—a
victory which is in reality defeat, since it means the end of
resistance and warfare to one who can exult only in resistance
and war. "Why cannot such a night be longer?" he laments.

> If Alectryon could forget himself, why cannot the sun be
> equally sympathetic? Still, it is over now, and I hope never
> to see her again . . . Now all resistance is impossible, and
> only as long as that is present is it beautiful to love; when
> it is ended there is only weakness and habit. I do not wish
> to be reminded of my relation to her . . . I will have no
> farewell scene with her; nothing is more disgusting to
> me than a woman's tears and a woman's prayers which
> alter everything, and yet really mean nothing. I have loved
> her, but from now on she can no longer engross my soul.
> [*EO, 1,* 439–40]

The military concepts and imagery which pervade these passages seem to be so well suited to character and situation that
one might easily overlook the fact that they belong to a well-
established literary tradition and are embedded in language it-

self; or the fact that Kierkegaard pressed them into the service of existential subjectivity. Gods or goddesses of love have always used the implements of war to wound their victims, and many an old ballad compares the city beleaguered by its enemies to the woman wooed and conquered by her lover, or the deer stalked by the hunter to female innocence in flight from its armed pursuer. If Racine's poetry shows so great an economy of language, this economy could be achieved in part because the vocabulary of love is largely identical with that of war. But what is remarkable in the Seducer's use of this literary topos is that it is not Cordelia's defeat at which his strategy aims but rather a surrender on her part of such a nature that she would appear to be the pursuer and in defeat would seem victorious. In his *Søren Kierkegaard and French Literature,* Ronald Grimsley perceptively discusses a parallel situation found in Laclos's *Les Liaisons dangéreuses.*[17] It is immaterial for this comparison whether Kierkegaard was familiar with the French novel, though this may well have been the case. Its value lies rather in the fact that it gives emphasis to certain elements which might otherwise go unnoticed. What it most strongly reveals is the Kierkegaardian concept of subjectivity that pervades Johannes' diary as compared to the letters of Valmont in *Liaisons.* Valmont is as much the reflective Seducer as Johannes. He, too, uses military imagery to describe his advances upon an unsuspecting and innocent woman. He, too, wants the woman's surrender to be "in the strictest sense freedom's gift."[18] But while Valmont plays the role of the roué above all in order to be applauded by a roué society and particularly to gain the approval of Madame Merteuil, Johannes remains strictly his own audience. His

17. Ronald Grimsley, *Søren Kierkegaard and French Literature: Eight Comparative Studies* (Cardiff, University of Wales Press, 1966), pp. 26–44.

18. Ibid., p. 30.

triumphs are seen only by him. He is the individual in complete isolation. When he acts as the ironist and dons his diverse masks, he does so merely for his own enjoyment. He never plays the hypocrite for he has gained total ironic freedom and has thereby, like Schlegel's Julius, suspended the ethical. Yet, being presented as but one aspect of a dialectic, as the Either Kierkegaard was to confront with an Or, he could get off unpunished.

Because the Seducer sees love, moreover, as that power which, like irony, can eliminate the past, he emphasizes the present. The present tense is, of course, also the tense of existence and quite naturally that of a diary. "I seek the immediate," he confesses. "It is the eternal element in love that the individuals first exist for one another in the moment of love" *(EO, 1, 376)*. Woman is to him, indeed, altogether a creature of the present. Since she was taken from Adam's rib and not his brain, she belongs to the category of Nature, according to the Seducer *(EO, 1, 425)*. "This being of woman (for the word *existence* is too rich in meaning, since woman does not persist in and through herself)" he writes (and Lowrie explains that Kierkegaard plays here on the word *exist/ex-sisto: appear, come forth*), "is rightly described as charm, an expression which suggests plant life . . . Woman is, namely, substance, man is reflection . . . Woman's essential being is being for another . . . Hence it is that the moment has here such infinite significance; for a being for another is always a matter of a moment" *(EO, 1, 426–27)*. And thus Kierkegaard stresses again, in this indirect way, man's, that is, the individual's essential separateness from the Other.

But even the diary of an existential Seducer and ironist may permit elements which transcend the present and reach into the past as well as the future. We have seen Johannes introducing glimpses of the future into dramatic scenes that are very much of the moment. He is equally successful in associating glimpses of the past with events of the hour, thereby altering their significance: "When now after what I have learned, I think back upon the impression that first meeting made upon me, I find my ideas about her are considerably modified, to her advantage as well as to my own. It is not quite usual for a young girl to go out alone or for a young girl to be so introspective. I subjected her to my strict criterion: charming. But charm is a very fleeting factor, which is as yesterday when it is past. I had not imagined her in the environment in which she lives; least of all had I pictured her so unreflectingly familiar with the stormy side of life" *(EO, 1,* 340). Such observations are apt to reveal also the fleeting quality of existence which, according to Kierkegaard, is forever a "becoming." It is perhaps because of this particular quality of the Kierkegaardian view of life that the Seducer never becomes a static figure, never is clearly shown as the hypocrite or the seducer; that he always seems the artist engaged in the process of creating himself.

But it is neither the Seducer's egocentricity and contempt for women nor his aesthetic attitude towards life and love that wholly account for his actions. What they reflect in the last analysis is the virtual inability of an existent to understand another existent. And here the choice of the diary and the human situation it reveals express this philosophical truth aesthetically. Since the diarist cannot enter the mind of others (and no existent can do this in the eyes of Kierkegaard), his observations of them merely scratch the surface of their being. His bold attempts to envision Cordelia's reactions remain, in spite of his shrewdness and obvious experience, mere generalities: "You are sixteen years old, you are a reader, that is to say, you read novels. You have accidentally, in going through your brothers' room, caught a word or two of a conversation between them and an acquaintance, something about Eastern Street. Later you whisked through several times, in order, if possible, to get a little more information. All in vain. One ought, it would seem, if one is a grown-up girl, to know a little something about the world" *(EO, 1, 313)*. This, of course, might fit any girl her age of that time. Johannes seems to know, to understand, but only as we seem to know about Nature, about which we have learned a few reassuring but rarely reliable laws based on observation. Such laws remain, in fact, hypotheses and conjectures: "I wonder how it is with her emotions. She has certainly never been in love, for her spirit is too free-soaring for that, nor is she by any means one of those theoretically experienced maidens, who, long before their time, are so familiar with the thought of being in the arms of a loved one. The figures she has met in real life have hardly been able to bring her to confusion about the relation of dreams to reality. Her soul is still nourished by the divine ambrosia of ideals" *(EO, 1, 340)*. Even if he ventures into psychological analyses, he does so but in general terms and moves in general categories: "Our relationship is not the tender and loyal embrace of understanding, not attraction; it is the repulsion of misunderstanding. My relationship to her is simply nil; it is purely intellectual, which means it is simply nothing to a young girl" *(EO, 1, 347)*.

As a consequence, though calculating every move, he can never be sure of its effects: "So now I am engaged; so is Cordelia, and that is about all she knows about the whole matter. If she had a girl friend she could talk freely with, she might perhaps say: 'I don't really understand what it all means . . . He has a strange power over me, but I do not love him'" *(EO, 1, 371)*. This is what he conjectures, but what she really thinks remains a mystery to him. On one occasion he decides to talk to her "like a book" because he wants to confront her with the same challenge of interpretation that a book would require. Her reaction is one of surprise. This much he had expected, but beyond it his power of analysis fails him: "To describe how she looked is difficult. Her expressions were so variable, indeed much like the still unpublished but announced commentary to my book, a commentary which has the possibility of any interpretation . . . Curiously enough. When in the days preceding I surveyed the affair, I was rash enough and confident enough to believe that taken by surprise, she would . . . That shows how much thorough preparation amounts to" *(EO, 1, 370)*.

The Kierkegaardian concept of the individual's incomprehension of the Other has found perhaps its most poetic expression in a diary entry wherein Johannes likens the relationship beween himself and Cordelia to a dance:

> I am watching the birth of love within her. I am even almost invisibly present when I visibly sit by her side. My relation to her is that of an unseen partner in a dance which is danced by only one, when it should really be danced by two. She moves as in a dream, and yet she dances with another, and this other is myself, who, in so far as I am visibly present, am invisible, in so far as I am invisible, am visible. The movements of the dance require a partner, she bows to him, she takes his hand, she flees, she draws near him again. I take her hand, I complete her thought as if it were completed in herself. She moves to the inner melody of her own soul; I am only the occasion for her movement. [*EO, 1, 376*]

This image of the dance for two danced by only one, this inability of Kierkegaard's fictional world to contain valid human interrelationships stresses again the fundamental aesthetic dilemma that confronted him and that I shall now consider from another angle.

Thus far my concern with the interplay of content and form has been restricted to the body of the "Diary." But this interplay also affects the "Diary's" framework. In this respect, an important formal element is the anonymous and pseudonymous editor, A.

Because of his presence we are enabled to gain, both directly and indirectly, information about events and characters which the Seducer himself could not have conveyed to us in his own intimate notations. It is through A that we learn how the Seducer appeared to others, for A had known him personally. He tells us that Johannes had led, on the surface, a rather colorless existence; that he had developed, however, a "talent for discovering the interesting in life . . . had known how to find it," and thereby had tried "to realize the task of living poetically" *(EO, 1,* 300). But A not only conveys to us judgments concerning the Seducer, he also pronounces judgment upon the diary itself, declaring it, as we have seen, "neither historically exact nor simply fiction, not indicative but subjunctive," and belonging therefore to the realm of the aesthetic, that is, to the realm of possibility. Its poetic qualities are, according to A, due to the author's temperament rather than to any conscious intent on his part to publish it as a work of fiction. "The poetic," A feels, "was constantly present in the ambiguity in which he passed his life" *(EO, 1,* 302). As editor, A therefore not only situates the protagonist and judges him from his own, that is, an outside point of view, but also critically defines the quality and genre of the work.

And A functions in yet another way: he serves to enlarge the work's perspective because he also knew Cordelia and possesses some evidence of her reactions to the events and situations. Evidently A's acquaintance with Cordelia cannot directly add to our understanding of her, for he is as incapable of entering her mind as is the Seducer, or any other existent for that matter. He, too, stops at conjectures:

> Poor Cordelia! For her too it will be difficult to find peace. She forgives him from the bottom of her heart, but she finds no rest, for then doubt awakens: it was she who broke the engagement, she who was the cause of the disaster, it

was her pride which craved the uncommon. Then she repents, but she finds no rest; for then the accusing thoughts acquit her: it was he who so subtly put this plan in her mind . . . It is hard for her that he has deceived her, even harder, one might almost be tempted to say, that he has developed the many-tongued reflection within her, that he has developed her aesthetically so far that she no longer listens to one voice but is able to hear many voices at one time. [*EO, 1,* 305]

But what helps us to round out the picture we have of Cordelia is the fact that A can publish, with the diary, letters that Cordelia had written to her Johannes and that had been returned to her unopened, as well as a letter she had addressed to A. The letters she wrote to Johannes reveal her as a person of feeling and intelligence, even if she "did not possess the compass she admired in her Johannes" *(EO, 1,* 309). The letter to A about her fiancé is proof of her own awareness of the fact that she is incapable of understanding him, the Other she would have most wanted to understand:

Sometimes he was so intellectual that I felt myself annihilated as a woman. At other times he was so wild and passionate, so filled with desire, that I almost trembled before him. Sometimes he was like a stranger to me, sometimes he was devotion itself; when I then flung my arms about him, sometimes everything was suddenly changed, and I embraced the cloud . . . I think all my thoughts in connection with him. I have always loved music; he was a matchless instrument, always responsive; he had a range such as no musical instrument has; he was the epitome of all feelings and moods, no thoughts were too lofty for him, none too despairing, he could roar like an autumn gale, he could whisper soundlessly. No word of mine was without

> effect; and yet I cannot say that my word did not fail of its effect; for it was impossible for me to know what effect it would have. With an indescribable but mysterious, blissful, inexpressible dread I listened to this music I had myself evoked, and yet did not evoke. [*EO, 1*, 305–06]

There is still another perspective which A's presence adds to the work, because Cordelia also entrusted to him a few of the letters Johannes had sent to her. As A inserts them in the diary in those spots where, because of specific references, they seem appropriate, he not only intensifies our impression of the Seducer as an aesthete in the process of creating a work of art, but also makes us believe in him as a man with whom a young girl might well fall passionately in love—something the diary with its air of cold calculation could not convey. For these letters are jewels of imaginative charm and poetry, as a few samples will prove:

> My Cordelia! Because I have loved you so short a time you almost seem to fear that I may have loved someone before. There are manuscripts on which the trained eye immediately suspects an older writing which in the course of time has been superseded by insignificant foolishness. By means of chemicals, this later writing may be erased, and then the original stands out plain and clear. So your eye has taught me to find myself in myself. I let forgetfulness consume everything which does not concern you, and then I discover an exceedingly old, a divinely young, original writing, then I discover that my love for you is as old as myself. Thy Johannes. [*EO, 1*, 396]

> My Cordelia! One reads in ancient tales that a river fell in love with a maiden. So my soul is like a river that loves you. Sometimes it is peaceful and reflects your image deeply

and quietly; sometimes it imagines that it has captured your image; then its waves rise up to prevent your escaping; sometimes the surface ripples softly, playing with your image; sometimes it has lost it, then its floods are black with despair.—Such is my soul: like a river which has fallen in love with you. Thy Johannes. [*EO, 1,* 402]

My Cordelia! Do you believe that he who lays his head on a fairy hillock sees the image of a fairy in his dreams? I do not know, but I do know this, that when I rest my head upon your breast, and then do not close my eyes, but peep up through my eyelids, then I see an angel's face. Do you believe that he whose head reclined on a fairy hillock cannot lie quiet? I do not believe it; but I know that when my head rests on your bosom, I am moved too strongly for sleep to close my eyes. Thy Johannes. [*EO, 1,* 415]

Without an editor this poetry as well as much external information would have been withheld from the reader who would have had to rely only on the point of view of the Seducer. A first-person account, whether in the form of a diary or a letter, is limited by the consciousness and knowledge of that person—especially if an existential point of view prevails, stressing the individual's isolation. In aesthetic terms, the introduction of A permitted Kierkegaard to present us with a combination of varied first-person views—each that of an isolated existent—so that by their sheer coexistence they form a world of interaction. One is reminded of Beckett's play entitled *Play,* in which each character is the narrator of his own individual story and the play results from the almost accidental overlapping of their accounts. In Kierkegaard's "Diary of the Seducer" each character is thus an author—as well as a hero or heroine—revealed in either Preface, letters, or diary. As soon as we are aware of this fact we also begin to see Kierkegaard's numerous pseudonyms in a new light and not merely as devices that conceal his identity, add ironic distance and aesthetic possibles. In order to make this apparent, "Diary of the Seducer" must be placed within the context of *Either/Or,* of which it is a structural part.

The entire *Either/Or* is edited by Victor Eremita—a fictitious being, a pseudonym for Kierkegaard. As Victor elaborately explains in the Preface to the work, it was "by sheer coincidence" that he found two sets of manuscripts "whose external differences were strongly marked." Irony in the form of exaggeration comes into play when Kierkegaard has him tell in detail that

> one of them was written in a kind of vellum in quarto, with a fairly wide margin . . . the handwriting was legible, sometimes even a little elegant, in a single place, careless . . . [that] the other was written on full sheets of foolscap with ruled columns, such as is ordinarily used for legal documents and the like. The handwriting was clear, somewhat spreading, uniform and even, apparently that of a business man. The contents also proved very dissimilar. One part consisted of a number of aesthetic essays of varying length, the other was composed of two long inquiries and one shorter one, all with an ethical content, as it seemed, and in the form of letters. This dissimilarity was completely confirmed by a closer examination. [*EO, 1, 7*]

Yet, in spite of such disparity, the two manuscripts obviously belonged together, because the "second series consists of letters written to the author of the first series" *(EO, 1, 7).* Victor Eremita's efforts to identify the two authors proved futile, and it was only the dissimilarity between the two manuscripts which provided him with some insight into their lives. What he learned about the author of the second, the ethical, part was mainly that he was a magistrate at some court and that he signed his letters "William." The name of the other, the aesthetic author, was nowhere revealed. For the sake of convenience, therefore, Victor

Eremita decided to refer to him as A and to the ethical author as B.

We are informed by Eremita of the amount of editing he found it necessary to undertake before publishing the manuscripts:

> Then I tried to arrange the papers as well as I could. In the case of those written by B this was fairly easy. Each of these letters presupposes the one preceding, and in the second letter there is a quotation from the first; the third letter presupposes the other two. . . . The arranging of A's papers was not so simple. I have therefore let chance determine the order, that is to say, I have left them in the order in which I found them, without being able to decide whether this order has any chronological value or ideal significance.

He explains that due to their lyrical form it seemed "proper to use the word Diapsalmata as the principal title" of the aphorisms, which he placed first because they provide "provisional glimpses of what the longer essays develop more connectedly" *(EO, 1, 7–8)*.

Victor Eremita's claim to be merely the editor and not the author of the two manuscripts provides him—or rather Kierkegaard—with obvious advantages: He is able to express an opinion about the authors as well as their relationship to their work and to each other. He can establish A as the aesthetic, B as the ethical author. He even has occasion to explain the apparent disorder of A's manuscript by stating that "a single, coherent, aesthetic view of life can scarcely be carried out" *(EO, 1, 13)*. He has, moreover, the opportunity of juxtaposing two different attitudes in the same volume without having to take sides:

> One sometimes chances upon novels in which certain characters represent opposing views of life. It usually ends by

one of them convincing the other. Instead of these views being allowed to speak for themselves, the reader is enriched by being told the historical result, that one has convinced the other. I regard it as fortunate that these papers contain no such information. Whether A wrote his aesthetic essays after having received B's letters, whether his soul continued to be tossed about in wild abandon, or whether it found rest, I cannot say, since the papers indicate nothing. Nor is there any clue as to how things went with B, whether he had strength to hold to his convictions or not. When the book is read, then A and B are forgotten, only their views confront one another, and await no finite decision in particular personalities. [*EO, 1,* 14]

A part of the work which Kierkegaard later published under the title of *Stages On Life's Way* was to represent equally contradictory views—as is clearly indicated by its first title *Right Hand and Left Hand.*[19]

Victor Eremita, claiming to be only the editor of *Either/Or,* can even afford to discuss with the reader his choice of title for the volume which is to contain both manuscripts:

It remained only to choose a title. I might call them Papers, Found Papers, Lost Papers, and so forth. A number of variants could be found, but none of these titles satisfied me. In selecting a title I have therefore allowed myself a liberty, a deception for which I shall try to make an accounting. During my constant occupation with the papers, it dawned upon me that they might be looked at from a new point of view, by considering all of them as the work of one man. I know very well everything that can be urged against this view, that it is unhistorical, improbable, un-

19. Søren Kierkegaard, *Stages on Life's Way,* trans. Walter Lowrie, (Princeton, Princeton University Press, 1940), p. 8; henceforth cited in the text as *S.*

> reasonable, that one man should be the author of both parts, although the reader might easily be tempted to play on words, that he who says A must also say B. However, I have not been able to relinquish the idea . . . As I let this thought sink into my soul, it became clear to me that I might make use of it in choosing a title. [*EO, 1,* 13]

The title, then, reflects not only two contrary views, but also a paradox within one individual presented in dialectical form.

As editor, Eremita can dwell, moreover, on the fact that author A had complicated his task by denying authorship of the part of his manuscript that forms "Diary of the Seducer" and ironically claiming to be merely its editor. He complains—tongue in cheek, no doubt—of what he calls "an old trick of the novelist" to which he would not object were it not for the fact that one author now "seems to be enclosed in another, like the parts in a Chinese puzzle box" *(EO, 1, 9)*. What makes him doubt the veracity of A's claim is the organic manner in which "Diary of the Seducer" seems to belong to the remainder of A's manuscript. The Seducer seems to be prefigured in two of A's essays which precede the *"Diary."* Though Johannes is a reflective seducer, he is, of course, an analogue to the Don Giovanni of the essay entitled "The Immediate Stages of the Erotic." Victor Eremita can inject here even his disapproval of the diary by stating that it seems to him "as if A had actually become afraid of his poem, [and] as if it continued to terrify him, like a troubled dream when it is told" *(EO, 1, 9)*. For even as the editor "twice removed from the original author," Eremita admits to strange feelings when "in the silence of the night, I have busied myself with these papers" *(EO, 1, 9)*.

But regardless of Eremita's objections to A's "trick," A's refusal to acknowledge his authorship of the "Diary" brings the number of authors up to five: Victor Eremita, A, B, the Seducer, and Cordelia—not to mention Kierkegaard, who stands behind it all pulling the strings, nor to consider the fact that the Seducer reveals himself as one person in his diary and as another in his letters to Cordelia. Not a single one of these five authors—whether pseudonymous or anonymous—could be omitted without omitting valid and valuable information and without altering the structure of the story—though Victor Eremita may be considered as serving mainly as a persona for Kierkegaard, he himself being unable to sign his name to a work of aesthetic rather than religious character. But even if we were inclined to disregard Eremita, we must not forget that it was Kierkegaard himself who claimed that each of his pseudonyms is a "poetically actual" individuality which, once created, exists independently of its author and produces its own views. This claim alone should caution us not to accept too readily the explanation given by some critics that Kierkegaard's use of pseudonyms was a mere imitation of the practice of German Romanticists. It is comforting, in fact, to find a scholar of the quality of Lowrie equally suspicious of such an explanation *(K,* 287*)*. Yet even Lowrie's assumption that Kierkegaard was playing a game of hide-and-seek with the reader appears unsatisfactory in the light of the author's own remarks and in view of the ironic exaggeration with which he introduces each new editor and each newly found manuscript. It is, indeed, Kierkegaard himself who provides us with an explanation of this form of irony. In his *Concept of Irony* he had recognized such "mystification" as "a certain inward infinity which seeks to emancipate one's work from every finite relation to oneself" *(CI,* 269*)*.

In his attempts at "mystification" Kierkegaard runs the whole gamut of his vivid imagination. What results is burlesque comedy. In *Either/Or,* Victor Eremita tells us painstakingly of the many coincidences that conspired to put him in possession of the two manuscripts he decided to publish under that title. There is, the fascinating old secretary he notices in a merchant's shop, admiring and desiring it for a long time before deciding to buy it. There comes the moment when this secretary is finally bought and installed in his apartment where he familiarizes himself with "its rich economy, its many drawers and recesses" which please him no end. There is the day "in the summer of 1836" on which he decides to take a trip to the country.

> The postilion was engaged for five o'clock in the morning, the necessary baggage had been packed the evening before, and everything was in readiness. I awakened at four, but the vision of the beautiful country I was to visit so enchanted me that I again fell asleep, or into dream. My servant evidently thought he would let me sleep as long as possible, for he did not call me until half-past six. The postilion was already blowing his horn, and although I am not usually inclined to obey the mandates of others, I have always made an exception in the case of the postboy and his musical theme. I was speedily dressed and already at the door, when it occurred to me, Have you enough money in your pocket? There was not much there. I opened the secretary to get at the money drawer to take what money there was. Of course, the drawer would not move. Every attempt to open it failed. It was all as bad as it could possibly be. Just at this moment, while my ears were ringing with the postboy's alluring notes, to meet such difficulties! The blood rushed to my head, I became angry. As Xerxes ordered the sea to be lashed, so I resolved to take a terrible revenge. A hatchet was fetched. With it I dealt the secretary a shattering blow, shocking to see. Whether in my anger I struck the wrong place, or the drawer was as stubborn as myself, the result of the blow was not as anticipated. The drawer was closed, and the drawer remained closed. But something else happened. Whether my blow had struck exactly the right spot,

or whether the shock to the whole framework of the secretary was responsible, I do not know, but I do know that a secret door sprang open, one which I had never before noticed. This opened a pigeonhole that I naturally had never discovered. Here to my great surprise I found a mass of papers, the papers which form the content of the present work. [*EO, 1,* 5–6]

To appreciate fully the vengeance with which Kierkegaard put the "trick of the novelist" to use in order to establish the "author's" anonymity, one must also keep in mind the method used in his *Stages on Life's Way,* which is if possible an even more burlesque and intricate one. The manuscripts of *Stages on Life's Way,* each representing one stage or, as Walter Lowrie has called it, Sphere or Existence Sphere, were supposed to have been forgotten in the shop of a bookbinder named appropriately enough Hilarius Bookbinder who, in total ignorance of their content, had bound them together while waiting for their rightful owner to claim them. They remained untouched and forgotten until a young man of some learning came across them and encouraged Hilarius Bookbinder to publish them, considering them of possible interest to other readers. Hilarius proceeded to follow his advice, but not without apologies to the reader: "That a bookbinder should desire to be an author could only awaken justifiable resentment in the literary world and contribute to bring the book into discredit; but that a bookbinder stitches, forwards to the press and publishes a book, that he also in another way than as a bookbinder seeks to benefit his fellowmen, no sensible reader will take amiss" *(S,* 24). The volume begins with a "Recollection" entitled "In Vino Veritas," said to have been "subsequently related by William Afham." It is the story of a banquet in which five people participated, among them a Ladies' Tailor, Johannes nicknamed the Seducer, Victor Eremita (both known to us from *Either/Or*), and Constantine Constantius. Afham recollects how the banquet was organized, tells a number of things concerning the apparent character of each participant, and, above all, reports to us the speeches each made under the motto *in vino veritas.* It is then that we hear each speaker individually and expressing himself in the first person, while Afham gives us some idea of their outward appearance. The banquet ends in the early morning, but instead of immediately returning to their respective homes, the participants invade the lovely abode of Judge William (the author of the ethical part of *Either/Or*), which they pass on their way, and surprise him and his good wife at breakfast. It is here that Victor Eremita discovers and steals a bundle of papers, "a manuscript written by a judge," which Victor considers it his duty to publish because he had published the previous one (meaning *Either/Or*). But before Victor can put the manuscript in his pocket, Afham takes it away from him, and it is then that he identifies himself to the reader: "But who am I? Let nobody ask. If it has not occurred to anybody to ask, I am relieved, for then I am over the worst of it. Besides, I am not worth asking about, for I am the most insignificant of all things, it makes me quite bashful to have people ask about me. I am 'pure being' and therefore almost less than nothing" *(S, 93)*. While this statement is clearly a take-off on Hegel, it also represents, no doubt, Kierkegaard's view of any author, or editor for that matter, as being ultimately a mere medium through which truth manifests itself.

The manuscript Afham publishes is entitled "Observations about Marriage." It is followed by yet another which is an account of "A Psychological Experiment" by Frater Taciturnus and bears the title "Guilty?/Not Guilty? A Passion Narrative." Frater Taciturnus appears not only as a factual poetic character but also as the experimenter and author. And again pseudonymity and polynymity are compounded by the fact that the object of his experimentation is the manuscript of a diary he found through a grotesque coincident and which he has proceeded to publish. It was during a boat excursion on a lake that he came across it:

> Wrapped in oilskin and provided with many seals was a rosewood box. The box was locked, and when I opened it by force the key lay inside—thus it is that morbid reserve is always introverted. In the box was a manuscript written with a very careful and clear hand upon thin paper. There was orderliness and neatness in it all, and yet an air of solemn consecration as if it had been written before the face of God. To think that by my intervention I have brought disorder into the archives of heavenly justice! But now it is too late, now I crave forgiveness of heaven and of the unknown author. Undeniably the place of concealment was well chosen, and Søeborg Lake is more trustworthy than the most solemn declaration which promises "complete silence," for the lake makes no such declaration. [S, 183]

The unknown author is referred to by Frater Taciturnus as Quidam, Latin for "a certain somebody." While Frater Taciturnus makes us believe at times that he may actually be the diarist, his real or assumed remoteness from the characters to whom the diary makes reference permits him to analyze them in the cold manner of a scientist (S, 363–64). The story that emerges is similar to that of "Diary of the Seducer," the poetic version of Kierkegaard's relationship to Regina. We find here again "the double reflection" of Either/Or, the pieces of the Chinese puzzle box with one author enclosed in another, and the publisher Bookbinder three times, Kierkegaard himself four times, removed from Quidam.

When Kierkegaard spoke in *Either/Or* of "the trick of the novelist," he proved himself, of course, aware of a tradition that seems to be as old as the novel itself. In some form or other it can, indeed, be traced back to the Middle Ages. Even then authors had claimed to be simply recorders or editors of stories they had either witnessed or had heard from eye witnesses. Later, when the art of writing became more widely known and when the printed book had made its appearance, more and more authors adopted the device, all pretending to have found manuscripts which they merely edited and published. By the time of Cervantes the technique had apparently been used to such excess that he ridiculed it in *Don Quixote*. With an irony and a burlesque willfulness, which may well have inspired Kierkegaard directly or indirectly, Cervantes interrupted his tale at the end of its eighth chapter, when Don Quixote and his valiant adversary have drawn swords to cleave each other in two. His reason: the manuscript—he had never mentioned that such a thing existed but had told the story as if it had happened in a Spanish town—suddenly ended. By sheer accident, however, and a number of fortunate coincidences, he finds one day an Arabic manuscript which is the precise continuation of Don Quixote's adventures told by the historian Cide Hamete Benengeli. It is this discovery that enables Cervantes to continue his account.[20]

During the seventeenth and eighteenth centuries fictitious authors and editors were frequently used in the rapidly developing genre of the novel. We have only to think of the anonymous French *Lettres Portugaises* whose publisher made the claim (now proven false) that they were real letters written by a real Portuguese nun and transmitted to him by her lover, to whom they were addressed. In the eighteenth century, such novelists as Marivaux, Crébillion, Swift, Defoe, Richardson, Sterne, Goethe, and many others of equal or smaller fame employed the same

20. Miguel de Cervantes, *Don Quixote*, chapters 8–9.

"trick." Richard Sympson, the fictitious publisher of *Gulliver's Travels,* declared Lemuel Gulliver to be his "ancient and intimate friend" who left the manuscripts in his hands "with the liberty to dispose of them as I should think fit." And neither the fictitiousness of Sympson nor that of Gulliver was self-evident to Swift's contemporary readers. "A letter from Captain Gulliver to his cousin Sympson," which was used as an introduction to the work, permitted Swift, moreover, to distance "the publisher" and thereby himself from the views of Gulliver. Defoe's use of the technique permitted him to present his *Robinson Crusoe* with the commendation that "the editor believes the thing to be a just history of fact." Usually the device was used for many reasons: to conceal authorship of a genre not considered serious literature; to induce credulity for a rather unlikely story; to give occasion for a statement that the immoral story presented is to be considered a deterrent rather than a model for imitation; to account for an author's acquaintance, which might otherwise seem improbable, with facts of startling intimacy; or to create a distance between the story's protagonist, writing in the first person, and the author, who did not wish to be identified with him.

But Kierkegaard, though availing himself of a well-known tradition, did not merely follow it. It is true, as we have seen, that he used the device for the sake of ironically distancing himself from his aesthetic work—a distancing for which he must have felt a special need because of the author-hero identification suggested by existential thought and because of his use of first-person writing which further emphasized this identity. Granted this need for distancing, however, one still has to account for his doubled and tripled pseudonymity and polynymity within the framework of his aesthetic writing. In view of our preceding discussions of *Either/Or* and *Stages on Life's Way,* the explanation for these given by Kierkegaard himself in "The First and

Last Explanation" appended to his *Concluding Unscientific Post-script* is eminently acceptable and enlightening. In this Appendix he first acknowledges "formally and for the sake of regularity" that he is "the author as people would call it, of *Either/Or* (Victor Eremita), Copenhagen, February 1843; *Fear and Trembling* (Johannes de Silentio) 1843; *Repetition* (Constantine Constantius) 1843; The *Concept of Dread* (Vigilius Haufniensis) 1844; *Stages on Life's Way* (Hilarius Bookbinder: William Afham, the Judge, Frater Taciturnus) 1845; *Concluding Postscript to the Philosophical Fragments* (Johannes Climacus) 1846; an article in *The Fatherland*, 1843, No. 1168 (Victor Eremita); two articles in *The Fatherland* January 1846 (Frater Taciturnus)" *(CUP,* Appendix, 554). He proceeds to explain that his "pseudonymity or polynymity has not had a casual ground in his person" but "has an essential ground in the character of the *production."* He makes it clear, moreover, that it was not fear of legal penalty of any sort which made him choose the pseudonyms and assures us, in fact, that he will accept all responsibility for them in any legal or literary sense. On the other hand, he insists on his detachment from these pseudonyms: "What is written therefore is in fact mine, but only in so far as I put into the mouth of the poetically actual individuality whom I *produced,* his life-view expressed in audible lines." Since the pseudonyms are authors, he considers his relationship with them even more external than that of other authors would be to the characters they have poetized and acknowledged as narrators in their prefaces. Kierkegaard thinks of himself as irrelevant under the circumstances, or one merely playing the part of the souffleur, the prompter, who produced authors who can write their own prefaces. He goes so far as to claim that not a single word of these works is truly his and that he has to read them like any other reader, as a third person. They are "doubly reflected communications." As regards *Either/Or,* he refuses to be identified with either the Seducer, Judge William, or the editor Victor Eremita. He considers Eremita a "poetically actual, subjective thinker, whom one encounters again in "In Vino Veritas" and who like each one of the other "poetized authors has his definite life-view" The lines attributed to these authors "which with this understanding of the case might possibly be significant, witty, arousing, would perhaps if put in the mouth of a definite factual individual man sound strange, ludicrous, disgusting," Kierkegaard maintains. Since he claims not to be the author of his pseudonymous books in the ordinary sense and merely the one who "has contributed to bring it about that the pseudonyms could become authors," he feels sorry for any reader who might mistakenly burden himself with the weight of his, Kierkegaard's, "personal reality" when he might and should enjoy the "doubly reflected, light ideality of a poetically actual author." His personal life is for the literary production totally irrelevant, and the importance of the pseudonyms consists ultimately in their "wanting to have no importance, in wanting (at a distance which is the remoteness of double reflection) to read solo the original text of the individual, human existence-relationship, the old text, well known, handed down from the fathers—to read it through yet once more, if possible in a more heartfelt way" (*CUP*, 554).

Kierkegaard, then, takes an attitude toward his pseudonymous authors comparable to that which more traditional novelists take to the characters within their fictional world. In *Either/Or,* for instance, each editor-author assumes a specific stance and expresses specific views. Yet all are taking part in a *comédie humaine* and, like Balzac's characters, may turn up again under different circumstances in other works. We do, in fact, encounter some of the characters, or rather authors, of *Either/Or* in *Stages on Life's Way.* Victor Eremita is there a speaker at the banquet, that is, actor and author. But he is also the would-be editor of another of Judge William's manuscripts. Judge Williams, who in *Either/Or* had remained almost a hypothesis who had gained reality only through the letters he had addressed to the Seducer, becomes in this later work a person of flesh and blood, seen in the midst of everyday existence with his wife by his side. Johannes the Seducer is likewise seen as participant in the banquet, taking a specific point of view in his talk, and being altogether part of the gaiety and seriousness of that night. While to Kierkegaard, the factual existent, each of these characters is but a "possibility" and belongs to the realm of aesthetics, each has poetic reality and actuality within that realm. Because of his view of the individual as limited by the horizons of his own consciousness, however, they can not enter into true communication with each other within that world. Nor can Kierkegaard as their author assume the role of omniscience and enter into their consciousnesses—as other nineteenth-century novelists were beginning to do. Each individual dances alone, as it were, and this is where they differ from the Balzacian *comédie humaine*.

A quick glance at the history of the novel would indicate that "pseudonymous authors" apparently disappeared from the serious novel at the same time that the omniscient author made his entrance. Vivienne Milne, in her careful study, *The Eighteenth-Century Novel,* considers *Les Égarements du coeur et de l'esprit* by Crébillon the first novel with a truly omniscient author, quite in contrast to other letter-novels of the time which usually respect the one-consciousness approach.[21] Deliberately objecting to this limitation of seeing others only from the outside and being able to present their thoughts and feelings only as conjectures, Crébillon had tried a different approach and apparently started a new development. For it seems that by the early nine-

21. Vivienne Milne, *The Eighteenth-Century Novel* (Manchester, Manchester University Press, 1965), p. 133.

teenth-century omniscient authors or narrators had become the vogue. But while the characters of an omniscient author are usually mere actors, put in motion, guided, and understood by a superior consciousness, Kierkegaard's heroes, once created poetically, could no longer be interfered with but had to assume their own aesthetic actuality. Being able to speak only in the first person, only for themselves, they willy-nilly had to be both authors and actors, that is, author-heroes, so that Kierkegaard's relationship to them was—exactly as stated in "A First and Last Declaration"—"that of being the author of the author of authors." (*CUP*, 554).

This fact reveals in aesthetic terms Kierkegaard's fundamental philosophical opposition to Hegel. The omniscient author can be fitted exceedingly well into the Hegelian system of thought. Hegel, as Sartre so acutely observed in his *Being and Nothingness*, could forget the limits of his own consciousness and study the relationship between other consciousnesses which, to him, were but a particular kind of object: a subject-object. "These consciousnesses from the totalitarian point of view which he has adopted are strictly equivalent to each other although each of them is separated from the rest by a particular privilege," Sartre wrote.[22] Hegel himself, as Sartre reminds us, considered Others from the point of view of the Absolute. It would seem therefore that a writer who, consciously or unconsciously is permeated by Hegelian philosophy, could assume an omniscient as well as an objective role. Kierkegaard's existential way of thinking, on the other hand, could not abstract itself into the point of view of the Absolute. He remained the individual, the "I." It was only in the realm of the aesthetic and as ironic possibilities that this "I" could become a third person and assume the mask of different "I's." Only in the realm of myth

22. Jean-Paul Sartre, *Being and Nothingness,* trans. Hazel Barnes (New York, Philosophical Library, 1956), p. 243.

could it find an objective correlative. Kierkegaard's awareness that even these aesthetic "I's" remain but aspects of his Self was beautifully expressed by him in his work *The Repetition*. "The individual has manifold shadows," he stated there, "all of which resemble him and from time to time have an equal claim to be the man himself" *(K,* 289, quoted by Walter Lowrie). However, not even these fictional "I's" which Kierkegaard created in their poetic actuality could be perceived by him in the manner of Hegel, that is, as equivalent subject-objects to be studied and to function as privileged consciousnesses in their relationship to others. None of these poetic actualities could itself adopt the Hegelian totalitarianism.

Kierkegaard's technique of enclosing one author in another "like the parts of a Chinese puzzle box" is therefore decidedly more than a game. It is rather his serious and imaginative attempt to save his aesthetic universe from solipsism. It represents an ingenious effort to create worlds within the realm of the aesthetic in spite of the individual's isolation. Because one author is enclosed in another an interaction is created between the manifold poetic actualities of the "I's." Ultimately, of course, the intricacy of the puzzle box points back to Kierkegaard himself and beyond him to the individual as such. It permitted the author, as Kierkegaard suggested in "A First and Last Explanation," in the "remoteness of double-reflection" to "read solo the original text of the individual human existence-relationship, the old text, well known, handed down from the fathers." It enabled him to refer to himself in the third person—not unlike Lisette, the character in Schlegel's *Lucinde* who is most expressive of Romantic irony —and treat his story as if it were that of another.[23] Because he

23. See Schlegel, p. 190:

> Es war eine von ihren vielen Eigenheiten, dass sie bei solchen Gelegenheiten in der dritten Person von sich sprach. Auch wenn sie erzählte, nannte sie sich nur Lisette, und sagte oft, wenn sie

enclosed one author in another, each speaking in the first person, he could reflect upon his life dialectically; could conjure up the Romantic hero's infinite variety of masks (Kierkegaard was aware of Eichendorff's Romantic revival of the picaresque novel in his *Life of a Ne'er-do-well*), without letting his own life dissolve in indefinite contours. He thus infused the old "trick of the novelist" with new and original meaning. The diversity, density, and perspective of the poetic world, which the omniscient author with the authoritarian point of view creates by introducing and analyzing a variety of characters, is established by Kierkegaard with the help of individual poetized authors, each guiding and interpreting only himself and merely conjecturing about others, but each capable of creating another author-hero with equal propensities.

It is obviously this author-hero who proved himself most expressive of Kierkegaard's existential thought. This seems to indicate once more his affinity with German Romanticism, but it is an affinity which proves deceptive upon closer investigation. Both the figure of the author-hero and the Kierkegaardian concept of "double reflection" conjure up the Künstlerroman, a form of fiction in vogue by the time of his writing, and whose generic designation testifies to its origin and its popularity. We must determine, therefore, to what extent Kierkegaard's author-heroes correspond to those of the genre which German Romanticism had produced and to what extent they differ from them. We must do so particularly in view of the fact that the author-hero has held extraordinary appeal for some of the most outstanding novelists of the twentieth century and has been strikingly reincarnated in Sartre's *Nausea*.

---

schreiben könnte, wollte sie ihre eigene Geschichte schreiben, aber so als ob es ein andrer wäre. Cf. also p. 202: "Auch er erinnerte sich an die Vergangenheit und sein Leben ward ihm, indem er es ihr erzählte, zum ersten Mal zu einer gebildeten Geschichte."

It was, of course, at the end of the eighteenth century that artistic genius came to be considered as "the highest human type" and to replace such "earlier ideal types as the hero, the 'sage,' the Saint, the *uomo universale,* the *cortigiano,* the *honnête homme,"* as Herbert Dieckmann has so keenly observed.[24] It is, therefore, in certain observations Friedrich Schlegel made about Romantic poetry, and which he published in 1798 as "Fragmente" in the *Athenaeum,* that we find an adumbration of the Künstlerroman. He stated that Romantic poetry (poetry in the German sense in which it includes the novel) had developed forms most receptive to and expressive of the author's mind, so that the Romantic novelist described himself in his work. Schlegel found Romantic poetry floating as it were midway between what is poetized and the poet, forever reflecting upon what had been reflected and multiplying it in a series of mirrors.[25] More appropriately yet, he felt the poetry of his time should combine artistic reflection with self-mirroring so that the poet inadvertently included himself in his presentations, thereby creating poetry as well as poetry of poetry.[26] Nor was it new to

24. Herbert Dieckmann, "Diderot's Conception of Genius," *Journal of the History of Ideas* 2 (1941), 151. See also Edith Kern, "The Modern Hero, Phoenix or Ashes?" *Comparative Literature* 10 (Fall 1958), 325–34 and *The Hero in Literature,* ed. Victor Brombert (Greenwich, Conn., Fawcett Publications, 1969), pp. 266–77.

25. Friedrich Schlegel states in his Fragment 116 that Romantic poetry

> kann gleich dem Epos ein Spiegel der ganzen umgebenden Welt, ein Bild des Zeitalters werden. Und doch kann auch sie am meisten zwischen dem Dargestellten und dem Darstellenden, frei von allem realen und idealen Interesse auf den Flügeln der poetischen Reflexion in der Mitte schweben, diese Reflexion immer wieder potenzieren und wie in einer endlosen Reihe von Spiegeln vervielfachen.

26. In Fragment 238, Friedrich Schlegel maintains that the poetry of his day should combine poetic matter "mit der künstlerischen Reflexion und schönen Selbstbespiegelung, die sich im Pindar, den ly-

the eighteenth century, as Oskar Walzel reminds us, "to divide the ego into an observing subject and an observed object."[27] Schlegel himself had presented Julius, the protagonist of his novel *Lucinde,* as a self-reflective author-hero. In the Prologue, Julius, specifically referring to Cervante's Prologue to *Don Quixote,* sends his "offspring" into the world. But within the work itself, interest is centered not so much on Julius as artist or author but rather on his desire to live poetically.

Julius' brief authorial appearance in the Prologue does not warrant the novel's classification as a Künstlerroman. Of such incidental self-portrayals, many examples can be found in art and literature long before the actual inception of the genre, as the reference to *Don Quixote* clearly indicates. To mention but a few, we may recall the well-known self-portrait of the medieval German poet Walther von der Vogelweide, who presented himself in the traditional pose of the Thinker, seated on a stone wth his legs crossed, his elbow on his knee, and chin and cheek resting in the hollow of his hand. We may think of Montaigne's disarmingly candid portrayal of himself. Velasquez might come to mind with his baroque presentation of his own figure in the process of painting the King and Queen of Spain whom we see mirrored in the picture entitled "Las Meninas." Or the manner in which Cervantes invites the reader directly to share his problems in composing the Prologue to his novel. Even Molière, whose personal feelings will probably remain forever unknown to us, managed to put his own likeness into *L'Impromptu de Versailles,* so that we have glimpses of him at work as playwright, actor, and director. Such attempts at self-portrayal

---

rischen Fragmenten der Griechen, und der alten Elegie, unter den Neuern aber in Goethe findet, vereinigen, und überall zugleich Poesie und Poesie der Poesie sein."

27. Oskar Walzel, *German Romanticism,* trans. A. E. Lussky (New York and London, Putnam, 1932), p. 24.

may create an atmosphere of irony, may place the work in an off-center baroque perspective, but are never central to the work.

In the truly representative Künstlerroman, however, the artist not only takes up the center of the stage but also lends the work his name. He is presented above all as a fictional not an auto-biographical character—though he may well elicit identification with the author. Among the first to produce such novels were two of Schlegel's closest friends, Tieck and Novalis, both engaged in writing in the genre at the very time when Schlegel expressed the theories that semed to foreshadow it and when he himself was working on his *Lucinde*. Schlegel's correspondence with these friends gives evidence of the close contact which then existed between them.[28] Tieck called his novel *Sternbalds Wanderungen (The Peregrinations of Sternbald)*, a title which suggests the artist-hero's development through travel and which clearly indicates that the Künstlerroman was also thought of as a Bildungsroman.[29] Novalis chose a medieval poet as the hero for his Künstlerroman and used the poet's name as title for his work. *Heinrich von Ofterdingen* is a highly lyrical, fictionalized biography of the poet, not only telling his life in episodic fashion but also showing him made incandescent by the spirit of poetry. The blue flower—symbol of poetry—which Heinrich sets out to find is to resolve magically all the difficulties and contradic-

28. *Friedrich Schlegel und Novalis: Biographie einer Romantiker-freundschaft in ihren Briefen,* ed. Max Preitz (Darmstadt, Gentner Verlag, 1957). See, for instance, pp. 156, 157, 159, 160, 225–31.

29. Tieck's unfinished *Sternbald* is a glorification of the individual and of genius. It is told in episodic form and is the fictional biography of an artist who begins by apprenticing himself to Dürer. In his wanderings he comes to know the great schools of painting of Italy and Holland, and art moves him to almost religious fervor. Novelistic and descriptive passages alternate with long theoretical disquisitions on painting. Today it is the novel's historical significance rather than its inherent value that deserves our attention.

tions of life. Poetry is to enable him to transcend time and space and to make all things an integral part of the great world harmony. In order to become a poet, Ofterdingen must decipher the hieroglyphs of Nature. Only then can he detect the unity underlying its manifoldness and transpose its language into the language of man.[30] Walzel has pointed out that Novalis' Romantic yearning for infinity, which he presents symbolically in the blue flower, had been portended in a letter Friedrich Schlegel had written to his brother Wilhelm in 1792 in which he specified the flower as a source of love both for God and woman. "It was the creed of a yearning which, about to soar into illimitable spaces beyond mere temporal existence, could nevertheless, find twofold satisfaction and peace in this world: in love and in poetry."[31] It is this almost priest-like conception of the poet, mystically united with the very ground of Being, which seems to have found an echo in such modern thinkers as Nietzsche and Heidegger.

The second part of Goethe's *Faust,* though obviously somewhere between a novel and a play, suggests a similar and equally modern conception of the artist. From its wealth of meanings one might easily isolate one that makes it a poet's epiphany. The play seems to show the poet in various guises and different stages of development. At its beginning, a Boy-Charioteer, taking part in the *Carnaval,* turns out to be a poet who, by dint of his rich

30. Since human conceptions of time are annulled in the novel, the adventures of Ofterdingen, those he experienced in the past and those he is to experience in the future, are recorded in a book he discovers in a hermit's cave. To become a poet, Ofterdingen must also learn to decipher the hermit's book. It is interesting to notice the tremendous influence here as elsewhere of Cervantes' *Don Quixote.* Ofterdingen's discovery of the hermit's book is obviously patterned after Cervantes' faked discovery of the Arabic manuscript that contained the exploits Don Quixote was to engage in.

31. Walzel, *German Romanticism,* p. 30.

imagination, can conjure up spangles and jewels for all. Goethe later referred to him as an "allegorical being" personifying poetry "which is bound neither to time, place, nor person." Euphorion, born of the union of Faust and Helena, is still another stage and aspect of the poet. Even less substantial than the Boy-Charioteer, he was to be capable of being "present everywhere and at all times."[32] Faust could father him only, upon having dared, in loneliness and fear, the descent to the Mothers, the very ground of Being—an adventure truly resembling the passage of a hero. In the realm of the Mothers, Faust had to face not only the mysterious powers of creation but also those of death and perpetual recreation. Yet, both as a poet and a man, Faust was yet to reach a maturer stage upon his encounter with Care. The symbolism of this encounter is derived from a fable by Hygius which tells of Care sitting by the river and playfully shaping man out of clay. When Jupiter breathes life into the creature, a quarrel ensues as to who owns him, and it is decided that Care has charge of him as long as he lives, that Jupiter may take possession of him upon his death, and that the Earth (*humus*), from which he was formed, may impose its name upon him: *homo*. At the end of Goethe's play, Care's touch makes Faust blind, but it symbolically turns him into the poet, the seer, and the sage. More recently, however, Heidegger, inspired by the same fable, has considered anguish and care essential to the authenticity of man.[33]

Though the author-heroes of Tieck, Novalis, and Goethe (we might have mentioned not only his Faust but also his Wil-

32. Wolfgang von Goethe, *Faust II,* ed. and trans. Bayard Taylor, 2 (Boston, Houghton Mifflin, 1898), 334–40.

33. K. Burdach, "Faust und die Sorge," *Deutsche Vierteljahrschrift für Literaturwissenschaft und Geistesgeschichte, 1* (1923), 1 ff. Cited by Martin Heidegger, *Being and Time,* trans. J. Macquarrie and Edward Robinson (London, SCM Press, 1962), p. 242.

helm Meister) were possibly known to Kierkegaard,[34] his own author-heroes, encased one in the other, are, as we have seen, of a different nature. Their functions are more circumscribed, their experiences more limited. We might presume that Kierkegaard, seeing a similar relationship between poetry and religion, might have felt himself in stronger agreement with German Romanticists, had he better understood them. But what is essential is that his heroes do not have to progress toward authorship. Their authorial qualities are never questioned. Since Kierkegaard, whose possibles they represent, did not wish to become an artist but a Christian, he would rather have them subservient to this task. They are, clearly, not created for their own sake and development but rather in order to add depth, density, and diversity to the universe of the isolated individual, ultimately engaged in becoming a "Knight of Faith." While it is essential in Kierkegaardian terms that they be authors and express their life-views in audible lines, they remain the poetically actual individualities Kierkegaard *produced.* Though each solo, these authors tell together of *his* quest and *his* religious concern.

Kierkegaard's author-heroes alone cannot, therefore, have occasioned Sartre's return to the Künstlerroman in *Nausea,* nor the widespread renascence of the genre in our time. In *Nausea,* the Romantic concept of the hero's becoming an author seems fused with the existential concept of man becoming authentic. Before turning to Sartre's novel, therefore, we should ascertain how this fusion was made possible. In attempting to do this, we cannot overlook the seminal parts played, at least in France, by Gide and Proust, with whose works Sartre was, of course, well acquainted.

Gide's own inclinations, his *culte du moi,* and his Symbolist friends, all had led him to Novalis, Goethe, and Nietzsche. At one time, he had planned to translate *Ofterdingen,* considering

34. Kierkegaard frequently refers to Goethe and his *Faust.* See, for instance, *CI,* 16, 17, 18, 20 ff., 226, 337, 338, 356, 394, 396, 407.

such a translation of the highest importance, though he actually never completed it.[35] It was apparently through him that the Künstlerroman, which seems to have held no appeal whatsoever to the scientifically and socially oriented nineteenth century, found a place in the French literature of his time.[36] Gide had acquainted himself not only with Goethe's *Faust II,* but also with his *Wilhelm Meister, Tasso,* and *Prometheus*—play, novel, play, and poem respectively, each having a poet-creator as protagonist. Gide's own work reflects in its entirety this preoccupation with the artist's, the writer's, becoming. His *Cahiers d'André Walter* (1891) represents his first tribute to this concern. As it shows Walter recording his *drame intime,* it also shows him as the author projecting a novel. *Traité de Narcisse,* published the same

35. By the end of the nineteenth century, Novalis' mysticism held strong appeal for the youth of France and especially the Symbolists. His thoughts seemed to be in the air so that even those who had not read his works were familiar with them. His writings were so steadily gaining in prestige that Maeterlinck and Gide divided them among themselves for the purpose of translating them. Gide, however, never completed his share of the task which he had assumed with much enthusiasm. Yet this was not for lack of appreciation, for he reminded himself in an entry in his *Journal,* dated 1893, that he should attend to this translation without delay. Cf. Renée Lang, *Gide et la Pensée allemande* (Paris, L. U. F. Egloff, 1949), esp. pp. 72, 19.

36. Cf. Susanne Howe, *Wilhelm Meister and His English Kinsmen* (New York, Columbia University Press, 1930), passim. In this history of the genre in the English literature of the nineteenth century, it appears that such writers as Carlyle, Disraeli, and Bulwer-Lytton adopted and maintained it. But the picture that emerges is an uninspired one: interest centers more and more upon the protagonist's moral development and there is less and less stress on his development as a poet or artist. In France the genre is almost totally unknown during the nineteenth century, unless we think of such works as Balzac's *Le Chef-d'oeuvre inconnu* or Zola's *L'Oeuvre* and his *Ébauche de l'Oeuvre,* which place artistic creation at the center of attention without, however, attempting to present the artist's development or his insight into his art. There are also works, of course, that show the artist in conflict with society, such as *Chatterton.*

year, portrays its protagonist as the poet in quest of form and discovering it in his own image as it is fleetingly and changeably reflected upon the water.[37] While Gide's interest in the genre prevailed through the years and found added expression in his decision to translate Rilke's *Notebooks of Malte Laurids Brigge,* also a Künstlerroman,[38] it was climaxed by *The Counterfeiters* (1926). But by the time of this novel's publication, Gide had undergone other powerful influences, that of Nietzsche and, most likely, that of Proust, which have undeniably shaped his work.

It was particularly in *The Birth of Tragedy* that Nietzsche had expressed notions on art and the artist which have not yet ceased

37. Lang, *Gide,* pp. 71, 84–85, 45.

38. Rilke had begun this diary of a poet in the years 1903–04 but did not complete it until 1908–10. His protagonist, Malte, is as "I"-centered as are those of Gide's *Cahiers* and *Narcisse.* When the poet started the work, he seems to have thought of it mainly in autobiographical terms. For he later wrote to a friend "Malte Laurids has developed into a figure which, quite detached from me, acquired existence and personality, and interested me the more intensely the more differentiated it became from myself" (Rainer Maria Rilke, *The Notebooks of Malte Laurids Brigge,* trans. H. Norton [New York, Putnam, 1958], p. 7). But the author's very attempt to dissociate himself from the author-hero seems only to emphasize their initial oneness. Critics have discovered parallels between Malte and early Gidean characters, and Rilke is said to have been highly flattered when the famous Gide, several years his senior, offered to translate the work into French. Unfortunately, Gide's intentions never materialized, perhaps because Rilke's poet-hero remained after all too foreign to the French author. In an attitude foreshadowing modern existential thought, Rilke's Malte stressed the importance of loneliness and death, and his first-person writing did not correspond so much to Gide's *culte du moi* but was rather an expression of the poet's conviction that the "third person" was a "ghost who never was . . . one of the pretexts of Nature who is always endeavoring to divert the attention of men from her deepest secrets" (*Malte,* p. 27). Even with his quest for a new language, Malte foreshadowed modern concerns of the writer rather than indulging in the symbolism of an André or a Narcisse.

to captivate the mind of writers and critics. Gide was well acquainted with the philosopher's work. In an article entitled "Lettre à Angèle" and published in *L'Ermitage* in 1898, he displayed considerable knowledge of Nietzsche's writings and made specific reference to *The Birth of Tragedy* (1871).[39] Although Nietzsche differentiated in his work between two strains of poetry, the Apollonian and the Dionysiac, and considered Greek tragedy the perfect union of both, he came to emphasize more and more strongly the importance of the Dionysiac. He considered Dionysus not only the god of music and poetry but also the prototype of all tragic Greek heroes who merely assumed different aspects in different tragedies. While Apollo, as the apotheosis and the principle of individuation, demanded "Know thyself," Dionysus represented an abandoning of the principle of individuation. Nietzsche saw in the mythical death and rebirth of the god of wine man's metaphysical consolation, his triumph over subjectivity and deliverance from Self. To him, artistic creativity of real depth could result only from such Dionysiac abandonment of the Self, and he felt that the distinction usually made between subjective and objective art had no

39. Translations of Nietzsche's work had appeared in France as early as 1877, and by about 1891 young French intellectuals proclaimed him in the pages of such periodicals as *La Revue Blanche, Le Mercure de France, Le Banquet* as the "new prophet" and eagerly spread what they considered his liberating thought. To those who could not read him in the original, he became available through these discussions as well as through translations. Fragments and outlines of his works were published. By 1893, the well-known French critic, Henri Albert, claimed that Nietzsche was so famous in France that one could not open a single periodical without encountering his name. Gide was, as is to be expected, in the forefront of those young men who had acquainted themselves with his writings, for in 1898, he published his "Lettre à Angèle" in *L'Ermitage,* wherein he displayed a considerable knowledge of the philosopher and particularly of his *Birth of Tragedy* (Cf. Lang, *Gide,* pp. 82, 83, 88).

true value in aesthetics—not even with regard to the lyric poet. For to the extent "that the subject is an artist," he maintains in *The Birth of Tragedy,* "he is already delivered from individual will and has become a medium through which the True Subject celebrates His redemption in illusion." The poet "may boldly speak in the first person," but "his 'I' is not that of the actual waking man, but the 'I' dwelling truly and eternally, in the ground of being." Nietzsche's own hallucinatory identification with Dionysus in his later years is well known, and it is quite in keeping with such thinking and feeling that *The Birth of Tragedy* turned out to be not only a remarkable hymn to Dionysiac art but also an adumbration of a new facet of the Künstlerroman. For Nietzsche claimed that our knowledge of art must remain illusory as long as we are mere objective "knowers": "Only as the genius in the act of creation merges with the primal architect of the cosmos can he truly know something of the eternal essence of art. For in that condition he resembles the uncanny fairytale image which is able to see itself by turning its eyes. He is at once subject and object, poet, actor, and audience."[40] The great twentieth-century novelists who have produced Künstlerromane have have tried to achieve precisely this understanding of their art by looking at themselves in the act of creation, though not all have surrendered their subjectivity in equal measure. Under the aegises of Novalis, Goethe, and Nietzsche, their protagonists have assumed the role of the Apollonian or Dionysiac poet, yet it seems mainly due to Nietzsche and, probably, Proust that they have become their own self-reflecting and critical audience. Their critical consciousness of their work sets these author-heroes apart from those of the Romanticists and their more immediate imitators.

40. Friedrich Nietzsche, *The Birth of Tragedy,* trans. Francis Golffing (Garden City, N.Y., Doubleday, Anchor Books, 1956), pp. 41, 39, 42; henceforth cited in the text as *BT.*

Edouard, Gide's protagonist of *The Counterfeiters,* is presented, in Gide's own image, as the writer in the process of writing a novel about a writer writing a novel. It is in the course of this endeavor that he gains insights into the process of artistic creation and perpetually reviews the work he has done. We would, of course, distort Gide's image were we to assume that he merely adopted the ideas of others and to overlook the extent to which these ideas harmonized with something innate in his own genius. Applying what one might call Proust's structural approach to criticism, Jean Hytier detects in this "reduplication of the object within itself" the essential quality of Gide's genius. As early as 1893, Gide had professed in his journal his predilection for seeing things artistically presented *"en abyme."*

> I like discovering in a work of art ... transposed to the scale of the characters, the very subject of that work. Nothing illuminates it better and establishes more surely all the proportions of the whole. Thus in certain paintings by Memling or Quentin Metsys, a tiny dark convex mirror reflects the interior of the room where the scene painted occurs. Similarly in Velasquez' Meninas (though in a different way). Finally, in literature, in Hamlet's play within a play, and in many other dramas. In *Wilhelm Meister,* the marionette scenes or the parties at the château. In *The Fall of the House of Usher,* the passage Roderick is reading, etc. None of these examples is entirely fair. What would be much more so, what would say much better what it is I wanted in my *Cahiers,* in my *Narcisse,* and my *Tentative,* is the comparison with that method in heraldry which consists of putting a second blazon in the center of the first, *en abyme.*[41]

41. Jean Hytier, *André Gide,* (Garden City, N.Y., Doubleday, 1962), pp. 214; 214–15.

It is a brilliant stroke of critical insight on the part of Hytier to have recognized that this self-confessed Gidean attitude towards life and art is reflected in the novelist's entire work and even in his style of writing. But Gide's own inclination seems to have found new nourishment in Nietzsche's *The Birth of Tragedy* and, most likely, in Proust's *Remembrance of Things Past.*

In the *Counterfeiters* the author gives, in general, evidence of Nietzschean thought not yet discernible in his earlier work. In her *Histoire du Roman français* Claude-Edmonde Magny expresses her bewilderment at the statement of Edouard, Gide's author-hero, that he wants to free the novel of all that is extraneous to it and that he designates as such exterior events, realistic dialogue, even the description of characters, in brief, all that is accidental.[42] Indeed, Edouard's statement becomes plausible only in the light of *The Birth of Tragedy.* Gide had recognized in his "Lettre à Angèle" that the theater of his day needed a new ethics and could find it in Nietzsche. He himself had attempted to write such theater in his *Roi Candaule,*[43] and he obviously tried to apply Nietzschean theories along such lines in *The Counterfeiters.* Nietzsche had criticized the theater of his own time, claiming that it "tried to resolve the tragic dissonance in terrestrial terms: after having been sufficiently buffeted by fate, the hero was compensated in the end by a distinguished marriage and divine honors." This, he considerd a deplorable departure from the Dionysiac spirit of tragedy, which conceived of life and death as the perpetual renewal of Being. The metaphysical solace contained in this conception had been replaced, he felt, with genteel domestic drama and with denouements by a *deus ex machina.* He also regretted that poets had come to delineate character so finely that the particular had won

---

42. Claude-Edmonde Magny, *Histoire du Roman français depuis 1918* (Paris, Editions du Seuil, 1950), pp. 243–44.
43. Lang, *Gide,* p. 103.

out over the general, and underlying myths had been forgotten
(*BT*, 88, 106–07). Edouard speaks in pure Nietzschean terms
when he declares that there is a kind of tragedy "which has hitherto almost entirely eluded literature. The novel has dealt with
the contrariness of fate, good or evil fortune, social relationships,
the conflicts of passions and of character—but not with the very
essence of man's being." We detect Nietzschean echoes in his
desire to present an "ideal reality, removed from what is accidental in life"; in his contempt for precise psychological analyses
of character, and his appreciation for Racine's manner of presenting the universal rather than the particular.[44] Edouard, as
Hytier has so well observed, was to be the poet extracting his
novel from the chaos of reality.[45] He searched in the Nietzschean
manner for "an unvarnished expression of truth" and was willing
to "cast away the trumpery garments worn by the supposed reality of civilized man," and to sacrifice the entire phenomenal
world in favor of a search for the eternal core of things (*BT*, 53).
This distinction between the true and the counterfeit is, of
course, at the very heart of the novel, as its title implies. In
terms of the novelist it meant, above all, the task of distilling the
truth of art from the confusion and deception of the phenomenal
world.

Gide's Edouard is so imbued with Nietzschean thought that
he uses, at times, the very concepts and imagery employed by
the philosopher. Thus we find him stating: "The only existence
that anything (including myself) has for me, is poetical—I restore this word in its full signification." He becomes the Dionysiac artist whom Nietzsche envisioned as looking at himself
in the act of creation: "It seems to me sometimes that I do not
really exist, but that I merely imagine I exist. The thing that I

44. André Gide, *The Counterfeiters*, trans. J. O'Brien (New York,
Knopf, 1959), pp. 112, 172, 174, 171.

45. Ibid., pp. 64–65; Cf. *BT*, 106.

have the greatest difficulty in believing in, is my own reality. I am constantly getting outside myself, and as I watch myself act I cannot understand how a person who acts is the same as the person who is watching him act, and who wonders in astonishment and doubt how he can be actor and watcher at the same moment."[46] Edouard seems, indeed, to divest himself of his Self in the process of creation in order to grasp the essence of his art. It is almost inadvertently, through looking at himself in this manner, that he produces a novel, or perhaps an anti-novel— as Sartre has called it in his preface to Nathalie Sarraute's *Portrait of a Man Unknown.*

It is, however, in *Remembrance of Things Past* that, prior to *Nausea,* Nietzsche's adumbration of the Künstlerroman finds its most striking expression, and Gide may well have been familiar with the conception of the author-hero which Proust develops in this novel and which he brings to culmination in its last volume. There is no doubt that Proust knew Nietzsche and that Schopenhauer, moreover, was one of his favorite philosophers. Both are mentioned in his correspondance, where he also makes reference to Goethe's *Wilhelm Meister.*[47] It is equally well known that, since the appearance of the first part of *Remembrance* in 1913, Gide and Proust had become friends. For Gide, as director of La Nouvelle Revue Française, had come to see his mistake in rejecting the work. Even if the publication of Gide's *Counterfeiters* preceded that of Proust's last volume (which appeared five years after his death in 1927), the central problem

46. Gide, *The Counterfeiters,* pp. 64–65.

47. Cf. Walter A. Strauss, *Proust and Literature, The Novelist as Critic* (Cambridge, Harvard University Press, 1957), pp. 160–61. Also Milton Hindus, *A Reader's Guide to Marcel Proust* (New York, Farrar, Straus and Cudahy, 1962), pp. 4, 72, 124–26, 132; Harold March, *The Two Worlds of Marcel Proust* (Philadelphia, University of Pennsylvania Press, 1948), p. 17.

and vision of *Remembrance* was most likely discussed between the two authors.

Marcel, the author-hero of Proust's novel, represents a subjectivity which transcends itself by descending into the depths of the involuntary memory which Nietzsche would designate as Dionysiac rather than Apollonian. One might say of Marcel what Proust says elsewhere of the valid critic: he "dies instantaneously in the particular and begins immediately to float and live again in the general. He lives only by means of the general: it animates and nurtures him. . . . But while he is alive, his existence is but ecstasy and felicity."[48] Proust's protagonist regains lost time, as he slowly and intermittently comes to understand the essence of life and art and of his own vocation as an artist. He descends into the depths of his subconscious mind—accessible only to involuntary memory—in order to find there the "reality" of the world. His narration, like that of the Nietzschean poet, is therefore both subjective and objective. "I now recaptured," he tells us in the course of his development as an artist, "by an instinctive and complete act of recollection, the living reality. That reality has no existence for us, so long as it has not been created anew by our mind."[49] People and objects are for Proust's author-hero only what the mind makes of them. The world is that which is interiorized in the individual, and the artist's vision alone can fuse its disparate parts into a meaningful unity. "I had too often," Marcel realizes, "experienced the impossibility of discovering in physical form what was in the depths my being" *(R, 2, 999)*. He therefore comes to interpret the sensations which his subconscious has registered "as indications

48. Marcel Proust, *Contre Sainte-Beuve* (Paris, Gallimard, 1954), p. 303.

49. Marcel Proust, *Remembrance of Things Past*, trans. F. A. Blossom, 2 (New York, Random House, 1932), p. 1013; henceforth cited in the text as *R*.

of corresponding laws and ideas," and he decides: "I must try to think, that is, to say, bring out of the obscurity what I had felt, and convert it into a spiritual equivalent" (R, 2, 1000). Usually, he finds, involuntary memories are apt to be crowded out by voluntary concerns and recollections, "but if the setting of sensations in which they are preserved be recaptured, they acquire in turn the same power of expelling everything that is incompatible with them, of installing alone in us the self that originally lived them" (R, 2, 114). Such recapturing, however, is the process which Marcel recognizes as artistic creation (R, 2, 1001).

Again it is in Nietzschean terms that the Proustian author-hero thinks of the artist as one who gains understanding of his art by looking at himself in the act of creating and being at once "subject and object, poet, actor, and audience." Referring to nineteenth-century French writers whom he admires, Marcel describes them literally as "watching themselves at work as though they were at once author and critic," and he claims that they "have derived from this self-contemplation a novel beauty, exterior and superior to the work itself, imposing upon it retrospectively a unity, a greatness which it does not possess" (R, 2, 490). The authors he singles out are, above all, Balzac, who retrospectively saw his series of novels as The Human Comedy; Hugo, whose heterogeneous poems afterward appeared to him as The Legend of the Ages; and Baudelaire, whose verses assumed for him the aspect of Fleurs du Mal, that is, Flowers of Evil or Flowers of Suffering. What seems to him crucial, however, is that this unity, though ulterior, was not fictitious— "otherwise it would have crumbled into dust like all the other systematizations of mediocre writers" (R, 2, 491)—but rather "a unity that has been unaware of itself, therefore vital and not logical" (R, 2, 491). It is, indeed, the "irreducibly individual existence" of the artist's soul which becomes visible in the work of art and which its author detects as he looks at himself in the moment of creation. The art of a composer (Vinteuil), a painter (Elstir), or a writer (e.g. Racine) "makes the man himself apparent, rendering externally visible . . . that intimate composition of those worlds which we call individual persons and which, without the aid of art, we should never know" (R, 2, 559). As he considers the work of great writers, Marcel is more and more convinced that they have produced but one work and "refract through various mediums an identical beauty which they bring into the world" (R, 2, 643–44). He who knows to read their works—be he critic or the author himself—will recognize in it the *phrases types* that epitomize the essence of their self.

It is this fundamentally Nietzschean vision of the self-reflecting artist which is personified in Proust's author-hero himself and which makes him more original and complex than any author-hero created before him. Even the difference between Proust's earlier novel *Jean Santeuil* (written in 1896 but published only posthumously in 1952) and his mature work is to be accounted for mainly by the profound grasp of the unity of existence and art which such self-contemplation affords Marcel and for which Proust may well have found inspiration in the works of Nietzsche and Schopenhauer. For, with regard to a large number of its episodes, *Jean Santeuil* may be considered a prefiguration of *Remembrance*. If it falls short of the greatness of the later work, this is precisely because its protagonist, not being a self-reflecting artist, fails to attain a unified vision of existence and art. The French critic Bernard Dort seems to me to have been wrong, therefore, when he refers to *Remembrance,* in a mixture of admiration and scorn, as "cette tentative admirable et insensée de l'oeuvre pour être à elle-même son propre objet, son principe et son produit, sa cause et sa vérité,"[50] and

50. Bernard Dort, "A la Recherche du Roman," *Cahiers du Sud, 42* (1955), 347: "that admirable and insane attempt of a work to be its own object, its own principle and product, its cause and its truth."

speaks of its autotelic character as indicative of the novel in full crisis. It would seem rather that the intuitive insights which Marcel attains at the end of the novel rival in character and importance those of Descartes' cogito and Newton's law of gravity. The artistic epiphany at which the author-hero arrives permits of that meaningful integration of human existence at which all philosophic and scientific endeavor is aimed. Indeed, Proust makes an indirect plea that it be granted the same importance (*R, 2,* 1008).

Like Nietzsche's Dionysiac poet, Proust's Marcel sees art as a redemption of life. The six specific arts which make their appearance in *Remembrance*—drama, sculpture, architecture, painting, music, and literature—all lead to Marcel's final vision and illumination. Perhaps a seventh art should be added, that of criticism. They all lead him to realize that "this work of the artist, to seek, to discern something different underneath material experience, words, is exactly the reverse of the process which, during every minute that we live with our attention diverted from ourselves, is being carried on within us by pride, passion, intelligence and also by our habits, when they hide our true impressions from us by burying them under the mass of nomenclatures and practical aims which we erroneously call life. After all, that art, although so complicated, is actually the only living art" (*R, 2,* 1013). Marcel comes to despise, therefore, the life of habit as well as that of immediate purpose, realizing, like Nietzsche's Dionysiac poet, "that everything that is generated must be prepared to find its painful dissolution." He too forces us "to gaze into the horror of individual existence," nevertheless providing us with the "metaphysical solace" that the death of the particular means—the continuation of the soul, that is, of the artist's essence. This solace "lifts us above the whirl of shifting phenomena," as Nietzsche puts it, and leads man to the recognition that it is not the "I" that ultimately counts, not the individual appearance and phenomenon, but rather the "fecundity of the world will of which he is but a part" (*BT*, 102–03).

Like the medieval alchemist, the Proustian artist transforms his individual impressions and finds the underlying substance that binds them all. In this spirit Proust, like Nietzsche, rejects all art which is conceived merely as an imitation of reality. "Some," Marcel states, "wished the novel to be a sort of cinematographic parade. This conception was absurd. In reality, nothing is farther removed than this cinematographic view from what we have perceived ... [and] literature which is satisfied to 'describe objects,' to give merely a miserable listing of lines and surfaces, is the very one which, while styling itself 'realist,' is the farthest removed from reality" (*R*, 2, 1003–05). It is also quite in keeping with Nietzschean thought that Marcel believes that it is music (considered by Nietzsche the art of Dionysus) that is the purest expression of the essence of existence, making man's feelings "visible" and representing those that are impenetrable by intelligence. "This music," he says of a piece by Vinteuil, "seemed to me to be something truer than all the books that I knew. Sometimes I thought that this was due to the fact that what we feel in life, not being felt in the form of ideas, its literary (that is to say an intellectual) translation in giving an account of it, explains it, analyses it, but does not recompose it as does music, in which the sounds seem to assume the inflexion of the thing itself" (*R*, 2, 642). Nietzsche, emulating Schopenhauer, had proclaimed that music renders, above all, *das Ding an sich*, the object in its very essence and *sine materia* (*BT*, 99). Likewise, Marcel wants to "extract the real essence of life in a book," (R2:1112) because, next to music, writing has become to him "the most real of all things," the justification of his own existence and that of the universe.

Proust's narrator speaks—as does Nietzsche's Dionysiac poet —"boldly in the first person," and it is equally true of him that "his 'I' is not that of the actual waking man, but the 'I' dwelling truly and eternally in the ground of being." We know that Proust's choice of a first-person narrator for *Remembrance* was a conscious one and represents a departure from *Jean Santeuil* as well as from the original plan of his later novel. Indeed, his entire conception of the artist as the individual storing up the essence of his particular world within the realm of his involuntary memory, where it becomes communicable only through art, cannot be separated from a first-person experience. At the same time, as Proust differentiates between voluntary and involuntary memory, so he distinguishes between the writer as man and as artist or author. His novel abounds in situations which give striking evidence of the obvious separation of these two aspects of the creative individual. Almost all the artist figures which it contains—writers, painters, and musicians—border in their personal existence on the trivial, the insignificant, the absurd, while their works speak the language of genius. The same may be said of the novel's protagonist, who, only through his ultimate artistic vision, is lifted from the realm of ordinary social snobbery into the isolation of genius. In his literary criticism and criticism of criticism Proust has equally emphasized the separation of man and artist. He severely censured Sainte-Beuve for having judged Baudelaire the poet by Baudelaire the man, concluding that an individual may be completely ignorant of what the poet who lives within him desires.[51]

Because of this paradoxical view of the author's subjectivity as essential to the work of art and yet being that of a *moi* other than that of the man, Proust was faced with technical problems of narration not unlike those of Kierkegaard—though for different reasons. While the first-person narrative of his author-hero clearly established a sort of identification with the author himself, this identification was not allowed to include Proust the

51. Proust, *Contre Sainte-Beuve*, p. 176.

man. This paradoxical attitude is reflected in the ironic form of the novel. The "I" of the author-hero is only belatedly, as if inadvertently, identified as Marcel, which is, of course Proust's first name. In an equally offhand manner the author-hero refers to a study on Ruskin in which he is engaged which is actually a study that Proust himself published. Outside the novel Proust created the same ambiguous situation with regard to any identification between author-hero and actual author qua man. For instance, in an article which Proust wrote on the style of Flaubert,[52] he refers to his novel's protagonist as saying "I" although he should not always be considered identical with him. In the novel itself, the same distinction between Marcel-hero and Marcel-narrator is maintained and explained above all in terms of time. "If the reader," Marcel-narrator comments at one point, "has no more than a faint impression of these [his sentiments], that is because, as narrator, I reveal my sentiments to him at the same time as I repeat my words . . . I was but imperfectly aware of the nature which guided my actions; at present I have a clear conception of its subjective truth." For its objective truth he cannot vouch even then (*R, 2, 624*). Indeed, the multiformity of character which in terms of both time and vision belongs to the Proustian world and accounts for its three-dimensional psychology, adds to the ambiguity and hence the irony of narrative technique. As many critics have observed, the figures of Swann, Charlus, and Bloch parallel and complement that of Marcel in *Remembrance.* Proust himself has metaphorically given expression to this distribution of an authorial subjectivity. He compares Swann, who recalls a dream wherein he is both actor and observer, to a novelist who has "distributed his own personality between two characters, him who was the 'first person' in the dream, and another whom he saw before him" (*R, 1, 379*). One

52. Marcel Proust, "A propos du 'style' de Flaubert," in *Chroniques* (Paris, Gallimard, 1927), p. 210.

almost sees duplicated here the fictional technique of a Kierkegaard: Proust has invented a Marcel-narrator who tells the story
told to Marcel-hero by Swann, who is himself both actor and
observer in this dream-story within the story.

If we turn our attention now to Sartre, his indebtedness to his
two French predecessors, Gide and Proust, becomes only too
obvious. Indeed, when writing *Nausea,* he may well have been
acquainted with some of the great Künstlerromane written in
other languages, such as Rilke's *Malte Laurids Brigge,* some of
Thomas Mann's or Herman Hesse's novels,[53] James Joyce's

53. In the self-reflective manner suggested by Nietzsche, Thomas
Mann—beginning with *Tonio Kröger* and through *Doktor Faustus,*
Lotte in Weimar, and *Felix Krull*—presented the artist in what seemed
to him the three most important aspects of artistic existence: as a man
partaking of divine harmony, as a holy sinner who has sacrificed his life
and happiness to the daemonic in art, and as a being who has understood the playfulness and lightness of art. Dionysiac abandon and Apollonian harmony seem to hold sway alternately, but it is usually Apollonian clarity which prevails.

Hermann Hesse, whose protagonists are almost all artists or writers,
established his affinity with Novalis by entitling one of his early
stories "Der Novalis" (1907). He also stressed the link between his
own *Magister Ludi* and Goethe's *Wilhelm Meister* by calling one of its
protagonists Knecht (servant) in contrast to Meister (master). The
problem of art and the artist so preoccupied Hesse that he wrote two fictitious autobiographies, both allegories of the artist. The first, *Childhood
of the Magician,* identifies art with magic and the artist with the magician. The second, *Brief Vita,* has as its hero the fictionalized author who
defies and overcomes social inroads on his freedom with the power of
his imagination. Having been convicted and imprisoned for having
seduced a young girl, the octogenarian poet paints on his prison wall a
beautiful mountain landscape traversed by a train and regains his freedom by boarding this train. Ralph Freedman (*The Lyrical Novel,*
[Princeton, N.J., Princeton University Press, 1963], pp. 57, 80–81) has
called attention to the frequency with which Hesse both identifies with
and dissociates himself from his heroes by giving them his own name,
his initials, or even pseudonyms which he himself used previously.

Portrait of the Artist, or even Virginia Woolf's work[54]—all

———

Freedman has also observed to what extent the novelist adopted Novalis's notion that each "I" consists of innumerable persons, as the following quote indicates: "Instead of narrowing your world, of simplifying your soul, you will have to become always more world" (quoted by Freedman, from Hesse's *Steppenwolf*). Hesse's concept of the artist is perhaps best illustrated by the "Treatise" which is given to the author-hero of *Steppenwolf* (1927). It makes the artist aware of the fragmentation inherent in existence and leads him beyond his initial concept of a dual Self. True art—and drama in particular—should, according to Hesse, never "assume an enduring form of the Self," as the Greeks did, but should rather, "like the Indian epic, present all of its characters as aspects of a single Self" (Freedman, p. 80). As the author-hero transcends fragmentation, he becomes the many in One: the whole man and the whole artist. Almost all of Hesse's author-heroes, though speaking in the first person, are thus engaged in overcoming what Nietzsche would have called the "principium individuationis," the principle of individuation.

54. It was especially in his *Portrait of the Artist as a Young Man* (1914–16) that James Joyce created an author-hero in whom art triumphed over subjectivity in the manner of Nietzsche's Dionysiac artist. Yet Joyce's source of inspiration may have to be sought elsewhere. In his "Dante . . . Bruno. Vico . . . Joyce" (in *Our Exagmination Round His Factification For Incamination of Work in Progress* [1961]), Samuel Beckett pointed out the ideational link that exists between Joyce and Vico. Yet to the extent that they affect the author-hero, Vico's notions easily fuse with those of Nietzsche. Beckett quotes him, for instance, as considering "individuality . . . the concretion of universality, and every individual action . . . at the same time superindividual. The individual and the universal cannot be considered as distinct from each other" (p. 7). Stephen, Joyce's author-hero, gives theoretical expression as to what he considers the role of the author with regard to his work, and it is necessary here to quote the well-known passage in some detail. He sees "the simplest epical form . . . emerging out of lyrical literature when the artist prolongs and broods upon himself as the centre of an epical event." He sees this form progressing "till the centre of emotional gravity is equidistant from the artist himself and from others." Then "the narrative is no longer purely personal. The personality of the artist passes into the narration itself, flowing round and round the

showing a revival of Romantic notions of the artist infused with

persons and the action like a vital sea." Using as an example the old English ballad *Turpin Hero,* which begins in the first person and ends in the third person, Stephen maintains that "the personality of the artist, at first a cry or a cadence or a mood and then a fluid and lambent narrative, finally refines itself out of existence, impersonalizes itself, so to speak . . . The mystery of aesthetic like that of material creation is accomplished. The artist, like the God of creation, remains within or behind or beyond or above his handiwork, invisible, refined out of existence, indifferent, paring his fingernails" (*Portrait of the Artist* [New York, Viking Press, 1960], pp. 214–15). Leon Edel, somewhat disagreeing with Joyce, has interpreted the passage in almost Nietzschean terms and has claimed that the Irish writer "is not quite right in saying that the artist has been, by this process, refined out of existence." Edel finds him to remain "after all, within, behind, above, or beyond the work—and not too far beyond . . . like those dreams we have in which we are both the actor and the audience; in which we act and also stand by watching ourselves in action" (*The Modern Psychological Novel* [New York, Grove Press, 1955], p. 120).

Writing Künstlerromane in the same language as Joyce, Virginia Woolf seems to have been equally concerned with the passage from the artistic Self to depersonalization. Her views on this matter, which have found expression in almost all of her novels, were discussed theoretically in her essay, "The Narrow Bridge of Art" (1927). These views contain many Nietzschean, notions, although they may not have been derived from him directly. Like him, she rejects psychological motivation of character and environmental influences, opting for a literature concerned with man's primary problems of life and death rather than with his falling in and out of love. She envisioned a novel of a vaster scope and a more impersonal approach, concerned with ideas, dreams, imagination, poetry, and peopled with mythlike characters. Ralph Freedman has pointed out with much acumen that in *To the Lighthouse,* for instance, the seemingly realistic marriage of the Ramseys must be seen rather as the archetypal union of the sterile, intellectual male and the fecund, sense-directed female (*Lyrical Novel,* pp. 188, 228 ff.). This marriage, imbued as it is with such mythical motifs as lighthouse, skull, and water, becomes the artistic catalyst for the development of the young artist dwelling in the midst of its atmosphere, participating, observing, and creating aesthetically.

Nietzschean concepts. There can be no doubt that the Sartrean author-hero Roquentin, shown in the process of becoming an artist, is the poet looking at himself in the act of creation and becoming cognizant of the essence of art. Yet Roquentin, as we shall see, symbolizes at the same time existential man at his most authentic, so that he proves both an affirmation and a modification of the Kierkegaardian author-hero.

SARTRE

Ostensibly Sartre did not think of himself as an existentialist until Gabriel Marcel and other French journalists, toward the end of the second World War, conferred the epithet upon him. He had employed the term neither in the title nor the body of his first comprehensive philosophical work, *Being and Nothingness,* which had been called by him rather *L'Étre et le Néant, essai d'Ontologie phénoménologique* (1943).[1] When he wrote this work, the terms "existentialism" and "existentialist" were probably as little known to him as they were to Simone de Beauvoir who, as we have seen, registered amazement at hearing them used in reference to herself.[2] By 1945, as she recorded in her Memoirs, her novel *Le Sang des Autres,* had been catalogued as *roman existentialiste,* a label which was subsequently attached to all her works as well as those of Sartre.[3] Merleau-Ponty insists that Sartre protested at first, but finally doubted his right to ob-

1. We shall refer henceforth to the English translation: *Being and Nothingness,* trans. Hazel Barnes (New York, Philosophical Library, 1956).

2. Kern, *Sartre,* pp. 2–3; Simone de Beauvoir, *The Prime of Life,* trans. Peter Green (Cleveland and New York, World Publishing Co., 1962), p. 433.

3. Simone de Beauvoir, *La Force des Choses* (Paris, Gallimard, 1963), pp. 49–50. See Richard Howard's English translation:

Blood of Others was published in September [1945] . . . It was

ject to the way in which Others saw him.[4] Such yielding on his
part is understandable, moreover, because *Being and Nothingness* deals so prominently with the problem of existence that the
epithet "existentialist" does not seem inappropriate or alien to
its spirit. Even in Sartre's early novel, *Nausea,* existence is of
central concern, and there are echoes of Kierkegaardian and
Heideggerian thought—though often imbued with new meaning. Since his deliberate adoption of the term existentialism—
in a talk given in 1945 and published a year later under the title
Existentialism Is a Humanism[5]—Sartre has been considered the
existentialist par excellence.

As a philosopher of existence or an existentialist, Sartre—like
Simone de Beauvoir and Merleau-Ponty—has stressed the affinity
between his philosophy and literature. To a philosophical school
that endeavors to see man not in the abstract, not statically, but
as a dynamic being plunged into the midst of his universe, fiction
in its capacity of being ambiguous and inconclusive serves as a
more appropriate means of expression than the philosophical

---

labeled not only a "Resistance novel" but also an "Existentialist
novel." Henceforth this label was to be affixed automatically to any
work by Sartre or myself. During a discussion organized during the
summer by the Cerf publishing house—in other words, by the
Dominicans—Sartre had refused to allow Gabriel Marcel to apply
this adjective to him: "My philosophy is a philosophy of existence;
I don't even know what Existentialism is." I shared his irritation.
I had written my novel before I had even encountered the term
Existentialist; my inspiration came from my own experience, not
from a system. But our protests were vain. In the end, we took the
epithet that everyone used for us and used it for our own purposes.
[*The Force of Circumstance* (New York, Putnam, 1965), pp.
37–38].

4. Maurice Merleau-Ponty, *Sense and Non-Sense,* trans. Hubert L.
Dreyfus (Evanston, Illinois, Northwestern University Press, 1964), p.
47.

5. Jean-Paul Sartre, *Existentialism is a Humanism,* trans. Bernard
Frechtman (New York, Philosophical Library, 1947).

essay, expected to be based on premises and logical proofs. Sartre has ostensibly been drawn as much to the novel, the short story, and the drama as to theoretical exposition. And as if this were not enough to bring him to the attention of literary criticism, he himself has indulged in such criticism and has particularly challenged it by maintaining that "A fictional technique always relates back to the novelist's metaphysics" and that it is "the critic's task . . . to define the latter before evaluating the former."[6] What, then, is the relationship between Sartre's metaphysics and his fictional techniques? Again—as in the case of Kierkegaard—not all facets of his philosophy are of equal relevance to this question and we shall restrict ourself to the discussion of those of which his fictional techniques seem expressive.

If we consider Sartrean thinking in this perspective, we find that it owes much to Kierkegaard and almost as much to Heidegger, though it has transcended these sources by finding its own originality. All three philosophers are concerned with authenticity, but the term may mean integrity, a search for the Truth of Being, an acceptance of the absurdity of existence, faith, or—in specifically ethical terms—man's assumption of what Dostoevsky's Grand Inquisitor called his "terrible freedom" and his burdensome responsibility to make decisions rather than conform to prevailing rules and theoretical systems. All three are concerned with man as the existent individual in his relationship to the universe as well as to others: the Other. Thinking of man as an existent, Sartre conceives of him, as Heidegger does, as Being-in-the-world, a world that reveals itself to him and that he establishes with the help of language, which is as much a part of Being as man himself. Since the writer is an existent who aesthetically creates fictional existents, Sartre's metaphysics have presented him with problems quite similar to

6. Jean-Paul Sartre, "On the Sound and the Fury: Time in the Work of Faulkner," p. 84.

Kierkegaard's concerning his fictional techniques. Yet some new insights gained by modern thought allow the novelist more leeway and a greater variety of formal solutions within the framework of existential thought.

It is interesting in this regard to look, first of all, at the formal similarities and dissimilarities between Kierkegaard's "Diary of the Seducer" and Sartre's first published novel, *Nausea.*[7] Both have a narrator who is at once protagonist and witness. Writing in the first person, he makes us see others, the world of objects around him, and himself through his own consciousness and within the range of that consciousness. Both have fictitious "editors." But while Kierkegaard's editors are very much in evidence and willing to put forth certain views and hypotheses, Sartre's do not emerge as definite individuals but rather—like Sartre himself—completely efface themselves behind the narrator. As a consequence, there are in *Nausea* no editorial or authorial comments; no explanations are given, or transitions established between the events recorded in Roquentin's diary. Kierkegaard's Seducer keeps a diary because this is appropriate to the poetic existential actuality which his author has given him. Roquentin, though likewise the keeper of a diary, is more than a diarist, however. He is a writer, and to him writing becomes an existential necessity.

Nausea was published in 1938, although according to its fictitious editors it had been written in 1932. While its conception therefore seems to antedate by several years the time when the term existentialism was coined and propagated, the completion of the novel coincides in part with that period of Sartre's life which he spent as a student of philosophy in Germany, in an intellectual climate, that is, permeated with the thinking of Husserl, Kierkegaard, and Heidegger. Although Sartre did not

7. Jean-Paul Sartre, *Nausea,* trans. Lloyd Alexander (New York, New Directions, 1959); henceforth cited in the text as *N.*

weave around his work as elaborate and intricate a web of editors upon editors as did Kierkegaard, he did pretend that Roquentin's notebooks and a few loose sheets preceding them were published by "editors." These editors are in no way identified, nor are we told how Roquentin's papers fell into their hands. It remains a matter of conjecture on the part of the reader whether the diary was found by chance, whether Roquentin disappeared, or whether he died. Within the fictional world established by Sartre all this remains unknown and unresolved—perhaps in order to evoke the manner in which actual life leaves questions unanswered. Giving no evidence of ever having known the diarist and failing to express any comments concerning the account given by him, the editors seem to have no function other than that of dating the work and noting certain lacunae in the text.

One might wonder, therefore, why Sartre employed "the old trick of the novelist" (see p. 51) in a work which, in many ways, takes issue with traditional techniques of novel writing. In his autobiography, *Words*,[8] published many years later—in 1964 to be precise—Sartre justifies obliquely the existence of these "editors." He speaks there both of his delight in identifying himself with Roquentin and his simultaneous desire to distance himself from any and all of his literary creatures. "I *was* Roquentin," he writes. "I used him to show, without complacency, the texture of my life. At the same time, I was *I*, the elect, the chronicler of Hell, a glass and steel photomicroscope, peering at my own protoplasmic juices" (*W*, 251–52). Underneath such statements we detect the concept of Kierkegaardian subjectivity which considers the author and his protagonist as essentially identical. This

8. Jean-Paul Sartre, *The Words*, trans. B. Frechtman (New York, George Braziller, 1964); henceforth cited in the text as *W*. Since the correct translation of this title should be *Words* rather than *The Words*, I shall refer to this work as *Words* throughout this study.

conviction seems to permeate all existential writing and has, on occasion, been given explicit expression. Camus, for instance, maintained quite emphatically "That the idea of an art detached from its creator is not only outmoded; it is false."[9] But we detect in Sartre's statement also a need—not unlike Kierkegaard's—to counteract such implicit and explicit identification by means of distancing irony. Another passage in *Words* makes this even more evident. As he relates his first childish encounters with literature and his spontaneous desire to identify with all the heroes of the books he has read, Sartre also reminisces about his early imitative writings and his attitude toward the fictional heroes he created: "As author, the hero was still myself; I projected my epic dreams upon him. All the same, there were two of us: he did not have my name, and I referred to him only in the third person. Instead of endowing him with my gestures, I fashioned for him, by means of words, a body that I made an effort to see. This sudden 'distancing' might have frightened me; it charmed me. I was delighted to be *him* without his quite being me" *(W,* 146–47). (Kierkegaard's discussion of Romantic irony comes to mind, and the Romantic protagonist's propensity for splitting himself into "an observing subject and an observed object," see above, pp. 56–82). *Nausea,* of course, is not a third-person narrative. By its very nature it must be a first-person account. Sartre needed, therefore, a distancing device, even though his protagonist neither bears his name nor has his appearance. In spite of their unobtrusiveness—their existence being established merely by a few prefatory statements and a small number of explanatory footnotes—the editors serve this purpose.

Because of the editors, the protagonist of *Nausea* is twice removed from his author so that an additional obstacle is placed

9. Albert Camus, *The Myth of Sisyphus,* trans. Justin O'Brien (New York, Random House, Vintage Books, 1955), p. 71.

in the way of the reader's inclination to identify the author and his hero. Unlike Kierkegaard however, Sartre wants to counteract such existential identification not for religious but for aesthetic reasons. It is in his essay on Imagination that he re fers to the artistic dilemma facing a novelist who writes a first-person narrative. While aiming at an atmosphere of intimacy, he must at the same time keep the actual world apart from that of fiction. He must prevent the world of reality from invading and thereby corrupting the realm of the imaginary to which the novel belongs.[10] In *What Is Literature?* Sartre likewise stressed the need for such a *recul esthétique,* aesthetic distance, in two directions. On the one hand, "the reader must be able to make a certain withdrawal," on the other, the reader must not "suspect the artist of having written out of passion and in passion," lest his confidence in the work vanish. An author's decision to write, Sartre maintained, "supposes that he withdraw somewhat from his feelings, in short, that he has transformed his emotions into free emotions as I do mine while reading him."[11] Devices of distancing are then as important to Sartre as they were to Kierkegaard, though for different reasons.

To Roquentin the first-person account is perhaps even more essential than to the Seducer. If Kierkegaard's Seducer was shown to uncover and record, allegedly for his own satisfaction, the mainsprings and movements of his scheming and his ultimate victory in the game of seduction, his actions were such that their effect could also be observed by others and even judged by them. Roquentin, on the other hand, gives account of an inner development and an ultimate vision that are attainable by and concern

10. Jean-Paul Sartre, *The Psychology of Imagination,* trans. B. Frechtman (New York, Philosophical Library, 1948), pp. 248, 249–50.

11. Jean-Paul Sartre, *What is Literature?* trans. B. Frechtman (New York, Washington Square Press, 1966), pp. 34–35; henceforth cited in the text as *WL.*

only the individual experiencing them. They could not possibly be objectified and permit of no outside witness. His very first notes jotted down on loose, undated sheets, which precede the actual diary, indicate that his is to be a record of his urgent and intimate quest to ascertain the meaning of his strange attacks of Nausea. The problem started inexplicably one day on the beach when he had picked up a pebble and, wanting to pitch it into the sea, had to stop short because a sweetish liquid suddenly filled his mouth. From that day on, bouts of Nausea assailed him more and more frequently and mysteriously remained part of his daily existence. They were with him on his lonely rounds about the city, whether he visited the public library, paced his room, loitered in cafés and restaurants, or rode on streetcars. Though physical in nature, these attacks did not seem to be symptoms of any physical or even mental disorder. Roquentin is certain that he is not insane. His Nausea is, as he eventually comes to realize, a "metaphysical trouble" (*N*, 143). One cannot easily imagine an omniscient author entering the mind of Roquentin during this gradual road toward understanding. It is essential that he himself stumble through events and conversations in which he plays a part he does not understand, that he encounter sensations he cannot analyze. Truth comes to him not through reasoning but rather by revelation, and revelations are strictly individual and personal experiences. He alone can write: "And suddenly, suddenly, the veil is torn away, I have understood, I have *seen*" (*N*, 170).

As his metaphysical trouble is of an existential nature, Nausea reveals to him the meaning of *existence* through a vision (the French word used is *illumination*). The experience is not only intensely personal but almost mystic:

> So I was in the park just now. The roots of the chestnut tree were sunk in the ground just under my bench . . . I was sitting, stooping forward, head bowed, alone in front of this

black, knotty mass, entirely beastly, which frightened me. Then I had this vision ...

Never, until these last few days, had I understood the meaning of "existence." I was like the others, like the ones walking along the seashore, all dressed in their spring finery ... Even when I looked at things, I was miles from dreaming that they existed: they looked like scenery to me. I picked them up in my hands, they served me as tools. I foresaw their resistance. But that all happened on the surface ... And then all of a sudden, there it was, clear as day: existence had suddenly unveiled itself. It had lost the harmless look of an abstract category: it was the very paste of things, this root was kneaded into existence. Or rather the root, the park gates, the bench, the sparse grass, all that had vanished: the diversity of things, their individuality, were only an appearance, a veneer. This veneer had melted, leaving soft, monstrous masses, all in disorder—naked, in a frightful, obscene nakedness ... All things, gently, tenderly, were letting themselves drift into existence ... If you existed, you had to *exist all the way,* as far as mouldiness, bloatedness, obscenity were concerned ... little, heat-mists floating in the cold air, a red-haired man digesting on a bench: all this somnolence, all these meals digested together, had its comic side ... We were a heap of living creatures, irritated, embarrassed at ourselves, we hadn't the slightest reason to be there. [*N,* 170–72]

The veil which had been torn for Roquentin in the course of his vision was the veil which habit, conceptual schemes, and the indolent complacency of man forever spread over the true nature of existence. It can be torn only by the individual. But once he has torn it, the entire order of a man-centered universe comes to be questioned. If the diversity of things and their individuality are conceived of as "appearances," all forms begin to fluctuate and the dizzying underlying chaos has to be faced. Nausea is the inevitable result. "I can't say I feel relieved or satisfied;" Roquentin continues to record, "just the opposite, I am crushed. Only my goal is reached: I know what I wanted to know; I have understood all that has happened to me since January. The Nausea has not left me and I don't believe it will leave me so soon; but I no longer have to bear it, it is no longer an illness or a passing fit: It is I" (N, 170). When Roquentin feels at one with the "heap of living creatures," when he realizes the extent to which his existence resembles theirs, the sensation of being *de trop*, totally superfluous, invades him. To an apparent refusal of objects to be classified there is added a sense of the futility of human existence. As Roquentin records his vision, the word of *absurdity* comes to his pen (N, 173).

> Absurdity was not an idea in my head, or the sound of a voice, only this long serpent . . . Serpent or claw or root or vulture's talon, what difference does it make. And without formulating anything clearly, I understood that I had found the key to Existence, the key to my Nausea, to my own life. In fact, all that I could grasp beyond that returns to this fundamental absurdity . . . I understood the Nausea, I possessed it . . . The essential thing is contingency. I mean that one cannot define existence as necessity. To exist is simply *to be there*. {N, 173, 176]

Roquentin's Nausea, being a metaphysical trouble, so violently shakes the established and rational way of perceiving the universe that objects begin to show themselves to him in a thingness totally impervious to human rationality. As a consequence, he can no longer be satisfied with their known classifications. He becomes aware of the inadequacy of ordinary language to render their very paste. They defy the rationality of the word. A root may be *described,* in terms of its function, or by words approximating its color, but its existence overflows all these words. This is the more perturbing to Roquentin the more he realizes that existence in all its irrationality is ubiquitous, timeless, and something of which one is inevitably a part. He waxes lyrical under the unsettling impact of this realization: "The tips of the branches rustled with existence which unceasingly renewed itself and which was never born . . . All was fulness and all was active, there was no weakness in time, all, even the least perceptible stirring, was made of existence. And all these existents which bustled about this tree came from nowhere and were going nowhere. Suddenly they existed, then suddenly they existed no longer: existence is without memory . . . Existence everywhere, infinitely, in excess, for ever and everywhere; existence—which is limited only by existence" (*N*, 178).

There are Pascalian accents in this vision of the universe in the midst of which the individual finds himself a thinking reed whose existence is ignored and who remains incapable of penetrating the eternal silences. There are Kafkaesque echoes in Roquentin's comparison of the futile busyness of Nature with that of an insect fallen on its back. There are, above all, affinities with the thought of Nietzsche: Roquentin is as aware as Nietzsche's Dionysiac man of the "constant proliferation of forms pushing into life" and the painful dissolution that awaits everything which is generated (*BT*, 102). Having looked, like Hamlet, "into the true nature of things," Nietzsche's Dionysiac man has "understood" and is therefore "loath to act" (*BT*, 51). "The truth once seen," Nietzsche wrote in his *Birth of Tragedy*, "man now detects everywhere nothing but the ghastly absurdity of existence . . . : nausea invades him."[12] It is noteworthy that the terms "absurdity" and "nausea" are used both by Nietzsche and Sartre

12. *BT*, 52. Golffing's version is here too far removed from the original so I have given my own more literal translation, based on *Die Geburt der Tragödie* (Stuttgart, Alfred Kröner Verlag, 1945), p. 82.

and that both thinkers see man's experiencing of them as result-ing in inaction. Analogous to the Dionysiac man who is "loath to act," Roquentin concludes: "I know very well that I don't want to do anything: to do something is to create existence—and there's quite enough existence as it is" (N, 231).

Yet the very affinities one may discover in this respect between Pascalian, Nietzschean, and Sartrean thought underline the new dimension arrived at by the fictional form of Nausea. Form here is not something accidental, something arbitrarily imposed upon thought. It is rather itself expressive of thought. If we are deeply stimulated by Pascal's Pensées, by their intellectual depth and the rhythm of their language, if we are carried away by the pas-sionate pace and feeling of Nietzsche's writing, Sartre's fictional hero Roquentin involves us in a more immediate manner be-cause he lives absurdity. We identify with him to the extent to which the real world of the reader and the imaginary world of the hero let us do so. He not only draws us into the intimacy of his "I" but, since he is always en situation, into his very existence. He is Being-in-the-world. As Simone de Beauvoir was to point out,[13] theoreticians arrive at conclusions, they deduce meanings, but they do so in a manner which remains abstract and by neces-sity is too "systematic" to remain in touch with human reality. But the novelist evokes existence and meanings in their concrete singularity. Roquentin's quest becomes for us a concrete, singular reality, distantly echoing Sartre's and at the same time challeng-ing, as Sartre would put it, the freedom of the reader so that he in turn may grant it that reality.

Roquentin's concept of absurdity differs, of course, from that of Kierkegaard. To the Danish philosopher it was Abraham, the Knight of Infinite Resignation, and ultimately the Knight of

13. Simone de Beauvoir, "Literature and Metaphysics," Art in Action 10th anniversary issue (New York, Twice a Year Press, 1948), pp. 86–93.

Faith, who engaged in the absurd because he believed and because belief by its very nature is absurd. Looked at through rational eyes, the behavior of a father ready and willing to sacrifice his son can only be considered that of a murderer. Abraham's willingness was both unethical and absurd. It was justifiable—in defiance of all logical explanation—only on the basis of faith. In the biblical and in Kierkegaard's versions of the story, however, it was because of Abraham's faith that his son was returned to him. Faith, then, in Kierkegaard's way of thinking, annuls absurdity because of its absurdity. Such faith cannot be described or analyzed. Even if presented in the intimacy of a diary, its profession would appear tasteless and inane and would offend the reader. Kierkegaard rightly chose myth as the objective correlative for its literary presentation. But to Roquentin existence itself is absurd. Absurdity to him is everywhere. He can escape it as little as he can escape existence. His profoundest experience of fundamental absurdity is, therefore, also his most deeply felt consciousness of existence, of its fullness, its inescapability, and of his own partaking in it. "You couldn't even wonder," he muses, "where all that sprang from, or how it was that a world came into existence, rather than nothingness . . . There had never been a moment in which it could not have existed." Even "to imagine nothingness you had to be there already, in the midst of the World." Existence "was there, in the garden, toppled down into the trees, all soft, sticky, soiling everything, all thick, a jelly. And I was inside, I with the garden" (N, 180–81). Yet out of this oneness is born, paradoxically, Roquentin's awareness of himself as a part and yet a separate part of existence. He has a momentary sensation of what Sartre has called the prereflective cogito. No myth could tell of such a moment. Only the reflective "I," which grows out of it, can later record it. Protagonist and teller must be one and the same person. Stories of such a nature are truly first-person narratives.

Roquentin's cogito is, as has been generally observed, the reversal of the Cartesian. The awareness of his body precedes his consciousness of this awareness. Whereas Descartes' first certainty was his thinking, his body being something whose existence had to be proved afterwards, Roquentin's first intuitive certainty is the existence of his body. At a certain moment the sensation of Nausea and his realization that it is *his* Nausea, a secretion of *his* body are one and the same thing. Indeed, it is not only through Nausea but as Nausea that his body's functioning discloses itself to him as being *his:* "I exist. It's sweet, so sweet, so slow. And light: you'd think it floated all by itself. It stirs, it brushes me, melts and vanishes. Gently, gently. There is bubbling water in my mouth. I swallow. It slides down my throat, it caresses me—and now it comes up again into my mouth. Forever I shall have a pool of whitish water in my mouth—lying low—grazing my tongue. And this pool is still me. And the tongue. And the throat is me" (*N,* 134). (*Nausea* seems to be a uniquely appropriate title for the Sartrean novel, and one is startled to learn from Simone de Beauvoir's memoirs that the original title given it by Sartre was *Melancholia* and that Gallimard's suggestion of the change was at first opposed by her because it seemed to suggest a naturalistic novel. *Melancholia,* on the other hand, establishes the novel's link with Romanticism— a link already observed by Robert Champigny.)[14]

As Roquentin contemplates certain parts of this body which he senses to be his, as he looks at his hands, for instance, he has

14. Simone de Beauvoir, *The Prime of Life,* p. 239; Robert Champigny, *Stages on Sartre's Way, 1938–52* (Bloomington, Indiana University Press, 1959), p. 38: "Nausea reminds us of Romantic ennui, of Laforgue's disgust." See also Henri Peyre, *French Novelists of Today,* (New York, Oxford University Press, Galaxy Books, 1967), who states that a previous, more philosophical version was written by Sartre in 1930–31 and that this version bore the title of *La Légende de la Vérité* [*The Legend of Truth*] (259).

a similar sensation of I-ness. Looked at in a totally detached manner, a hand on a table may seem like an animal turned upside down. But Roquentin soon has to tell himself: "I am these two beasts struggling at the end of my arms ... It pulls a little, softly, insinuatingly it exists ... I can't suppress it, nor can I suppress the rest of my body, the sweaty warmth which soils the shirt, nor all this warm obesity which turns lazily, as if someone were stirring it with a spoon, nor all the sensations going on inside ... quietly vegetating from morning to night" (N, 134). Yet this body vegetating and producing its own juices may well be like those of others.

What makes it different from those of others is Roquentin's realization that it is not only *his,* but indeed *himself.* And bound up with this realization is the reflection that it is *he* who is thinking that he exists, indeed, that he is forced to think he exists, even if doing so exhausts him. *"I exist,* I am the one who keeps it up. I. The body lives by itself once it has begun [and, we might add, as long as it is alive]. But thought—I am the one who continues it, unrolls it. I exist" (N, 135). Even if he were to tell himself to stop thinking, it would still be he who would have to do so. "I think I don't want to think. I mustn't think that I don't want to think. Because that's still a thought" (N, 135). There is no escaping it then: he is a paradox, a thinking individual who forever pulls himself from the nothingness to which he aspires (N, 136). His thereness is the *en-soi* (in-itself) from which a *pour-soi* (for-itself), negativity, surges up and becomes consciousness of the world it is in and, more intimately, of itself. Even Descartes, though writing as a philosopher and not as an individual *en situation,* could speak of existence only in first-person terms— as the grammatical form of the cogito clearly indicates. To Roquentin, in whom physical I-ness precedes the intellectual consciousness of himself, such first-person writing and the diary form appropriate to it seem inevitable.

The Sartrean cogito, however—being a reversal of the Cartesian—permits of the presumption that the world exists objectively and that man's consciousness merely reveals it. Sartre accepts Heidegger's notion of man as Being-in-the-world, and explains that, in this sense, being means "to open oneself toward the world, to begin with the nothingness of the world and of consciousness in order to emerge as consciousness-in-the-world."[15] According to Heidegger, man partakes of Being. He is that part of Being which throws a light upon Being and thereby allows it to become visible in its temporalization and localization in and through him. Heidegger speaks of man as a "clearing" (like the clearing in a forest which permits the light to enter and fall upon what there is, although "clear" and "light" here also imply understanding), within whose horizon man himself and the world about him show themselves in their diversity. In and through man, Being becomes historical, as it discloses itself in time and space. The individual, therefore, does not conjure up phenomena, but makes it possible for them to appear to him as what they are, and the more authentic he is, the closer he is to Being, the more authentically they will appear. Referring to man as *Dasein,* that is, the here and now of Being, Heidegger states that man "ec-sists": the word's root "sist" meaning "to be there" and designating the thereness of man, and the prefix "ec" (out) indicating that he transcends his thereness. Transcendence, in this sense, does not mean any other-worldliness, but rather man's openness to and awareness of what there is in the world as well as his ability to bear witness to it through language.[16] Although Sartre's division of man into an en-soi and a pour-soi seems to be more dualistic than the Heideggerian ec-sisting Dasein, the two

15. Jean-Paul Sartre, "Une Idée fondamentale de Husserl," *Situations I* (Paris, Gallimard, 1947), p. 33.

16. Martin Heidegger, "Letter on Humanism," trans. E. Lohner, in *Philosophy in the Twentieth Century,* ed. W. Barrett and H. D. Aiken, 3 (New York, Random House, 1962) pp. 278–79, 281.

concepts resemble each other closely. For it is due to the pour-soi, peculiar only to man, that the Sartrean existent transcends himself, can open himself toward the world, and can "begin with the nothingness of the world and of consciousness in order to emerge as consciousness-in-the-world."

What interests us in particular is the resemblance of this existentialist image of man as consciousness in and of the world, of which he is a part, with that of the Dionysiac poet of Nietzsche who turns his eyes in order to look at himself and understand the essence of his art. This resemblance becomes especially striking, if we recall that, to Heidegger, poet and thinker are closer to Being and are therefore the most authentic in their disclosure of it. When writing *Nausea,* Sartre apparently was in agreement with Heidegger that man's authenticity consists in revealing existence (Being in its here and now) and himself as a part of it.[17] In an interview he was to give many years later to Madeleine Chapsal, he literally declared that "what all people want, some without being aware of it, is to be witness to their time, their lives, and above all themselves."[18] To Heidegger, Care was the essential catalyst in man's development toward such authenticity. He let himself, quite consciously, be guided here by the fable of Hygius, which he knew had inspired Goethe.[19] In Sartre's novel, Nausea obviously assumes a catalystic function analogous to that which Care assumed for Faust, as it induces Roquentin to break the crust of habit and complacency in order to *see* and to become authentic as an individual and a writer. It is, then, as if

17. As World War II progressed, Sartre came to adopt a different conception of authenticity. Simone de Beauvoir says in *The Prime of Life* that he decided to take part in politics after the war and to engage in political action, so as to "assume his situation" (346; 380).

18. Madeleine Chapsal, *Les Écrivains en présence* (Paris, Julliard, 1960), pp. 230–33.

19. See above, p. 63.

in striving for authenticity, existential man, by his very nature, becomes an author-hero resembling that of the Künstlerroman. Since he is not only the artist, however, but Being-in-the-world, his concerns must be more inclusive, and even the essence of his art cannot but be informed by existential concerns. This will become apparent, as we follow Roquentin on his road toward human and authorial authenticity.

It is only through a conscious preference for loneliness that Roquentin becomes a witness to existence; that is, less and less blinded by prevailing prejudices and clichés. In *Nausea*, Roquentin is not just incidentally and regrettably but essentially alone. Not only is he a stranger in town, knowing no one except the Self-Taught Man, but he is also without family, friends, or even property in Bouville or anywhere else. He thinks of himself as a man who hangs around cafés. "I live alone," he realizes, "entirely alone. I never speak to anyone, never; I receive nothing, I give nothing. The Self-Taught Man doesn't count. There is Françoise, the woman who runs the *Rendez-vous des Cheminots*. But do I speak to her? Sometimes after dinner, when she brings my beer, I ask her: 'Have you time this evening?' She never says no and I follow her into one of the big rooms on the second floor" (*N,* 14). But even such loneliness—much as it corresponds to that of Descartes when he developed his method—eventually cannot suffice Roquentin. He comes to blame himself for having remained only on the surface of solitude, still resolved to take refuge in the midst of people in case of any emergency. "Up to now I was an amateur at heart," he realizes at the beginning of his diary *(N,* 16). He resolves therefore to attain a more decided loneliness in order to "get rid of plausibility" and tear the veil of maya.

Such isolation on the part of his protagonist has the effect of limiting the fictional universe of the novelist—unless, of course, he assumes the attitude of omniscience or of a privileged point of view. Since Sartre does neither and since his "editors," unlike Kierkegaard's, divulge no information about Roquentin, he had to find indirect ways of transmitting that information to us. We glean some facts concerning his appearance, his habits, his character from casual and incidental remarks made by those few individuals with whom he engages in conversation. Through his encounter with Anny, his former girl friend, certain isolated facts about his past come to the fore. His conversations with her reveal, for instance, that she had considered him as unchangeable as the platinum stick that represents the standard French meter —the earthly thing closest to the permanence of a Platonic Idea. Since he actually has undergone profound changes when they meet again after many years, this judgment is invalidated almost as soon as it is uttered. What would, in fact, discourage any precise delineation of Roquentin's character is Sartre's underlying existential conviction—Kierkegaard thought along similar lines —that only the dead can be evaluated and labeled with a certain finality, while "human reality eludes direct knowledge to the degree that it *makes itself.*"[20] If we learn from Roquentin that he is a "red-haired man who hung around cafés," it is because that is what he assumes Others to have thought of him. Even when he looks into the mirror and describes his flabby cheeks, his high forehead, and the flame of red hair crowning it, our factual information about him is not greatly enriched by this fictional technique, usually so effective in first-person narratives.[21] For the mirror soon ceases to reflect a true portrait. As Roquentin approaches his reflection in the glass more and more closely, we begin to see with him a seemingly surrealistic, lunar world of feverish, swelled lips, crevices, and mole holes (N, 28). As he

20. Jean-Paul Sartre, *The Problem of Method,* trans. Hazel Barnes (London, Methuen, 1963), p. 170.

21. Cf., for instance, Virginia Woolf, *To the Lighthouse* (New York, Harcourt, Brace, 1927), pp. 13–14.

tells us, only people who live in society *see* themselves in mirrors because they see themselves as they appear to their friends (*N*, 29). By being without human "mirrors," as it were, Roquentin's life in all its loneliness becomes more and more freed of preconceived notions: unlabeled, not yet realized, free to change. The manner in which he sees his own face borders on the surrealistic precisely because he sees things out of the context established by tradition and habit. His description must not be understood, therefore, as that balance between the conscious and subconscious world which Breton had designated as *vases communicants*. It is not Roquentin's subconscious which surrealistically blurs or heightens the intensity of his world. A distinction between man's unconscious and conscious world would contradict Sartre's conception of man as en-soi and pour-soi (*WL*. 119). This means also that Roquentin's first-person account must not be seen as an interior monologue intended to draw the reader into his peculiar psychic reality or his subconscious (see *WL*, 98, n. 11). Nor should we understand him as seeking the fantastic or the unreal. Roquentin's seemingly surrealistic description of his own face is rather an important stage on his road toward an authenticity that rejects habitual patterns of seeing the world. Each stage turns him further into an authentic Being-in-the-world which reveals that world as it shows itself to him. Because of that, the world about him emerges at times in as dramatic a fashion as it did in the diary of Kierkegaard's Seducer, even if the motivation, manner, and effect of the two diarists differ. This becomes strikingly evident in the respective descriptions they give of their town on a Sunday morning. While Johannes the Seducer, living the life of a nineteenth-century aesthete, conveyed to us the intensity of his pleasure at observing a young woman who passes in her Sunday finery and is teased by the wind, we see Roquentin in the process of detaching himself from the crowds of Bouville who have never doubted plausibility. Seen through the eyes of his growing authenticity, others look like puppets on a string, engaged in totally meaningless and automation-like activities. Because of his detachment, their commonplace behavior takes on the appearance of a grotesque spectacle:

You must not be in a hurry on the Rue de Tournebride: the families walk slowly. Sometimes you move up a step because one family has turned into Foulon's or Piégeois. But, at other times, you must stop and mark time because two families, one going up the street, the other coming down, have met and have solidly clasped hands. I go forward slowly. I stand a whole head above both columns and I see hats, a sea of hats. Most of them are black and hard. From time to time you see one fly off at the end of an arm and you catch the soft glint of a skull; then, after a few instants of flight, it returns. At 16 Rue Tournebride, Urbain, the hatter, specializing in forage caps, has hung up as a symbol, an immense, red archbishop's hat whose gold tassels hang six feet from the ground.

A halt: a group has collected just under the tassels. My neighbor waits impatiently, his arms dangling: this little old man, pale and fragile as porcelain—I think he must be Coffier—president of the Chamber of Commerce. It seems he is intimidating because he never speaks. He lives on the summit of the Coteau vert, in a great brick house whose windows are always wide open. It's over: the group has broken up. Another group starts forming but it takes up less space: barely formed, it is pushed against Ghislaine's window front. The column does not even stop: it hardly makes a move to step aside; we are walking in front of six people who hold hands: "Bonjour, Monsieur, bonjour cher Monsieur, comment allez-vous? Do put your hat on again, you'll catch cold; Thank you, Madame, it isn't very warm out, is it? My dear, let me present Doctor Lefrançois; Doctor, I am very glad to make your acquaintance, my husband always speaks of Doctor Lefrançois who took such care of him, but do put your hat on, Doctor, you'll catch cold. But a doctor would get well quickly; Alas! Madame, doctors are the least well looked after; the Doctor is a remarkable musician. Really, Doctor? But I never knew you play the violin? The Doctor is very gifted." . . . On the other side of the street a gentleman, holding his wife by the arm, has just whispered a few words in her ear and has started to smile. She immediately wipes all expression from her chalky, cream colored face and blindly takes a few steps. There is no mistaking these signs: they are going to greet somebody . . . A bowing shadow passes them: but their twin smiles do not disappear immediately: they stay on their lips a few instants by a sort of magnetism. The lady and gentleman have regained their impassibility by the time they pass me. [N, 62–64]

Without launching into any analysis or passing any specific judgment, simply by writing down the scene as it presents itself to him, Roquentin reveals to us mass man in contrast to the individual (the Kierkegaardian "public" and the Heideggerian "everyman"—German: *man*). Because his Nausea makes his sight keener, he also senses that even among these crowds which are oozing out togetherness, there is no real communication. If they seem comfortably entrenched in their lives, if they are less anguished than Roquentin, it is because they are so busy devising their own little games and playing within the great human comedy the parts society has assigned to them. They bow and smile, they exchange inanities, they eat their Sunday dinner at the usual hour in their habitual restaurant. They either never experienced the fundamental absurdity of existence or try to conceal such experiences from themselves, too cowardly to face them. They do not live up to their essence as human beings.

As Being-in-the-world, Roquentin reveals not only himself in the process of becoming authentic but also the inauthenticity of those anonymous crowds about him. Even beyond the occasion of their Sunday promenades and dinners, Roquentin envisions the Bouvillians as an unindifferentiated mass of people entrenched in habit to the extent that they are unable to *see* reality, conceiving of it only in terms of verbal clichés or supposedly scientific laws which they learned and memorized in school.

> They come out of their offices after their day of work, they look at the houses and the squares with satisfaction, they think it is *their* city, a good, solid bourgeois city. They aren't afraid, they feel at home. All they have ever seen is trained water running from taps, light which fills bulbs when you turn on the switch, half-breed, bastard trees held up with crutches. They have proof, a hundred times a day, that everything happens mechanically, that the world obeys fixed, unchangeable laws. In a vacuum all bodies fall at the same rate of speed, the public park is closed at 4 p.m. in winter, at 6 p.m. in summer, lead melts at 335 centrigrade, the last streetcar leaves the Hotel de Ville at 11.05 p.m. They are peaceful, a little morose, they think about To-morrow, that is to say, simply a new today.

Roquentin comes to the conclusion that "cities have only one day at their disposal and every morning it comes back exactly the same" (*N,* 211–12). One can think of people living in them only as "they," blindly doing things in unison without ever realizing what it is all about: "They make laws, they write popular novels, they get married, they are fools enough to have children. And all this time, great, vague nature has slipped into their city, it has infiltrated everywhere, in their house, in their office, in themselves" (*N,* 212). Roquentin, who is no longer blind in the same manner, knows that they merely live under a delusion when they think of Nature as being tamed and obedient: "I know it has no laws: what they take for constancy is only habit and it can change tomorrow" (*N,* 212).

The novel's images of blind and unthinking man lost in large crowds reflect a world view Sartre inherited largely from Heidegger. The German philosopher has differentiated between "the subject of everyday-ness" and the "authentic Self." While he has considered it part of the essence of man that he is "Being-with-Others," he sees implicit in this essential situation man's potential loss of individuality, his becoming "inconspicuous," "indistinguishable," and subject to "the dictatorship of the they," while —as a member of the crowd—exerting in turn such a dictatorship upon others. This, as Heidegger stated, represents a perpetual "leveling down" of the manifold "possibilities of Being." For out of the "everyday Being-among-one-another" grow "distantiality, averageness . . . publicness." The individual fails to stand by his own Self.[22] If it was Heidegger who developed these views even before Sartre embraced them, both may well have found their inspiration in Kierkegaard's work where such problems are touched upon, though in a manner less systematic than that of Heidegger. In his review of a novel entitled *The Present Age,* Kierkegaard likewise spoke of a "leveling process" to be observed in a society ruled by "the public" and therefore less and less composed of authentic individuals. He envisioned with horror that "more and more individuals, owing to their bloodless indolence, will aspire to be nothing at all—in order to become the public, that abstract whole formed in the most ludicrous way, by all participants becoming a third party (an onlooker)."[23] It is

22. Martin Heidegger, *Being and Time,* trans. J. Macquarrie and E. Robinson, (London SCM Press, 1962), pp. 164–65, 166.

23. Søren Kierkegaard, "The Present Age: A Literary Review," in *A Kierkegaard Anthology,* ed. R. Bretall, (New York, The Modern Library, 1946), pp. 258 ff., 267.

obvious that the three existential thinkers here meet on common ground, even if Heidegger puts more emphasis on man's relationship with Being than does either Kierkegaard or Sartre. But because his foremost concern was Being, because he saw implicit in the "leveling down" of the individual Self a reduction of the possibilities of Being, Heidegger saw in it also a danger to language—something also present in Kierkegaard's thought. The problem of language endangered by inauthenticity has been further developed by Sartre, and Roquentin's diary is replete with it.

Heidegger's conception of language understood and employed authentically is perhaps best illustrated by his own use of the word "Dasein." Convinced that language is a part of Being and that the Truth of Being, as expressed by language, is sometimes hidden underneath the grime of everydayness, Heidegger proceeded to uncover this Truth in the word "Dasein." What he found was that this common German noun meaning "existence" consists of two parts: *da* (there; also possibly, here and now) and *Sein* (Being). If the noun is considered as designating human existence, then it indicates to him by its very form that man, as a part of Being, represents that part of it which is temporalized and localized in the here and now. It is then quite obvious that the here and now of Being consists not only of man and the objects about him but also of Others and, above all, of language. Language, seen in this manner, becomes the "house wherein man dwells" and of which he is at the same time the "guardian." Language, belonging uniquely to human existence, comes to light in the *da,* and there "brings to light" Being, of which both man and language partake. The closer man is to Being, that is, the more authentic he is, the more he will uncover the Truth of language and with it the Truth of Being (as I have earlier suggested). If he looks at such words as "Dasein" in the manner of Heidegger, in the manner of a poet or a philosopher, he will rescue both language and Being from the "groundlessness and nullity of inauthentic everyday-ness" into which they have been plunged by "idle talk" and "gossip."[24]

The "they" whom Roquentin observes in Bouville (Mud-town), where he has come to live, have plunged precisely into that groundlessness and inauthenticity. As Roquentin's more and more frequent attacks of Nausea lead him closer and closer to authenticity and away from the "careful little actions" he used to indulge in, he not only becomes progressively aware of the in-authentic everydayness of his fellow citizens but also of the idle-ness of their talk. While he is eating his Sunday dinner at the Brasserie Vézeline, his mind registers the conversations taking place all around him as people eat their "usual Sunday sauer-kraut."

"The stockbroker has taken a chair opposite the clean-shaven, lugubrious-looking old man. The clean-shaven old man immedi-ately begins an animated story," Roquentin notices. But he is also aware of the fact that the stockbroker does not listen to him: "They never listen to each other" (N, 65–66). There are, for in-stance, his neighbors, a middle-aged couple:

> My neighbors had been silent ever since I had come, but, suddenly the husband's voice . . . amused and mysterious . . .:
> "Say, did you see that?" The woman gives a start and looks, coming out of a dream. He eats and drinks, then starts again, with the same malicious air:
> "Ha Ha!"
> A moment of silence, the woman has fallen back into her dream.
> Suddenly she shudders and asks: "What did you say?"
> "Suzanne, yesterday."
> "Ah, yes," the woman says, "she went to see Victor."
> "What did I tell you?"

24. Heidegger, *Being and Time,* pp. 210–12, 223, 220.

The woman pushes her plate aside impatiently. "It's no good."

The side of her plate is adorned with lumps of gristle she spits out. The husband follows his idea. "That little woman there . . . " He stops and smiles vaguely. Across from us, the old stockbroker is stroking Mariette's arm and breathing heavily. After a moment: "I told you so, the other day."

"What did you tell me?"

"Victor—that she'd go and see him. What's the matter?" he asks brusquely with a frightened look, "don't you like that?"

"It's no good."

"It isn't the same any more," he says with importance, "it isn't the way it was in Hécart's time. Do you know where he is, Hécart?"

"Domremy, isn't he?"

"Yes, who told you?"

"You did. You told me Sunday."

She eats a morsel of crumb which is scattered on the paper tablecloth. Then, her hand smoothing the paper on the edge of the table, with hesitation: "You know, you're mistaken, Suzanne is more . . ."

"That may well be, my dear, that may well be," he answers distractedly. He tries to catch Mariette's eyes, makes a sign to her. "It's hot."

. . . . .

My neighbors are silent . . . You might think that silence was their normal state and speech a fever that sometimes takes them. [N, 68–71]

This speech can no longer be considered a dialogue. Language here no longer serves people as a means of communication or as something which is capable of revealing the Truth of Being or carries this Truth within itself. It has lost all significance. It has become absurd, aimless, empty chatter.

As a piece of writing, this entry in Roquentin's diary antedates the theatre of the absurd of Tardieu or Ionesco. Yet it is the language of the "they" which is merely recorded by Roquentin. When Sartre has Roquentin speak in his own voice, he has him proclaim the absurdity of existence in logical and lucid language. If Roquentin's style acquires at times a concrete density, this is never achieved at the expense of clarity. Sartre himself has frequently made a plea for clarity of language and precision of meaning. He seemingly adopted the Heideggerian concept that language is not something independent of man but "the house of Being wherein man dwells." But he has adapted this concept. For Sartre it is not the poet who is closest to the Truth of Being but the prose writer. It is he who is inside of language, who is *"en situation* in language," and "invested with words" which are "the prolongations" of his senses, "his pincers," "his antennae," "his eyeglasses." Sartre thinks of man as being "within language as he is within his body," maintaining that "we *feel* it spontaneously while going beyond it toward other ends, as we feel our hands and our feet; we perceive it when it is the other who is using it, as we perceive the limbs of others. There is the word which is lived and the word which is met" (*WL,* 12–13). According to Sartre, man is hardly conscious of this verbal body by which he is surrounded "and which extends his action upon the world."[25] Heidegger, admiring the poet as being capable of

25. *WL,* 6. Marc Bensimon has discussed with great acumen Sartre's further development of the writer's attitude toward language and has rightly referred to the passage in *The Problem of Method* (p. 113) which shows Sartre's awareness of man's dependence on a language that society tenders him ready-made. (Marc Bensimon, "D'un Mythe à l'autre: Essai sur *Les Mots* de J.-P. Sartre," *Revue des Sciences Humaines* [1965], 422).

unveiling the Truth of Being which is concealed in the etymon of words, has often adopted the poet's approach and proved his points not through logic but through juxtaposition of words, and skillful toying with semantics—in the manner of Mallarmé, Joyce, or even the Surrealists.[26] Sartre, on the other hand, clearly has considered prose utilitarian (*WL,* 11). He has excluded from its realm all concerns other than that of revealing truth. To him the language of poetry is removed from such truth, because the poet is rather "outside of language" and treats words not as signs pointing toward something but as if they themselves were objects he can touch, test, and handle at will (*WL,* 6). A poet may even believe, with some of the Surrealists, that words "make love."[27] The prose writer, on the contrary, is to Sartre "a man who makes use of word" (*WL,* 11). "The art of prose is employed in discourse; its substance by nature signifies; that is, the words are first of all not objects but designations for objects; it is not first of all a matter of knowing whether they please or displease in themselves, but whether they correctly indicate a certain thing or a certain notion" (*WL,* 12). It would seem therefore that, to Sartre, speech and all that pertains to the intelligence of man becomes absurd and deviates from logic only when it has become inauthentic, when it fails to grasp the essence of the universe and of objects and when a spade is no longer called a spade.

The impression Roquentin gives of the groundlessness and inauthenticity of the Sunday crowd's language is heightened by the fact that, while listening to their chatter, he is reading Balzac's *Eugénie Grandet.* The passage before him is that of a conversation between Eugénie, her mother, and their servant. In it, every word seems meaningful and relevant. A complex situation is revealed: the young girl's budding love, the older woman's indulgent and yet reluctant consent to her "madness" in wishing to

26. Heidegger, "Letter on Humanism," passim.

27. Julien Gracq, *André Breton ou l'Ame d'un mouvement* (Paris, Fontaine, 1958), p. 149.

serve the young Parisian visitor strong coffee for breakfast, with cream and sugar to boot, and the father's avarice which controls life in the household down to the smallest detail, even when he is absent. In Balzac's novel all characters are presented in the light of subtle psychological analyses. All is well arranged and well plotted. The author conveys to us what is going on in the mind of the mother as well as in that of the daughter. Having created and manipulated them in accordance with certain psychological laws, he makes the reader see them function according to those laws. Obviously the philosophy that informed Balzac's fictional technique acknowledged an orderly, rational universe (as did that of Kierkegaard). But Balzac's universe also permitted of omniscient and privileged authors—whether human or divine—quite unlike the existentialist author who witnesses and reveals and is yet unable to understand what he sees. But even if the Balzacian world of clearly outlined relationships and rational dialogues is more reassuring than the idle talk of the "they" in the brasserie, it can satisfy Roquentin as little as the "orderly" world of the Municipal Museum of Bouville. To Roquentin, both Balzac and the Municipal Museum are artificial. Because he has experienced the fundamental absurdity of existence, they do not reveal but rather conceal the true character of existence. As fear and trembling set Abraham apart from the "they" to whom he could not have explained what he was about to do and whom he had to disregard in order to become a Knight of Faith; as anxiety and Care set Dasein apart from the "indistinguishable" crowd and from "everyday-Being-among-one-another" to make man find the Truth of Being and thereby of language; so Nausea makes Roquentin reach that state of illumination which individualizes him and makes him *see* the "unjustifiable existence of his fellow men," their sham dignity, the cowardly manner in which they falsify reality so as to conceal the absurdity of existence, and their failure to use language as an instrument in the quest for truth.

At the beginning of his diary we find Roquentin desperately

trying to reveal truth in terms of the verbal categories at his disposal and realizing with dismay that the language of the "they" is not equal to his task: "Here is a cardboard box holding my bottle of ink. I should try to tell how I saw it *before* and how now I [the editor's note tells us that a word has been omitted in the diary]. Well, it's a parallelopiped rectangle, it opens—that's stupid, there's nothing I can say about it" (*N,* 7). Before Nausea had assailed him, he had conceived of things around him in traditional terms, that is, in traditional categories, and in terms of the function they have in man's universe: "points of reference which man had traced on their surface." When first seated before the chestnut tree and as long as the moment of his illumination had not yet arrived, he had still put all he saw into "harmless abstract categories" (*N,* 171). He had still been very much one of the "they" who perceive the world exclusively in human terms: failing to see the world in a perspective other than its purposefulness, "they" think of objects in terms of tools and utensils. Even to Heidegger's Dasein, a tree means above all the wood it yields for building or burning. But Roquentin has begun to look at objects, at a tree, for instance, mainly with the eyes of someone who wants to see them in order to know what they *are.*[28] As his fits of Nausea increase, objects refuse more and more obstinately to be fitted into the established human categories. Sartre himself has expressed the dilemma in theoretical terms in his *The Problem of Method:* the individual is inside culture and inside language.

> In order to *manifest* what he uncovers, he therefore has at his disposal elements both too rich and too few. Too few: words, types of reasoning, methods, exist only in limited quantity; among them there are empty spaces, lacunae, and his growing thought cannot find its appropriate expression.

28. Sartre, Madeleine Gobeil, "Playboy Interview: Jean-Paul Sartre," *Playboy Magazine, 12* (1965), 69–76.

Too rich: each vocable brings along with it the profound signification which the whole epoch has given to it. As soon as the ideologist speaks, he says more and something different from what he wants to say; the period steals his thought from him. He constantly veers about, and the idea finally expressed is a profound deviation; he is caught in the mystification of words.[29]

In *Nausea* this dilemma has been ingeniously concretized. For it is on a day when fog has invaded Bouville—this is perhaps a distant echo of Unamuno's novel *Niebla* (Mist)—that Roquentin finds objects most unwilling to adapt themselves to the categories of usefulness and the rational vocabulary society has assigned to them. Fog conceals and metamorphoses. Fog lends to objects mysterious instability, rendering them gaseous, dissolving them chaotically. (It is significant that the etymon of "gas" is "chaos.") Thus Nausea and fog combine to deprive objects of their last remnants of servility to man. Things begin to take on an unnatural look, and it is only by the power of his gaze that Roquentin can "reduce them to their everyday aspect" and by telling himself forcibly, "This is a gaslight, this is a drinking fountain" *(N,* 108). Yet once things have started to overflow the categories imposed upon them by man, they continue to defy labels, even in broad daylight and on sunny days.

It is quite natural, then, that at such moments Roquentin's world takes on a surrealistic aspect, sharing with Surrealism the fluidity of objects and their tendency toward metamorphosis. His own image in the mirror may assume, as we have seen, the aspect of a weird landscape. An ordinary seat in a streetcar may reveal itself as a dead animal floating in a river:

> I lean my hand on the seat but pull it back hurriedly: it exists. This thing I'm sitting on, leaning my hand on, is

29. Sartre, *The Problem of Method,* p. 113.

called a seat. They made it purposely for people to sit on, they took leather, springs and cloth, they went to work with the idea of making a seat and when they finished, *that* was what they had made. They carried it here, into this car and the car is now rolling and jolting with its rattling windows, carrying this red thing in its bosom. I murmur: "It's a seat," a little like an exorcism. But the word stays on my lips: it refuses to go and put itself on the thing. It stays what it is, with its red plush, thousands of little paws in the air, all still, little dead paws. This enormous belly turned upward, bleeding, inflated—bloated with all its dead paws, this belly floating in this car, in this grey sky, is not a seat. It could just as well be a dead donkey tossed about in the water, floating with the current, belly in the air, in a great grey river, a river of floods; and I could be sitting on a donkey's belly, my feet dangling in the clear water. Things are divorced from their names. They are there, grotesque, headstrong, gigantic and it seems ridiculous to call them seats or say anything at all about them: I am in the midst of things, nameless things. Alone without words, defenceless, they surround me, are beneath me, behind me, above me. They demand nothing, they don't impose themselves: they are there. [N, 168–69]

But in spite of its surrealistic echoes, here, too, Roquentin's vision is of a different nature. The scene's significance does not lie in the symbolical annulment of objects, of which Sartre was to accuse Surrealism (*WL*, 120). Nor is Roquentin concerned with a "symbolical annulment of the self by sleep and automatic writing." On the contrary, what he strives for is a meaningful relationship between object and word. While the Surrealists, according to Sartre, destroyed language by telescoping words, hashing them together, and having them shatter as they clash against one another, Roquentin wants to use language as an instrument to reveal truth (*WL*, 89).

Had Roquentin been created by Sartre in the image of a Surrealist poet, he would have reveled in the newness of his experience and poetically rendered the unwonted world he perceived while riding on the streetcar. He might have composed what Sartre has called an "object-poem" which would have *been* the "bench-donkey" rather than "signifying beyond itself" (*WL*, 4–12). Roquentin's experience, on the contrary, does signify beyond itself. Such words as "exorcism," "nameless things," and "defenseless" must be seen as keywords in his account.[30] Rather than wishing to render a "poetic" world of dreamlike distortion, he longs for a world which is truly and authentically named, but, because of that, may appear just as distant from the world falsified by habit. Only a world seen authentically would be worthy of man. Ernst Cassirer speaks in his *Language and Myth* of man's "emergence from the fulness of existence into a world of clear, verbally determinable forms" as the difference "between chaos and creation," and he considers speech as making "the transition from the featureless matrix of Being to its form and organization."[31] Even in biblical terms, it is the word of God which separates light from darkness and thereby creates heaven and earth, while it is left to Adam, to man, to give a name to all the creatures (Gen. 2:19). "In this act of appellation," which corresponds precisely to the exorcism of which Roquentin speaks, "man takes possession of the world both physically and intellectually—subjects it to his knowledge and his rule," Cas-

---

30. Claude-Edmonde Magny has brilliantly analyzed this in her *Sandales d'Empédocle* (Switzerland, Boudry, Editions de la Baconnière, 1945). See also "The Duplicity of Being," in Kern, *Sartre,* pp. 21 ff.

31. Ernst Cassirer, *Language and Myth,* trans. S. K. Langer (Dover, Dover Publications, 1946), pp. 81–82.

sirer states.[32] In Sartre's atheistic view of the world, the stress is put, of course, on man's role in this process.

Now it is obvious that the world with which Roquentin has to cope is a world already named and it is only because of his Nausea that he has become aware of the inauthenticity of its naming and the inauthenticity of the language employed in the process. "I was like the others," he tells us upon his moment of revelation before the chestnut tree. "I said, like them 'the ocean *is* green; that white speck there *is* a seagull,' but I didn't feel that it existed or that the seagull was an 'existing seagull.'" Like others he had used the verb "to be" without thinking of or evoking the objects in their very existence. He had rather classified them as *belonging to* a group: "the sea belonged to the class of green objects" or "green was part of the quality of the sea" (*N*, 171). Did the word "black" actually describe the root against which his heel had scraped?

> I felt the word deflating, emptied of meaning with extraordinary rapidity: Black? The root *was not* black, there was no black on this piece of wood ... I looked at the root: was it *more than* black or *almost* black? But I soon stopped questioning myself because I had the feeling of knowing where I was. Yes, I had already scrutinized innumerable objects, with deep uneasiness. I had already tried vainly to think something *about* them: and I had already felt their cold, inert qualities elude me, slip through my fingers. [*N*, 175].

This is the recognition of the "empty spaces" in language which Sartre was later to discuss in his *Problem of Method*. As Nausea reveals to Roquentin the meaning, or rather the absurdity, of existence, chaos begins to reign for him as it did until, by virtue

32. Ibid., p. 83.

of the word, the world was "created." To "create" it again, he would have to find a new language, more authentic than that of the "they," a language capable of rendering the essence of existence. It would have to be a language that would be, in Nietzsche's words, "an unvarnished expression of truth" because it has "cast away the trumpery garments worn by the supposed reality of civilized man" (*BT*, 53). Gide, as we have seen, also strove for such essential expression—without as yet doubting the ability of language as such to achieve it.[33]

In the years following the publication of *Nausea* Sartre expressed even more concern for the authenticity of words. He maintained that they should "correctly indicate a certain thing or a certain notion" (*WL*, 12). By virtue of naming authentically, language seemed to him capable not only of revealing but even of changing reality. "Anything one names," he asserted in a somewhat paradoxical and yet convincing manner, "is no longer quite the same; it has lost its innocence." The word "love" may well be inherent in a situation, but once it is spoken it both reveals and changes that situation by giving it a reality which it did not have previously. The ability of changing the world, which Sartre accredited to language, made him speak of it as a mode of *action* and made him aware of the writer's importance. Sartre realized that—even if unwittingly—the writer was *engaged* and decided that he had better determine consciously what form such commitment was to take—especially if he spoke in social and political terms (*WL*, 14–15). Indeed, in reading *Words*, his autobiography, or his biographies of Baudelaire and Genet, one cannot escape the impression that Sartre saw inherent in language also an almost mystical power to conjure up realities that previously did not exist even as potentialities. A child reading a story might put himself in the place of its hero, but beyond that he might become a writer, simply because a

33. See above, p. 71.

friend of the family "predicted" it and labeled him, as it were. Genet might become a thief not so much because, as a child, he had stolen, but rather because, having done so, he had been labeled a thief. Even if we are willing to accept Sartre's explanation that what is at stake here is the child's fundamental decision to be a writer or a thief, we cannot overlook the power and importance conferred upon the word in his thinking. The fact alone that Sartre chose *Words* as the title of his autobiography seems to reveal and underline this tendency on his part. So does the choice of his title for his Genet biography: *Saint Genet, Comedian and Martyr*. This title evokes the seventeenth-century play, *Saint Genest* in which an actor, who plays the part of a saint and pronounces words of saintliness, becomes what he pretends to be.[34] Both for Genet and his seventeenth-century namesake the word creates reality: it becomes flesh.

This belief in the power of the word strongly affected Sartre's presentation of character in fiction as well as in biography. For if language establishes a reality as it reveals it, it also has the power of solidifying this reality. This is in direct contradiction to Sartre's notion that human reality is not static but in a perpetual process of making itself. The biographer, in using words to situate and describe his subject, by necessity turns him into something statuesque. The same thing might happen to the novelist in presenting his characters, unless he is aware of this pitfall and consciously tries to avoid it. Victor Brombert has shown with great acumen the extent to which the possibility or impossibility of writing biography has permeated Sartre's entire work, since this question touches upon the very nature of man and the notion he has of his destiny. If man is essentially free to choose his essence, any choice, once made, represents a limitation of this freedom. His freedom is equally challenged by any judgment man makes of himself, or that is made of him by Others—even

34. Jean Rotrou, *Saint Genest,* IV. 5.

if the Other is his biographer. The biographer, moreover, must deal with a past that, having been recorded, has lost its potential of being reinterpreted by a future.[35]

It is obvious that some of these considerations already pre-occupied Sartre when he wrote *Nausea,* for they enter directly or indirectly into Roquentin's decision to abandon work on the biography of M. de Rollebon, who through him had come to life again and through whom his own life had, for a while, been filled with purpose. What is crucial in Roquentin's decision is his growing awareness that, in spite of all the documents at his disposal, Rollebon's reality remains to him unattainable and might emerge only if the facts were transposed to the realm of the imaginary:

> He [Rollebon] could have done all that, but it is not proved: I am beginning to believe that nothing can ever be proved. These are honest hypotheses which take the facts into ac-count: but I sense so definitely that they come from me, and that they are simply a way of unifying my knowledge. Not a glimmer comes from Rollebon's side. Slow, lazy, sulky, the facts adapt themselves to the rigour of the order I wish to give them; but it remains outside of them. I have the feeling of doing a work of pure imagination. And I am certain that the characters in a novel would have a more genuine appearance, or, in any case, would be more agree-able. [*N,* 23]

In the biographies he himself wrote, Sartre continued to cope with the question of whether imaginative or discursive writing more readily renders human reality. Having discussed certain events in Genet's life, for instance, he concludes, as Brombert has pointed out, by unexpectedly lapsing into the role of the novelist:

35. Victor Brombert, "Sartre et la Biographie impossible," *Cahiers de l'Association Internationale des Etudes françaises, 19* (1967), 155–66.

"This happened this way or otherwise." On other occasions, he enters into the role of the intruding novelist of the nineteenth century, fully armed with the judgment of the outsider, competent to give a factual account, yet indirectly confirming that he remains forever the Other and that Genet remains ultimately opaque to him. Thus he may exclaim: "I profoundly admire that child." Or he may maintain omnisciently: "But while he steals in innocence, while he modestly longs for the palm of the martyr, he unwittingly forges for himself a destiny."[36]

In *Nausea,* Sartre's author-hero Roquentin unequivocally turns from biography to fiction, a change of direction prompted not only by the conviction that it is impossible to write a biography, but also by his steadily emerging awareness of another world that is neither absurd nor gratuitous, neither contingent nor lawlessly proliferating, but rather pure, harmonious, and well ordered: the world of music and abstraction. "In another world," he tells himself, "circles, bars of music keep their pure and rigid lines. But existence is a deflection" (*N,* 172). The realm of existence is separated in his view from the realm of explanations, while "a circle is not absurd, it is clearly explained by the rotation of a straight segment around one of its extremities" (*N,* 174). This is because a circle does not exist. Music in particular holds for Roquentin that abstract "arid purity" he finds gratifyingly opposed to the viscosity of nature. As he listens to a recording, its "purity" fills him with a happiness quite in opposition to the Nausea with which he associates existence:

> The voice, deep and hoarse, suddenly appears and the world vanishes, the world of existence. A woman in the flesh had this voice, she sang in front of a record, in her finest get up, and they recorded her voice. The woman: bah! she existed like me, like Rollebon, I don't want to know her. But here

36. Ibid., pp. 162–63. The translations are mine.

it is. You can't say it exists. The turning record exists, the air struck by the voice which vibrates, exists, the voice which made an impression on the record existed. I who listen, I exist. All is full, existence everywhere, dense, heavy and sweet. But, beyond all this sweetness, inaccessible, near and so far, young, merciless and serene, there is this . . . this rigour. [*N*, 139–40]

The music has become "a little jewelled pain which spins around above the record and dazzles me . . . it spins gaily, completely self-absorbed; like a scythe it has cut through the drab intimacy of the world . . . It does not exist." He realizes that he could not reach *it*, even if he were to get up and break the record. "It is beyond—always beyond something, a voice, a violin note. Through layers and layers of existence, it veils itself, thin and firm, and when you want to seize it, you find only existents, you butt against existents devoid of sense. It is behind them: I don't even hear it, I hear sounds, vibrations in the air unveil it. It does not exist . . . It *is*" (*N*, 233). Elsewhere Sartre was also to state that music has its own, internal time. A symphony, he maintained, is not at all "within time." It does not exist, nor is it like an essence "outside of time and space: it is outside the realm of the real, outside of existence. I do not truly hear it, I hear it in the realm of the imagination." Only its analogues enter our realm of reality. When we listen to music, we ignore these analogues and are transported into the realm of the imaginary.[37]

In this pure realm beyond existence, Roquentin envisions his deliverance from Nausea, but also his "justification" for existence (*N*, 237). Deliverance might come to him through writing a book—not a history, nor a biography of an Other or even himself, but a book that would render the *essence of his life* in the manner in which the song rendered that of the people who wrote

37. Sartre, *The Psychology of Imagination*, pp. 280–81.

and sang it. He visualizes the composer's life as ugly, full of loneliness, grime, and suffering. He imagines him sweaty in the heat of a New York summer. But transfigured into song, the man's suffering and sweat become moving to Roquentin *(N,* 236). The book he plans to write is to represent a similar transfiguration of his own life: "You would have to guess, behind the printed words, behind the pages, at something which would not exist, which would be above existence. A story, for example, something that could never happen, an adventure. It would have to be beautiful and hard as steel and make people ashamed of their existence" (*N,* 237).

Roquentin shows himself at this point largely the heir of early German Romanticism, and of Schopenhauer, Nietzsche, and Proust.[38] Tracing the emphasis on music as the salvation of man and the highest of all arts from its Romantic origins to the present, Erich Heller has seen in it the artist's increasing desire for inwardness and has labeled the entire trend "the artist's journey into the interior." He felt with Heine that this tendency aimed perhaps at "nothing less than the dissolution of the whole material world." To Heller, this attitude seems to be epitomized in Rilke's assertion that "Gesang ist Dasein" (song is existence), and he explains that Rilke's poetic desire to see the world *aufgehoben* in song implied the triple meaning of the German word as "preserved," "raised to a higher level," and "removed" or "dissolved."[39] Rilke's singing set itself the contradictory task of rescuing the visible world by negating it and transposing it into inwardness. His endeavor approached that of a religious transubstantiation of reality into art. A similar claim can be

38. See above, p. 77. Also Walzel, *German Romanticism,* pp. 123 ff.

39. Erich Heller, *The Artist's Journey into the Interior* (New York, Random House, 1965), pp. 129, 170. I have taken the liberty of slightly changing Heller's translation, preferring "dissolved" to his "brought to an end" as one of the three possible meanings of the word *aufgehoben.*

made for Proust and, since it could not be put into more suc-
cinct and appropriate language than that used by Beckett in
his *Proust,* I shall quote it:

> Music is the catalytic element in the work of Proust. It
> asserts to his unbelief the permanence of personality and
> the reality of art. It synthesises the moments of privilege
> and runs parallel to them. In one passage he describes the
> recurrent mystical experience as "a purely musical impres-
> sion, non-extensive, entirely original, irreducible to any
> other impression . . . sine materia." The narrator . . . sees
> in the red phrase of the Septuor . . . the ideal and immaterial
> statement of the essence of a unique beauty, a unique world,
> the invariable world and beauty of Vinteuil, expressed tim-
> idly, as a prayer, in the Sonata, imploringly, as an inspira-
> tion, in the Septuor, the "invisible reality" that damns the
> life of the body on earth as a pensum and reveals the mean-
> ing of the word: "defunctus."[40]

Beckett is clearly aware here of the relationship between Proust
and Schopenhauer, using not only the vocabulary of both but
also making specific reference to the latter.

It is significant to realize, therefore, that Schopenhauer's views
on art and music also largely inspired Nietzsche in his *Birth of
Tragedy,* and that Roquentin's notions echo them as much as do
those of *Remembrance of Things Past.* Speaking of Dionysiac
man, Nietzsche observed that, if nauseated by the absurdity of
existence, he finds himself in a paroxysm, unable to see any significance in action, then, "in the supreme jeopardy of the will,
art, that sorceress expert in healing, approaches him; only she
can turn his fits of Nausea into imagination with which it is

40. Samuel Beckett, *Proust* (New York, Grove Press, 1931), pp. 71–
72.

possible to live" (*BT*, 52; VII).[41] As I have mentioned before, Nietzsche considered art—especially in the combination of poetry and music that is to be found in Greek tragedy—the highest human task. Concerning music, he adopted that part of Schopenhauer's conception which declared it a universal language in the highest degree, "related to the universality of concepts, much as these are related to particular things." Like Schopenhauer he considered the universality of music to be "by no means the empty universality of abstraction," but rather to resemble "geometrical figures and numbers, which are the universal forms of all possible objects of experience and applicable to them all a priori and yet are not abstract but perceptible and thoroughly determinate . . . Melodies reproduce the very soul and essence as it were without the body"—sine materia (*BT*, 99; XVI).

The parallels between Sartre's Roquentin, Proust's Marcel, and Nietzsche's Dionysiac man are striking. Roquentin longs to free himself from the world of existence and phenomena and aspires to that of pure geometric figures and music: of melodies which reproduce the very soul and essence as it were, without the body. To him, as to Nietzsche and Proust, music is not "a copy of the phenomenon" but the "metaphysical of everything physical in the world, and the thing itself of every phenomenon" (*BT*, 99; XVI). That is why Roquentin turns away from his nauseate inactivity and decides to write a book about himself, a novel that would "drive existence out of" him, would "rid the passing moments of their fat . . . twist them, dry them," and purify and harden his existence so as to make it "give back at last the sharp, precise sound of a saxophone note" (*N*, 234). Yet now that I have established such historical relationships and analogies between Roquentin on the one hand and Marcel and Nietzsche's poet on the other, I must also point out that Roquentin differs from them.

41. The Roman numerals within the parentheses refer to the sections of the work.

The unassuming popular song, "Some of these days," which inspires Roquentin, can hardly be compared to Rilke's concept of *Gesang,* redolent of almost religious elevation. Merleau-Ponty, Sartre's longtime friend, felt called upon to point out that Sartre's choice of the simple, popular American tune was not accidental, but was consciously made to reject in advance the religion of art and its consolations and to proclaim the validity of all art, not merely that with a capital "A," as man's means to transcend himself through creativity.[42] But this need for explanation which Merleau-Ponty felt, merely underlines Sartre's intrinsic ambiguity. One can only agree with Jean Wahl's observations, "A search for justification and the impossibility of justification are recurrent *motifs* in the philosophy of Sartre," and, "His philosophy is one of the incarnations of problematism and of the ambiguity of contemporary thought (for Man does seem, to the contemporary mind, to be ambiguous)."[43] For what matters here is not the simplicity of Roquentin's music, but rather his turning away from the lawlessness and absurdity of existence toward the order and abstractness of geometry and music. His turning away, however, is ambiguous because, unlike Rilke or Proust, Sartre does not wish to transfigure reality into poetic inwardness. While his author-hero, Roquentin, wants to rid the passing moments of their fat, he also wants to emerge as consciousness-in-the-world. If the fits of Nausea, which turn him into a more authentic consciousness-in-the-world and thereby a witness to existence and to himself, also imbue him with the desire to dissolve existence into poetry and music, he has become a paradox. For he can transcend existence through art only as the self-reflective author-hero who faces the problem of witnessing himself and reality authentically.

In his ambiguity, then, Roquentin represents a fusion of existentialist man and Dionysiac poet. But while gaining an

42. Merleau-Ponty, *Sense and Non-Sense,* p. 45.
43. Wahl, *Short History,* p. 30.

insight into the essence of his artistic creation seemed not much more than an intellectual game for Gide's Edouard, and while Proust's Marcel, at the end of a similar quest, incidentally gained metaphysical insights into existence and art, such insight is an existential inevitability for Roquentin and identical with his authenticity as a man and an artist. By the same token, the problems he encounters in his attempts to grasp the essence of his art are inevitably of an existential nature, which means that they touch upon his rendering of truth, of an unretouched reality. This accounts for Roquentin's intense preoccupation with language as a part of existence, as discussed earlier.[44] It also accounts for his preoccupation with the verbal rendering of reality in terms of tenses and the logical or chronological sequence or their absence in the telling of events. It affects, above all, the problem of the writer's understanding of the Other, both in his own fictional actuality and among the characters he wishes to create.

Having abandoned the biography of a historical figure as belonging to a past that forever escapes him, Roquentin wonders how he can render the present without letting it become a past in the very process of telling about it; how he can recapture its immediacy without falsifying it—as those young men do who sit together in cafés, telling each other about the events of the day, and who "bring you up to date in a few words" (*N,* 15). As the author-hero consciously concerned with fictional technique, Roquentin realizes that stories told are always plausible stories and, contrary to life, are never begun without their ending being known so that their ending mysteriously affects their beginning:

> You seem to start at the beginning: "It was a fine autumn evening in 1922. I was a notary's clerk in Marommes." And in reality you have started at the end. It was there, invisible

44. See above, pp. 118–19.

and present, it is the one which gives to the words the pomp
and value of a beginning. "I was out walking, I had left the
town without realizing it, I was thinking about my money
troubles." This sentence taken simply for what it is, means
that the man was absorbed, morose, a hundred leagues from
an adventure, exactly in the mood to let things happen
without noticing them. But the end is there transforming
everything. For us, the man is already the hero of the story.
His moroseness, his money troubles are much more precious
than ours, they are guided by the light of future passions.
And the story goes on in the reverse: instants have stopped
piling themselves in a lighthearted way one on top of the
other, they are snapped up by the end of the story which
draws them and each one of them in turn, draws out the preceding instant: "It was night, the street was deserted." The
phrase is cast out negligently, it seems superfluous; but we
do not let ourselves be caught and we put it aside: this is a
piece of information whose value we shall subsequently
appreciate. And we feel that the hero has lived all the details of his night like annunciations, promises, . . . blind and
deaf to all that did not herald adventure. We forget that the
future was not yet there; the man was walking in a night
without forethought, a night which offered him a choice of
dull rich prizes and he did not make his choice. [N, 57–58]

Roquentin, who would have liked to pattern his own life after a
story, realizes that you might as well "try to catch time by the
tail." Only the jotting down of events as they happen can give
an authentic picture of life in all its formlessness.

When one tells it, however, the endlessly repetitious sequence
of hours, days, and years becomes a fascinating adventure: "For
the most banal event to become an adventure, you must (and that
is enough) begin to recount it. This is what fools people: a man

is always a teller of tales, he lives surrounded by his stories and the stories of others" (N, 56). In fact man, as the teller of tales, often sees everything that happens to him through stories and "tries to live his own life as if he were telling a story" (N, 56), giving everything a coherence and structure that life does not have. Roquentin seems as aware as Kierkegaard of the quality of life that "separates and holds the various moments of existence discretely apart," a quality that implies both isolation and fluidity but one that is ignored and falsified by systematic thought. Within the fictional actuality of the author-hero looking at himself, Roquentin arrives at some of the same critical notions Sartre was to express in his essays on Dos Passos and Mauriac, notions he had apparently derived largely from the critic, Ramon Fernandez.

Fernandez had already maintained that the novelist should attempt to recapture the very moment of life, faithfully express its sinuosities and its rhythms, and make his intelligence merely subservient to its commands. Rather than present ideas in expository form, he should let them become apparent through a concrete situation.[45] In such a manner the novelist would create an atmosphere of the present rather than the past. Sartre's narrator Roquentin precisely adheres to such ideals. He records events as they happen and thereby avoids any impression of planned finality. The very form of the diary is expressive of discontinuity and openness. He uses, moreover, grammatical tenses that intensify this atmosphere, and his entries are frequently written in the present tense. Describing the vivid scene in the restaurant where he eats with the Self-Taught Man, he puts all verbs in that form, as if they were stage directions: "He turns . . . he contemplates . . . I read on his face" (N, 160). Even when he is alone in his room, he may record his activities in this man-

45. Ramon Fernandez, "The Method of Balzac," *Messages*, trans. Montgomery Belgion (New York, Harcourt, Brace, 1927), pp. 61–88.

ner: "I see my hand . . . it lives . . . it opens . . . I jump up" (*N*, 134–35). On other occasions he may lapse into the past definite or *passé simple:* "I got up (je me levai)," "I looked (je regardai)," "I seized (je pris)" (*N*, 106–07). But even this tense evokes the present, as Claude-Edmonde Magny explains. "The ordinary novel," she states, "wherein the characters are free and where they create their lives as they go along, because nothing has been arranged in advance, unrolls itself normally in the present tense; consequently, because of the lapse of time, the author tells us what has happened in the *passé simple,* which exactly corresponds to the present tense, the tense which grammarians call, if I remember correctly, 'the present in the past.'"[46]

The past, in fact, is something the self-critical author-hero Roquentin comes to consider as nonexistent and as being retained only by means of words emptied of their content. Roquentin still *knows* certain matters related to his own past, but it becomes more and more difficult for him to decide whether the scraps of images he can conjure up are fact or fiction. "Nothing is left but words: I could still tell stories, tell them too well" (*N*, 48). History, the books of Michelet, the Historical Museum of Bouville, Anny's notions of privileged moments, his own attempt to write a biography are but distortions of a present that no longer exists. It is only at one moment in the novel that, looking down upon the street from his window, Roquentin is capable of experiencing past, present, and future almost simultaneously. He sees an old woman cross the square below. She lumbers across it, stopping many times to adjust her windblown skirt and her kerchief. Seeing her advance and slowly pass makes Roquentin recognize the pattern of her project: her destiny. "She walks," he realizes, "she was there, now she is here . . . I don't

46. Magny, *Les Sandales d'Empédocle*, p. 137. The translation is mine. See also Sartre, "Camus' *The Outsider*," *Literary and Philosophical Essays*, p. 41.

know where I am any more: do I *see* her motions, or do I *foresee* them? I can no longer distinguish present from future and yet it lasts, it happens little by little, the old woman advances in the deserted street, shuffling her heavy, mannish brogues. This is time, time laid bare, coming slowly into existence, keeping us waiting, and when it does come, making us sick because we realise it's been there for a long time" (*N,* 46). Roquentin can see this past turning into a present and future; he can foresee the turn of events, because he is outside and above the woman. He looks at her life, or at least this small moment of it, the way a god, to whom past, present and future are as one, might do. But concerning his own existence, which is *in* time, only the present exists, while the future remains sheer possibility capable of being translated into infinite forms and yet as deprived of reality as is his past.

In his quest to recapture existence, the existential author-hero must face another crucial problem: the Other. Roquentin encounters it in his life as a fictional character and his own creative attempts. His relationship to the Self-Taught Man and those men and women he encounters in his daily endeavors is too casual to present him with true difficulties. But when a matter of greater intimacy with the Other is at stake, as in the case of Anny, he is doomed to failure. He cannot enter the consciousness of Anny any more than she can enter his. In spite of the attraction they feel for each other, in spite of the fact that they become reacquainted and even discover parallel developments in their lives, they cannot help one another. Roquentin's authorial relationship to the Other, to Rollebon, turns out to be even more problematic because his knowledge of the marquis is even less direct. It comes to him only through the eyes and reports of Others. This does not mean that there is any lack of information about Rollebon. On the contrary, Roquentin not only possesses documents concerning him that he acquired in Russia, but he can also consult a variety of sources in Bouville. People have written letters about him, have described his looks, his character, his preferences, even his successes in official and personal matters. And yet, Roquentin feels that the man more and more escapes him: "In the first place, starting from 1801, I understand nothing more about his conduct. It is not lack of documents: letters, fragments of memoirs, secret reports, police records. On the contrary I have almost too many of them. What is lacking in all this testimony is firmness and consistency. They do not contradict each other, neither do they agree with each other; they do not seem to be about the same person" (N, 22–23). Was he as boring as some report him to have been? Roquentin asks himself. Was he that great wit with a gift for mimicry, exuding infinite charm and exercising great power over women, that others thought him to be? Or was he perhaps nothing more than a low comedian?

> I was quite pleased that he lied to others but I would have liked him to make an exception of me; I thought we were thick as thieves and that he would finally tell me the truth. He told me nothing, nothing at all; nothing more than he told Alexander or Louis XVIII whom he duped. It matters a lot to me that Rollebon should have been a good fellow. Undoubtedly a rascal: who isn't? But a big or little rascal? I don't have a high enough opinion of historical research to lose my time over a dead man whose hand, if he were alive, I would not deign to touch. What do I know about him? [N, 81]

There hovers over Roquentin's quandary the existential view, fundamental to Kierkegaardian thinking, namely, that we cannot get hold of a reality external to ourselves, except through thinking it. Since we cannot make our Self into the Other, we cannot make his acting reality our own reality. The Other can remain for us only a possibility. Rollebon, having remained a mere possibility to those who knew him in real life (in the same way Roquentin's fellow men remain mere possibilities to him), is a possibility still further removed from Roquentin. He could not help but abandon Rollebon for the only concern of closest proximity: himself.

Is then the existentialist author limited to depicting only heroes in his own likeness, that is, heroes who are above all author-heroes? Many of Sartre's contemporaries seem to have been of this opinion, for modern fiction sports a multitude of author-heroes, intent on creating novels, and being rewarded for their tribulations by nothing more than an insight into their art and existence. Their abundance is too great to attempt to mention them. But, as we shall see, almost all of Beckett's fiction belongs in this category. Indeed, the pattern has gained so much favor in recent decades that it has affected even other genres as the theater and the film. In his *L'Impromptu de l'Alma,* for instance, Ionesco appears as the character Ionesco who is in the process of writing a play while he is besieged by critics. In Fellini's film $8\frac{1}{2}$, "the creator . . . dissatisfied to serve merely as his own model, proceeds to make not his likeness but the difficulty of creating a work of art out of that likeness the subject of the work of art," as Brendan Gill pointed out in reviewing the film. "The struggle to achieve something becomes the thing achieved; getting there is *all* the fun, or, more likely, all the anguish."[47] But Sartre, like Kierkegaard before him, must have felt the need to create fictional worlds of greater breadth and depth. Arrogating to himself, quite justifiably, the right to that perpetual change he considered essential to man's freedom, Sartre employed in his later fiction techniques that kept step with the widening horizons of his metaphysical and critical thinking. Whereas Kierkegaard

47. Brendan Gill, "The Current Cinema," *The New Yorker* (June 1963) 62.

had to resort to piling one fictional author upon another in order to introduce individual variety into his fiction, Sartre's metaphysics—though adhering to the same concept of the individual's fundamental isolation—opened up for him a greater variety of fictional possibilities, while his critical insights helped him to translate these into techniques.

Crucial in this development was Sartre's preoccupation with the fictional "point of view." We have already seen that the problem of the author-protagonist identification—which inadvertently affects the technique of the point of view—was something Sartre had been aware of since his early childhood. As already mentioned, he reminisces in *Words* about his childish joy at creating for his stories a hero who is really his double, though bearing a different name and being referred to in the third person. If the third-person mask was the child's game, it became a matter of serious exploration for the mature critic writing about Mauriac. In the famous essay Sartre wrote about the novelist he discussed the ramifications of the first-person/third-person narrative. With regard to Mauriac's ambiguous use of the third person, Sartre observed:

> In a novel, the pronoun "she" can designate *another*, that is, an opaque object, someone whose exterior is all we ever see—as when I write, for example, 'I saw *that she* was trembling.' But it also happens that this pronoun leads us into the intimacy which ought logically to express itself in the first person. 'She was astounded to hear the echo of her own words.' There really is no way of my knowing this unless I am in a position to say that I have heard the echo of my own words.[48]

48. Sartre, "François Mauriac and Freedom," *Literary and Philosophical Essays*, pp. 11–12. The translation here mistakenly reads "which ought logically to express itself in the third person."

Sartre defends this conventional pretense, this masking of a first-person situation, because it screens "the dizzying intimacy of the 'I,'" while it does not "demand of the reader an unreserved complicity." The third-person pronoun, moreover, gives the perspective of an opera glass. It "reminds us that the revealing consciousness is also fictional creation; it represents a viewpoint on the privileged point of view and fulfills for the reader the fond desire of the lover to be both himself and someone else." One is reminded of James Joyce's reference, in *A Portrait of the Artist as a Young Man,* to the old English ballad *Turpin Hero* which begins in the first person but ends in the third person. At the time he wrote his essay on Mauriac, Sartre had apparently reached a stage in his development as a writer and critic where he could accept the fact that the novelist may, to some extent, refine himself out of existence. For if he criticizes Mauriac, it is mainly because of the novelist's inconsistency in maintaining his point of view. He accuses Mauriac of unwarranted intrusion into the consciousness which tells the story, by analyzing and even judging it in the manner of an omniscient author. If such intrusion is avoided by the novelist, if the point of view is adhered to, Sartre can envision works of fiction with not only one but several consciousnesses revealing themselves in the third person. For he declares in his essay that "a novel is an action related from various points of view."[49]

Such a definition might seem to imply that Sartre abandoned the existential conception of the individual as being essentially isolated. But his own understanding of the point-of-view technique in the novel dispels such doubts. While different consciousnesses may relate the action in question in one and the same novel, they remain to each other as opaque as the Seducer's remained to Cordelia or Anny's to Roquentin. For Sartre defines point of view in the same essay as "the testimony of a participant" which "should reveal the man who testifies," while "the

49. Ibid., pp. 12–13, 15.

participants' interpretations and explanations will all be hypothetical." If the reader has "an inkling, beyond these conjectures, of the event's absolute reality . . . it is for him alone to re-establish it," yet even he could never get "beyond the realm of likelihood and probability."[50] It is interesting to realize that, in her book of memoirs, *The Prime of Life,* Simone de Beauvoir refers to such aesthetic principles as "the one rule" which both Sartre and she regarded as "fundamental" and prides herself on having let it govern the construction of her own novel *She Came to Stay.* "In each successive chapter," she explains, "I identified myself with one of my characters, and excluded any knowledge or notion beyond what he or she would have had" (269–73). If asked how the "I" of the author, that is, his own individual consciousness, is able to create a number of fictional existents each with his own, not the author's, point of view, one might answer that each of these existents is imagined as a possibility—not unlike Kierkegaard's "authors." Sartre's own answer would probably be that these existents are *within the field of the author's possibles.* For this is, in fact, the terminology he used in discussing Emma Bovary: he considered her one of Flaubert's possibles.[51]

The form of Sartre's later fiction shows the effect of such considerations. His collection of short stories, *Intimacy and Other Stories* (1939),[52] published the same year as his article on Mauriac, shows him translating into narrative techniques his newly gained critical insights. None of the protagonists of these stories is an author-hero. Though all narrators are first-person consciousnesses—even if often under the guise of the third person—their identity with the author is established only to the extent that they represent his possibles. In each story the assumed point of view is strictly adhered to, but a story may contain several points

50. Ibid., pp. 15–16.
51. Sartre, *The Problem of Method,* p. 141.
52. Jean-Paul Sartre, *Intimacy and Other Stories,* trans. Lloyd Alexander (New York, New Directions, 1948).

of view that come to the fore successively. These techniques, which Sartre uses as yet sparingly in the short stories, are more daringly exploited in his novel *The Roads to Freedom*—a development made clearer by a brief glance at the short stories.

In "Erostratus," the third story in the collection and one of its few first-person narratives, the protagonist reveals himself and the world about him. He discloses that he wants to be a "black," that is, a negative hero, emulating Erostratus, whose sole fame rests on his burning of the temple of Ephesus. Through the mad consciousness of this protagonist, a strange world emerges from which he is alienated in more than one sense. Like Roquentin, he hates the *salauds,* but not because of his own growing authenticity. His mad desire is rather to destroy and kill aimlessly. His animosity toward and isolation from society are constantly underlined, in grammatical terms, through a perpetual opposition of "I" and "they."

In "The Room," several first-person consciousnesses appear in third-person guise. Here various points of view come to the fore. Events and situations are first revealed through the consciousness of Madame Darbédat, who lives in a world of luxurious make-believe and remembrance of past happiness; then through Monsieur Darbédat, who thinks of himself as a realist but is totally ensconced in and blinded by conformity; and finally through Eve, their unfortunate daughter, who, defying her parents' world of narrowly selfish "normality," wants to share the chaotic universe of her mentally ill husband, Pierre. Yet she can enter his consciousness or his universe as little as she can her parents', or as they can enter hers. The object-ness things assume for Pierre, whose illness makes him see them outside the context in which society has placed them, remains unattainable to her, hard as she may try. Even Pierre, in spite of his growing madness, is aware of the wall that divides them and that she is unwilling to acknowledge. Through the story's alternating points of view, the desperate isolation of each consciousness is dramatically placed in relief. At the same time, one is aware of the extent to which Sartre's fictional world has been expanded through his use of more than one consciousness.

The same may be said of "Intimacy," which would totally lose its perspective and effectiveness if the simple story were merely told as the interior monologue of one person. But again, varying points of view—as if ironically to defy the story's title—stress the manner in which each consciousness remains immured within itself. What the characters consider their intimacy is only inauthentic simulation. As they "monologuize," they refer to themselves in the third person, though slipping occasionally into an undisguised "I." Lulu, the main character, for instance, reveals herself and her world in this manner: "She had closed her eyes and the blue discs began to turn, as they had done at the fair, I was aiming at the discs with rubber arrows, and there were letters which lit up, one at a time, and they formed the name of a town, he kept me from completing Dijon because of his mania to nudge me from behind, I detest it when someone touches me from behind."[53] Each time a character plunges in this manner from the third person into the first, he also seems to plunge into deeper isolation and inauthenticity.

In the tense atmosphere of "The Wall," all is told by a first-person narrator who accidentally is identified as Pablo. He is one of a group of political prisoners taken during the Spanish Civil War and condemned to death. The prisoners, under the surveillance of their enemy guards, spend their last night together. In this extreme situation of a man faced with death, each member of the group is alone. To the narrator, all that goes on remains incomprehensible as he observes himself and Others: the automatic reactions of their bodies which exude fear; his own "loyalty" (or is it sheer obstinacy?) to the friend for whom he dies and whose life he believes he will save by remaining silent. No admirable sentiments are expressed among the prisoners.

53. My translation, from *Le Mur* (Paris, Gallinard, 1939), p. 95.

There are none of the "privileged moments" which Anny, in *Nausea,* used to envision as accompanying death. All that happens is commonplace, disgusting, and even language descends to the depths of the situation. The story's powerful ending smacks of absurdity—not the fundamental metaphysical absurdity of Roquentin, but an absurdity transposed into human relationships and based on the odd coincidence that so preoccupied Camus.

Sartre introduced, however, in "The Wall" and especially in "The Childhood of a Leader" a fictional device based on views concerning the Other which he was to develop fully in *Being and Nothingness.* He accepted, of course, Kierkegaard's tenet that the Other remains to the individual mere conjecture. But Kierkegaard's view on this matter was restricted, as we have seen, to the plane of the ethical and the religious. In contrast to Heidegger or Sartre, Kierkegaard never developed a metaphysics. It was in his metaphysical reflections upon the Self and the Other that Sartre came to account for the fact that the Other is, nevertheless, a part of man's universe. Heidegger, unlike Descartes, never questioned the existence of the Other. He simply accepted the Other as a part of man's essential Being-with-one-another, as coming to light—like any other part of Being—within the horizon of the individual's consciousness. But Sartre, taking individual consciousness as his point of departure, had to prove the Other's existence. In *Being and Nothingness* he proved it ingeniously through the cogito, and thereby arrived at a unique conception of human interrelationships that does not deny man's essential separateness or his opaqueness to the Other. In proving the Other's existence, he uses the example of a person spying through a keyhole and being surprised by another. The presence of the Other makes itself felt to him, as he becomes aware of himself not in the manner in which he sees himself, but in the manner in which he is seen and judged by the Other. Because of the Other's Look, the cogito which surges up within himself is that of the Other and confirms the Other's presence. By his Look—whether actual or implicit—the Other, according to Sartre, deprives us of our freedom. For as he judges us, he labels and fixes us in what may be only one aspect of our Being. Sartre also conceives of the Other as depriving us of our world. As long as we are alone, we are the center of our universe which groups itself around us in the manner in which our consciousness organizes it. If an Other enters this world, he may at first appear to us as an object. But as soon as he emerges as an Other, he wraps our world around himself, imposing upon it *his* organization: "There is a regrouping in which I take part but which escapes me, a regrouping of all the objects which people my universe." Thus the man-object, Sartre concludes, by appearing in my world, has "stolen the world from me."[54] The Other, by being the human center of his object world, has decentralized mine.

To the Other conceived in this manner, I have become an object. His freedom is my limitation. It "is revealed to me across the uneasy indetermination of the being I am for him," a being I have not freely chosen. Sartre maintains that "I grasp the Other's Look at the very center of my *act* as the solidification and alienation of my own possibilities"[55] We are, then, not accidentally but essentially placed at the mercy of the Other's judgment which forever deprives us of our freedom. But we are at his mercy completely only by our death—whether this death is the termination of our life or the surrender of our moral prerogative to choose and change. In his play, *No Exit,* Sartre has found an analogue to this ambiguity by making hell look like a living room. The Other becomes hell only when his victim fails to assume his authenticity by asserting his freedom, rejecting the solidifying judgment of the Other, and insisting on making his own choices. By failing to do all this, the individual becomes an en-soi without a pour-soi—a thing not unlike the bronze statue

54. Sartre, *Being and Nothingness,* pp. 254–55.
55. Ibid., pp. 262–63.

in the living room of *No Exit*

In his collection of short stories, which preceded the publication of *Being and Nothingness* by about four years, Sartre used the Look as yet gropingly. In the moments before their death when language fails the prisoners in "The Wall" as a means of communication, a quasi-communication is established by the Look: prisoners and guards look at each other and are conscious of being looked at. But Sartre had not yet developed the device. In the collection's last story, "The Childhood of a Leader," however, it gains greater significance. Here the Look already represents the Other's judgment which, in the case of the protagonist Lucien, becomes his destiny. Stunted in his development since his early childhood, the inauthentic Lucien begins by thinking of himself as an adorable little girl, because Others designate him as such by their gestures and their remarks. As he grows up, he passes through a period during which he gropes for his identity. But he merely successively plays the roles of a candidate for suicide, a follower of Freud, a surrealist poet, and a homosexual. When he finds his "identity," it is not within himself but rather in the eyes of Others. It is there that he comes to admire himself at last as an aggressive, rich, young bully who hates Jews: a leader among his peers. Seemingly having made him free, the Looks of Others have turned him into their object.

There is drama inherent in the individual's relationship to the Other as revealed through the Look. And this drama becomes even more striking when it is singled out and transposed from the realm of actuality to that of the imaginary. The Look of the Other—partly reassuring and partly undermining existence—initiates struggles of the kind one finds in Racinian tragedies, as has been pointed out.[56] This drama was exploited extensively and ingeniously by Sartre in the three volumes of his projected

56. Jean Starobinski, "Racine et la poétique du regard," *Nouvelle Nouvelle Revue Française,* 5 (1957), 246–63.

tetralogy, *Roads to Freedom* (1945–49).[57] In this powerful work dealing with the period before and during World War II, Sartre is no longer concerned with one lone individual but presents us with an array of people and situations that prove him to be a novelist of genius and imagination. As the title indicates, the work revolves around the problem of freedom, a freedom of ethical nature based on the principle that, since there is no God, man is responsible. Sartre's concept of authenticity, which in *Nausea* meant above all the authenticity of witnessing and of language, has come to mean in *Roads to Freedom* mainly political decision and commitment. But the novel's characters are almost all inauthentic, with the exception of Brunet who becomes a Communist, and Mathieu, the protagonits, who seems to move toward a similar authenticity. In his *Stages on Sartre's Way,* Robert Champigny outlines what, in private conversation, Sartre had presented to him as the way in which he wanted to complete the fourth volume (two chapters of that volume appeared in 1949 in *Les Temps Modernes*):[58]

> From what we gathered in conversation with the author, here is what was to happen to the main characters in the last volume: on his return to France, Brunet, the Communist leader, was to discover that his line of action in the prisoner's camp was again congruent with the Party doctrine, in view of the German attack on Russia. Mathieu, who seemed to have been killed in volume three, but who had been only wounded, was to find at last a worthy oppor-

57. Jean-Paul Sartre, *The Age of Reason, trans.* Eric Sutton (New York, Knopf; London, Hamilton, 1947); *The Reprieve,* trans. Eric Sutton (New York, Knopf; London, Hamilton, 1947); *Troubled Sleep (Iron in the Soul),* trans. Gerard Hopkins (Knopf, New York, 1951; London, Hamilton, 1950).

58. Jean-Paul Sartre, "Drôle d'amitié," *Les Temps Modernes* (1949), 769–806, 1009–39.

tunity for committing his treasured freedom—thanks to the Resistance. Still intent on cultivating abjection and perversity, Daniel was to become a collaborator, then kill himself."[59]

Champigny concluded from his interview with the novelist that the projected continuation had become pointless because the postwar situation bore little resemblance to the one of significant choices and purposeful actions which Sartre had envisioned for his characters. Other hypotheses have been advanced for Sartre's failure to complete the fourth volume of *Roads to Freedom*. Henri Peyre writes in his *French Novelists of Today:* "The path to freedom and perhaps to heroism is an arduous one. (Sartre, remembering Gide's and Mauriac's warnings about the impossibility of portraying noble feelings and saints, must have been pondering lengthily his fourth volume, long overdue.)"[60] One should realize also, it seems to me, that Sartre, who by 1946 had moved toward the Communist Party, had come to see the impossibility of identifying with it completely. For, as Colette Audry points out, between the ontology of the individual as it is presented in *Being and Nothingness* and the Marxist dialectics of history there remained a gap which Sartre, in her view, breached for the first time in his *Critique de la Raison dialectique*.[61] It may well be that political problems of engagement and individual problems of choice clashed as bewilderingly for Sartre as they did for Brunet in the published excerpt of the

59. Champigny, *Stages on Sartre's Way*, p. 194.

60. Henri Peyre, *French Novelists of Today* (New York, Oxford University Press, 1967), p. 267.

61. Colette Audry, *Sartre, et la Réalité humaine* (Paris, Editions Seghers, 1966), pp. 10, 76–77. See also Simone de Beauvoir, *The Ethics of Ambiguity*, trans. B. Frechtman (New York, Philosophical Library, 1948), p. 23.

novel's fourth part, raising questions not only about the roads to freedom but about freedom itself.

But the considerations that may have kept Sartre from terminating his novel as well as any details of his characters' developments must here give way to the central concern of this study: the novelist's technique as it grew out of his metaphysics of the Other and the Look, and as it fused with his concept of the point of view. Since this technique has found its most striking expression in the novels second volume, *The Reprieve,* I shall, in the spirit of *pars pro toto,* single out this volume for closer inspection.

As we have seen, Sartre—like Kierkegaard before him—does not assume that an individual's character can be fully defined before his death. As a novelist, he could therefore not indulge in a delineation of character. But his use of the Look actually permits him to adhere to his position and yet to present the reader with layers upon layers of character delineations. An inauthentic man may well be aware of the manner in which his friends see him and may describe himself in that manner. Thus Daniel writes on one occasion to Mathieu:

> I have never known what I *am.* My vices, my virtues, are under my nose, but I can't see them, nor stand far enough back to view myself as a whole. I seem to be a sort of flabby mass in which words are engulfed; no sooner do I name myself than what is named is merged in him who names, and one gets no farther . . . For one instant, on that June evening when I elected to confess to you, I thought I had encountered myself in your bewildered eyes. You *saw* me, in your eyes I was solid and predictable; my acts and moods were the actual consequences of a definite entity. And through me you knew that entity. I described it to you in my words, I revealed to you facts unknown to you, which

had helped you to visualize it. And yet you saw it, I merely saw you seeing it . . . I then understood that one could not reach oneself except through another's judgment, another's hatred. And also through another's love perhaps.[62]

The individual, though undefined by the author, emerges as seen by the Other. But Daniel, who here represents an individuality Sartre would designate as inauthentic, also boasts that the relationship he describes is mutual: "Without me, you would be that same insubstantial entity that I am for myself," he writes in the same letter to Mathieu. "It is by my agency that you can at times get an occasional and doubtless rather exasperating glimpse of yourself—as you really are" (*R*, 405–06).

As he has Daniel describe to Mathieu how Mathieu should appear to himself as seen through the eyes of Daniel, the novelist affords the reader this twofold perspective of Mathieu: Mathieu's cogito surging up within him, not only as a result of his own awareness of himself, but also as revealed to him through Daniel's Look. Mathieu thus appears as "a rather limited rationalist, superficially self-confident, but fundamentally without convictions, well disposed to everything within the compass of your reason, blind and disingenuous towards anything else; rational by self-interest, naturally sentimental, by no means sensual; in brief, a cautious, moderate intellectual, an excellent middle-class product." Description and analysis which in a nineteenth-century novel might have been the task of an omniscient, intruding author, have here become "self-service." "If it be true," Daniel continues, "that I cannot get at myself without your agency, you need mine if you want to know yourself" (*R*, 405–06). In a more immediate manner, Ivich, sensing Mathieu's Look upon her, "felt like a precious, fragile object: a small dumb idol" (*R*, 393)—and

62. Sartre, *The Reprieve*, pp. 405–06; henceforth cited in the text as *R*.

the word idol is used here in the full sense of statuesque solidity. She finds the sensation both sweet and irritating. As in Racinian tragedy, Look may struggle against Look in dramatic fashion: Mathieu who has just met Irène, "scarcely listened: he *saw* her. A look. A vast look, an empty sky: she struggled in that look, like an insect in a shaft of light." And a moment later it is Mathieu who struggles against her Look, feeling himself judged, solidified, and objectified by it: "She looked at him intently, recovering her breath. 'But you are a bourgeois, aren't you?' . . . She sees me," he thinks *(R, 379)*. As Irène yields to Mathieu and they make love, he begins to feel himself immobilized and eternalized in the deep blackness of her eyes. "She has admitted me into her eyes," he tells himself, "and in that night I now exist: a naked man. I shall leave her in an hour or two and yet I shall remain in her forever. In her, in this nameless night" *(R, 388)*. The Look, which has the power to interfere with the Other's freedom by solidifying him, thus also has that of confirming his existence. An event or a person witnessed by an Other acquires a stronger reality. Daniel who, because he is inauthentic, is that much more in need of the Other as witness, sums it up as follows: "I am seen, therefore I am . . . he who sees me causes me to be . . . I am as he sees me"*(R, 406–07)*.

Since Sartre added his notion of the Other to his concept of the novel as "an action related from various points of view," his fictional technique was affected correspondingly. He was obviously no longer obliged to limit his fiction to a narrator-hero who was also an author. He could realize in the realm of the imaginary other possibles of himself and could present them as first-person consciousnesses, speaking in the third person and interacting by means of the Look. The first volume of his tetralogy, which began to appear in 1945, already reveals the universe through the eyes of Mathieu, Daniel, Boris, Marcelle, Ivich, and others. None of these consciousnesses is omniscient or privileged. As a result, the views of the universe which they share in part overlap and in part contradict each other, permitting insights and creating opaqueness. The world is at times clear and brightly lit and at other times intricate and dark. It is Sartre himself who has perhaps best analyzed this method, although he was speaking for the contemporary French novel in general rather than for his own work in particular:

> Since we were *situated,* the only novels we could dream of were novels of *situation,* without internal narrators or all-knowing witnesses. In short, if we wished to give an account of our age, we had to make the technique of the novel shift from Newtonian mechanics to generalized relativity; we had to people our books with minds that were half lucid and half overcast, some of which we might consider with more sympathy than others, but none of which would have a privileged point of view either upon the event or upon himself. We had to present creatures whose reality would be the tangled and contradictory tissue of each one's evaluations of all the other characters—himself included—and the evaluation by all the others of himself, and who could never decide from within whether the changes of their destinies came from their own efforts, from their own faults, or from the course of the universe. [*WL,* 155]

Quite in conformity with these theories, Sartre never appears as omniscient narrator or plays God to his creatures in *Roads to Freedom.* His characters are shown rather in their searching, their incomprehension of the world, and their helplessness before its absurdity. Not being limited to the monolithic ipseity of a Kierkegaard, who could only create author within author, Sartre's concept of the Look enabled him to create a variety of characters who shared a fictional world that showed itself to each of them under a different aspect.

In *Reprieve,* this technique seems to reach its culmination. As in the *Age of Reason,* which precedes it, and in *Troubled Sleep,* which follows it, the universe of *Reprieve* is disclosed by a variety of isolated consciousnesses, each placed *en situation.* The method of disclosing is not the diary; nor are there interior monologues exploring psychic depths, of the kind we find in Schnitzler or Joyce. No subconscious or dream world is probed. Stress is placed rather entirely upon events, action, and dialogue. All this creates an impression of immediacy and seems to exclude reflection (*WL,* 98, n. 11). Nothing is retrospective, nothing seems sifted. No explanations are given, no causal or psychological laws referred to. Nor is there room in *Reprieve* for any of the generalizations often found in traditional novels.[63] Innumerable activities and thoughts of innumerable individuals are placed side by side in such a way that they leave no room for interpretation or comment. *"Doing,"* as Sartre was to observe in *What Is Literature?* "reveals *being*" (*WL,* 165). It was in the same essay that he was to spell out for the contemporary novelist what he considered a new program, inspired by such writers as Saint-Exupéry and Hemingway. We did not want, he asserts, to write in a superior manner about a world already belonging to the past:

> no art could really be ours if it did not restore to the event its brutal freshness, its ambiguity, its unforeseeability, if it did not restore to time its actual course, to the world its rich and threatening opacity, and to man his long patience . . . We wanted to take it [our public] by the throat. Let every character be a trap, let the reader be caught in it, and let him be tossed from one consciousness to another as from one absolute and irremediable universe to another

63. Sartre objected elsewhere to such authorial intrusions as "Daniel, like all young people" or "Eve was quite feminine in that she" (*WL,* 96).

> similarly absolute; let him be uncertain of the very uncer-
> tainty of the heroes, disturbed by their disturbance, flooded
> with their present, docile beneath the weight of their future,
> invested with their perceptions and feelings as by high
> insurmountable cliffs. In short, let him feel that every one
> of their moods and every movement of their minds en-
> closes all mankind and is, in its time and place, in the womb
> of history and, despite the perpetual juggling of the present
> by the future, a descent without recourse toward Evil or an
> ascent toward Good which no future will be able to contest.
> [WL, 156]

Though Mathieu emerges as the protagonist of *Reprieve,* he remains, nevertheless, a voice in a large chorus of voices. The novel is not so much the story of an individual as it is that of a world in suspense during the week from September 23 to September 30—ignoring, dreading, or desiring a war that then seemed imminent, unacceptable, and yet unavoidable. The story is told without the benefit of a "primary" or "secondary" subjectivity acting either as author or intermediary narrator who "perceives and thinks the universe" *(WL,* 92). The reader is, as it were, brought into direct contact with each consciousness as it reveals itself and its world. The story seems to unroll itself: a composite of flashes or simultaneous consciousnesses, each lighted up momentarily, then falling back into darkness, their appearance regulated neither by logic nor chronological sequence. There is in *Reprieve* an "orchestration of consciousnesses" and a "multidimensionality of events," which Sartre considered the technical aim of the modern writer who wanted to restore to the living event all its value. The reader is forced to enter into the minds of the various subjectivities "as into a windmill" and "must coincide successively with each one of them" *(WL,* 158, n. 12).

Sartre apparently considered the past definite the tense best suited to creating an atmosphere of immediacy. It is the tense to which Claude-Edmonde Magny referred as "the present in the past" and the one she considered evocative of actions that are in the course of taking place and permit of a future not yet realized, a plot still unknown and hence not yet looked at in retrospect.[64] But in order to make the reader feel contemporary with the story, Sartre wanted to go beyond a mere changing of verb tenses. He wanted to revolutionize the technique of the story (*WL*, 98, n. 11). He did this in *Reprieve* by packing innumerable facts and characters not only into each chapter or paragraph of the novel but even into single sentences. In a sentence beginning with the subject pronoun *elle,* for instance, and clearly referring to Charles' nurse and her activities, this same pronoun, suddenly and without separating punctuation, may refer to Odette, a totally different person in a totally different locality and situation. As Odette speaks, Charles, in reacting to his nurse, may pronounce the very word which happens to be a reply to the question Odette has addressed to the person who is with her. As one comment made by one person ends on the word "no," the same word—as if in dreamlike association—may be the beginning of another comment made elsewhere and under different circumstances. This theme of simultaneity, which permeates the entire novel, is sounded from its very start: "Sixteen thirty o'clock in Berlin, fifteen thirty o'clock in London. The hotel stood bleakly on its hill, a desolate, solemn edifice with an old gentleman inside it. At Angoulême, Marseille, Ghent, and Dover, people thought: 'What can he be doing? It's past three o'clock, why doesn't he come out?'" (*R,* 3). It is as if an intelligence hovered over all events and situations and seeing them simultaneously associated them by means of coincidence of vocabulary or analogy of situation. At a certain moment, Milan Hlinka, a Czech in Czechoslovakia is prevented by his wife from hitting back at a

64. Magny, *Les Sandales d'Empédocle,* pp. 137–38. See above, p. 131.

Nazi who is throwing rocks into his apartment. "Milan!" she cries, "you don't have the right to do it. You are not alone." Remembering his responsibility to a pregnant wife and his unborn child, he mumbles to himself: "I am not alone. I am not alone." And, like an echo, the word "alone" reappears in the next statement: "Daniel was thinking: 'I am alone.'" Situation, characters, circumstances—all have changed, only the vocable is being echoed. On other occasions events seem to pivot around such a vocable. It is the word which seems to organize the pattern of actions and feelings. Ivich, alone in Paris and in Mathieu's apartment, suddenly is filled with the sensation that all life and excitement are "outside" in the street. But, once "outside" there, she feels that she is "outside" of everything and in the midst of a dreadful freedom *(R, 85, 362)*. At other times the associating link between otherwise disconnected events and people is a certain analogy of situation: Mathieu's making love to Irène in Paris is juxtaposed with a scene in another part of France where Boris embraces Lola. This intermingling of people, places, and events private and public is given perhaps its most artistic expression in a scene reminiscent of Flaubert's *Madame Bovary*. In *Reprieve*, Ivich submits to the advances of her lover, while highly placed politicians elsewhere decide the fate of Europe. The analogy with the love scene between Emma and Rodolphe against the clamor of the county fair is so striking that a quick glance at the two scenes may throw light upon the Sartrean technique. (The appropriate excerpts from the two works are annexed to this chapter.)

It would seem that Sartre, after all, played the role of the omniscient author able to be aware of all that happens in Berlin, London, Prague, or Angoulême and able to "coincide successively with each consciousness"; as if, similar to the artist as envisioned by Flaubert, he were "like God in creation, invisible, and all-powerful . . . felt everywhere but not seen." But between

Flaubert and Sartre there are essential differences as well as similarities, as the excerpts clearly indicate. Flaubert at times describes and narrates and at times shows, whereas Sartre always shows. Unlike Sartre, Flaubert links events, creates transitions, uses conjunctions such as "while" and "whereas." Sartre completely effaces himself. Individual consciousnesses are presented without transitions other than the "echoes" of a verbal or situational nature that we have referred to. Whenever an individual consciousness comes to the fore, it is through that consciousness that the world is revealed to us. No psychological inevitability governs Sartre's narrative. It adds up to a universal clamor of voices. If the author is at all present in the story, it is because each of these voices is one within the field of his own possibles. The voice heard most strongly within the novel, that of Mathieu, expresses perhaps situationally and poetically Sartre's own position vis-à-vis this work: "These four walls and that woman on the bed were an unimportant accident, a transitory vision of the night. Wherever night was, there was Mathieu, from the frontiers in the north to the Côte d'Azur; he was, indeed, absorbed into the night, and he looked at Irène with all the eyes of the night: she was no more than a faint flicker in the darkness" (R, 377–78). Sartre here resembles Kierkegaard in the manner in which he effaces himself before the aesthetic consciousnesses and actualities he has created, but by means of the Look—which is an essential part of his philosophy—he could make these isolated consciousnesses interact and thereby create a historical world. Abandoning the I-Roquentin identity of *Nausea*, Sartre could attain in the tetralogy—and especially in *Reprieve* —that orchestration of consciousnesses, that multidimensionality for which he had come to strive, proclaiming that "to our inner certainty of being revealers is added that of being inessential to the thing revealed" (WL, 23). In *Reprieve*, and the tetralogy in general, Sartre transformed himself, not unlike the dramatist envisioned by Nietzsche in *The Birth of Tragedy,* and spoke "out of strange bodies and souls" *(BT,* 55, *VIII).* Because of this, Sartre could express the hope that "our books remain in' the air all by themselves and that their words, instead of pointing backwards toward the one who has designed them, will be toboggans, forgotten, unnoticed, and solitary, which will hurl the reader into the midst of a universe where there are not witnesses, in short that our books may exist in the manner of things, of plants, of events, and not at first like products of man" *(WL,* 158). Sartre's desire to have the artist refine himself out of existence exceeds here even that of Joyce, but I am inclined to judge it in the manner in which Leon Edel judged Joyce's: "The dissociation is not complete. He remains, after all, within, behind, above, or beyond the work—and not too far beyond. He is like those dreams we have in which we are both the actor and the audience; in which we act and also stand by watching ourselves in action. So a work of fiction, if not autobiography of the artist, is still a particular synthesis created by him and by no one else."[65] This is, I think, in keeping with Sartre's own metaphysics which makes individual man the witness of Being, unable to enter other consciousnesses but capable of creating men aesthetically in the image of his own possibles.

Unlike the writer informed by Hegelian metaphysics, Sartre does not turn these consciousnesses into objects perceived and manipulated by the author from the point of view of the Absolute.[66] They remain subjective while at the same time transcending what Simone de Beauvoir has termed "the errors of subjective idealism and false objectivity." They reconcile, in fact, subjectivity and objectivity in the manner envisioned by Heidegger and embraced by both Simone de Beauvoir and Sartre: various truths reveal themselves through each situated

65. See Chapter 1, n. 54.
66. See Sartre, *Being and Nothingness,* p. 243.

individual, each expressing reality in its entirety.[67] "For *us* too," Sartre maintained "the event appears only through subjectivities. But its transcendence comes from the fact that it exceeds them all because it extends through them and reveals to each person a different aspect of itself and of himself" *(WL,* 158, n. 12).

67. *The Prime of Life,* pp. 269, 273.

Appendix: Flaubert/Sartre

Flaubert, *Madame Bovary*

Rodolphe, meanwhile, with Madame Bovary, had gone up to the first floor of the townhall, to the "council-room," and as it was empty, he declared that they could enjoy the sight there more comfortably. He fetched three stools from the round table under the bust of the monarch, and having carried them to one of the windows, they sat down by each other.

There was commotion on the platform, long whisperings, much parleying. At last the councilor got up. They knew now that his name was Lieuvain, and in the crowd the name was passed from one to the other. After he had collated a few pages, and bent over them to see better, he began:

"Gentlemen! May I be permitted first of all (before addressing you on the object of our meeting to-day, and this sentiment will, I am sure, be shared by you all), may I be permitted, I say, to pay a tribute to the higher administration, to the government, to the monarch, gentlemen, our sovereign, to that beloved king, to whom no branch of public or private prosperity is a matter of indifference, and who directs with a hand at once so firm and wise the chariot of the state amid the incessant perils of a stormy sea, knowing, moreover, how to make peace respected as well as war, industry, commerce, agriculture, and the fine arts."

"I ought," said Rodolphe, "to get back a little further."

"Why?" said Emma.

But at this moment the voice of the councilor rose to an extraordinary pitch. He declaimed:

"This is no longer the time, gentlemen, when civil discord ensanguined our public places, when the landlord, the business-man, the working-man himself, falling asleep at night, lying down to peaceful sleep, trembled lest he should be awakened suddenly by the noise of incendiary tocsins, when the most subversive doctrines audaciously sapped foundations."

"Well, some one down there might see me," Rodolphe resumed, "then I should have to invent excuses for a fortnight; and with my bad reputation ——"

"Oh, you are slandering yourself," said Emma.

"No! It is dreadful, I assure you."

"But, gentlemen," continued the councilor, "if, banishing from my memory the remembrance of these sad pictures, I carry my eyes back to the actual situation of our dear country, what do I see there? Everywhere commerce and the arts are flourishing; everywhere new means of communication, like so many new arteries in the body of the state, establish within it new relations. Our great industrial centers have recovered all their activity; religion, more consolidated, smiles in all hearts; our ports are full, confidence is born again, and France breathes once more!"

"Besides," added Rodolphe, "perhaps from the world's point of view they are right."

"How so?" she asked.

"What!" said he. "Do you not know that there are souls constantly tormented? They need by turns to dream and to act, the purest passions and the most turbulent joys, and thus they fling themselves into all sorts of fantasies, of follies."

Then she looked at him as one looks at a traveler who has voyaged over strange lands, and went on:

"We have not even this distraction, we poor women!"
"A sad distraction, for happiness isn't found in it."
"But is it ever found?" she asked.
"Yes; one day it comes," he answered.

"And this is what you have understood," said the councilor. "You farmers, agricultural laborers! you pacific pioneers of a work that belongs wholly to civilization! you men of progress and morality, you have understood, I say, that political storms are even more redoubtable than atmospheric disturbances!"

"It comes one day," repeated Rodolphe, "one day suddenly, and when one is despairing of it. Then the horizon expands; it is as if a voice cried, 'It is here!' You feel the need of confiding the whole of your life, of giving everything, sacrificing everything to this being. There is no need for explanations; they understand one another. They have seen each other in dreams!" He looked at her. "In fine, here it is, this treasure so sought after, here before you. It glitters, it flashes; yet one still doubts, one does not believe it; one remains dazzled, as if one went out from darkness into light!"

And as he ended Rodolphe suited the action to the word. He passed his hand over his face, like a man seized with giddiness. Then he let it fall on Emma's. She took hers away.

"And who would be surprised at it, gentlemen? He only who was so blind, so plunged (I do not fear to say it), so plunged in the prejudices of another age as still to misunderstand the spirit of agricultural populations. Where, indeed, is to be found more patriotism than in the country, greater devotion to the public welfare, more intelligence, in a word? And, gentlemen, I do not mean that superficial intelligence, vain ornament of idle minds, but rather that profound and balanced intelligence that applies itself above all else to useful objects, thus contributing to the good of all, to the common amelioration and to the support of the state, born of respect for law and the practice of duty—"

"Ah! again!" said Rodolphe. "Always 'duty.' I am sick of the word. They are a lot of old blockheads in flannel vests and of old women with foot-warmers and rosaries who constantly drone into our ears 'Duty, duty!' Ah! by Jove! one's duty is to feel what is great, cherish the beautiful, and not accept all the conventions of society with the ignominy that it imposes upon us."

"Yet—yet——" objected Madame Bovary.

"No, no! Why cry out against the passions? Are they not the one beautiful thing on the earth, the source of heroism, of enthusiasm, of poetry, music, the arts, of everything, in a word?"

"But one must," said Emma, "to some extent bow to the opinion of the world and accept its moral code."

"Ah! but there are two," he replied. "The small, the conventional, that of men, that which constantly changes, that brays out so loudly, that makes such a commotion here below, of the earth earthy, like the mass of imbeciles you see down there. But the other, the eternal, that is about us and above, like the landscape that surrounds us, and the blue heavens that give us light."

Monsieur Lieuvain had just wiped his mouth with a pocket-handkerchief. He continued:

"And what should I do here, gentlemen, pointing out to you the uses of agriculture? Who supplies our wants? who provides our means of subsistence? Is it not the agriculturist? . . .

The square as far as the houses was crowded with people. One saw folk leaning on their elbows at all the windows, others standing at doors, and Justin, in front of the chemist's shop, seemed quite transfixed by the sight of what he was looking at. In spite of the silence Monsieur Lieuvain's voice was lost in the air. It reached you in fragments of phrases, and interrupted here and there by the creaking of chairs in the crowd; then you suddenly heard the long bellowing of an ox, or else the bleating of the lambs, who answered one another at street corners. In fact, the cowherds and shepherds had driven their beasts thus far, and these lowed from time to time, while with their tougues they tore down some scrap of foliage that hung above their mouths.

Rodolphe had drawn nearer to Emma, and said to her in a low voice, speaking rapidly:

"Does not this conspiracy of the world revolt you? Is there a single sentiment it does not condemn? The noblest instincts, the purest sympathies are persecuted, slandered; and if at length two poor souls do meet, all is so organized that they cannot blend together. Yet they will make the attempt; they will flutter their wings; they will call upon each other. Oh! no matter. Sooner or later, in six months, ten years, they will come together, will love; for fate has decreed it, and they are born one for the other."

His arms were folded across his knees, and thus lifting his face toward Emma, close by her, he looked fixedly at her. She noticed in his eyes small golden lines radiating from black pupils; she even smelled the perfume of the pomade that made his hair glossy. Then a faintness came over her; she recalled the Viscount who had waltzed with her at Vaubyessard, and his beard exhaled like this hair an odor of vanilla and citron, and mechanically she half-closed her eyes the better to breathe it in. But in making this movement, as she leaned back in her chair, she saw in the distance, right on the line of the horizon, the old diligence the "Hirondelle," that was slowly decending the hill of Leux, dragging after it a long trail of dust. It was in this yellow carriage that Léon had so often come back to her, and by this route down there that he had gone for ever. She fancied she saw him opposite at his window; then all grew confused; clouds gathered; it seemed to her that she was again turning in the waltz under the light of the lusters on the arm of the Viscount, and that Léon was not far away, that he was coming; and yet all the time she was conscious of the scent of Rodolphe's head by her side. This sweetness of sensation pierced through her old desires, and these, like grains of sand under a gust of wind, eddied to and fro in the subtle breath of the perfume which suffused her soul. She opened wide her nostrils several times to drink in the freshness of the ivy round the capitals. She took off her gloves, she wiped her hands, then fanned her face with her handkerchief, while athwart the throbbing of her temples she heard the murmur of the crowd and the voice of the councilor intoning his phrases. . . .

Monsieur Lieuvain then sat down; Monsieur Derozerays got up, beginning another speech. His was not perhaps so florid as that of the councilor, but it recommended itself by a more direct style, that is to say, by more special knowledge and more elevated considerations. Thus the praise of the Government took up less space in it; religion and agriculture more. He showed in it the relations of these two, and how they had always contributed to civilization. Rodolphe with Madame Bovary was talking dreams, presentiments, magnetism. Going back to the cradle of society, the orator painted those fierce times when men lived on acorns in the heart of woods. Then they had left off the skins of beasts, had put on cloth, tilled the soil, planted the vine. Was this a good, and in this discovery was there not more of injury than of gain? Monsieur Derozerays set himself this problem. From magnetism little by little Rodolphe had come to affinities, and while the president was citing Cincinnatus and his plough, Diocletian planting his cabbages, and the emperors of China inaugurating the year by the sowing of seed, the young man was explaining to the young woman that these irresistible attractions find their cause in some previous state of existence.

"Thus we," he said, "why did we come to know one another? What chance willed it? It was because across the infinite, like two streams that flow but to unite, our special bents of mind had driven us toward each other."

And he seized her hand; she did not withdraw it.

"For good farming generally!" cried the president.

"Just now, for example, when I went to your house."

"To Monsieur Bizat at Quincampoìx."

"Did I know I should accompany you?"

"Seventy francs."

"A hundred times I wished to go; and I followed you—I remained."

"Manures!"

"And I shall remain to-night, to-morrow, all other days, all my life!"

"To Monsieur Caron of Argueil, a gold medal!"

"For I have never in the society of any other person found so complete a charm."

"To Monsieur Bain of Givry-Saint-Martin."

"And I shall carry away with me the remembrance of you."

"For a merino ram!"

"But you will forget me; I shall pass away like a shadow."

"To Monsieur Belot of Notre-Dame."

"Oh, no! I shall be something in your thought, in your life, shall I not?"

"Porcine race; prizes—equal, to Messrs. Lehérissé and Cullembourg, sixty francs!"

Rodolphe was pressing her hand, and he felt it all warm and quivering like a captive dove that tries to fly away; but, whether she was trying to take it away or whether she was answering his pressure, she made a movement with her fingers. He exclaimed—

"Oh, I thank you! You do not repulse me! You are good! You understand that I am yours! Let me look at you; let me contemplate you!"

A gust of wind that blew in at the window ruffled the cloth on the table, and in the square below all the great caps of the peasant women were uplifted by it like the wings of white butterflies fluttering.

"Use of oil-cakes," continued the president. He was hurrying on: "Flemish manure—flax-growing—drainage—long leases—domestic service."

Rodolphe was no longer speaking. They looked at one another. A supreme desire made their dry lips tremble, and softly, without an effort, their fingers intertwined.*

Sartre, *The Reprieve*

And now a hand; it moved lightly, almost casually down her side; fingers flicked over her stomach. "It's *nothing,*" she thought, "it's an insect, I'm asleep. I'm asleep. I'm dreaming. I shan't move."

Masarik took the map handed to him by Sir Horace Wilson. The territories to be occupied immediately by the German Army

*(New York, W. J. Black, 1904), 2, 177–78.

were marked in blue. He looked at it for a moment, then flung it on the table.

"I—I don't understand," he said, looking Mr. Ashton-Gwatkin in the eyes. "Are we still a sovereign state?"

Mr. Ashton-Gwatkin shrugged his shoulders, apparently to indicate that he had no say in the affair; but Masarik thought he was more moved than he cared to show.

"These negotiations with Hitler are very difficult," he observed. "You must take that into account."

"Everything depended on whether the great powers would stand firm," replied Masarik vehemently.

The Englishman flushed; then he stiffened and said gravely:

"If you don't accept this agreement, you must come to terms with Germany on your own." He cleared his throat and added in a milder tone: "Perhaps the French will say so in more elaborate terms. But, believe me, they share our views; if you refuse, they won't do any more for you."

Masarik laughed harshly and nothing more was said.

A voice whispered:

"Are you asleep?"

She did not answer, but she felt a mouth against her ear and then a whole body in contact with her own.

"Ivich," he murmured. "Ivich!"

She mustn't cry out or struggle. I'm not to be violated. She turned over on her back and said:

"No, I'm not asleep. What is it?"

"I love you," he said.

Oh for a bomb that would fall from fifteen thousand feet up and kill them on the spot! A door opened and Sir Horace Wilson appeared; he did not look at them; indeed, he was looking downwards. Since their arrival he kept his eyes averted when he spoke to them. Suddenly becoming aware of this, he raised his head and eyed them vacantly.

"Will you please come in now, gentlemen?"

The three men followed him down long, deserted corridors. A floor waiter was asleep on a chair; the hotel seemed dead.

He laid his burning chest on Ivich's breasts, and she heard a soft sound like a suction cup as the sweat poured off them.

"Let me go," she said, "I'm too hot."

"In here," said Sir Horace Wilson, receding into the background.

He did not move, one hand flung off the bedclothes, the other seized her shoulder, he was now upon her, kneading her shoulders and arms with vehement, predatory hands, as he murmured in a childish, pleading voice:

"I love you, Ivich darling—how I love you!"

It was a small, low room, brightly lit. Messrs. Chamberlain, Daladier, and Léger were standing behind a table scattered with papers. The ash-trays were full of cigarette butts, but no one was then smoking. Chamberlain laid two hands on the table. He looked tired.

"Good morning, gentlemen," he said with a genial smile.

Masarik and Mastny bowed without speaking. Ashton-Gwatkin stepped briskly away from them, as though he could no longer endure their company, and stood behind Mr. Chamberlain and beside Sir Horace Wilson. The two Czechs were now confronted by five men on the other side of the table. Behind them there was the door and the deserted corridors of the hotel. There followed an instant of oppressive silence. Masarik looked at them all in turn and then tried to catch Léger's eye. But Léger was putting some documents away in a portfolio.

"Will you sit down, gentlemen?" said Mr. Chamberlain.

The French and the Czechs sat down, but Mr. Chamberlain remained standing. . . .

"The other territories in which Germans predominate shall be determined by the International Commission, and occupied by German troops between this date and October 10th."

The monotonous voice rose up into the silence, in the center of that somnolent town. It stumbled, stopped, then quavered on; millions of Germans, as far as eye could reach, lay asleep, as it described how a historic murder was to be committed.

The pleading, whispering voice—Oh my dearest darling, how I love your breasts, I love the very smell of you, do you love me?

—rose into the night, and the hands beneath that burning body were *committing murder*.

"I should like to ask one question," said Masarik. "What are we to understand by 'territory in which Germans predominate'?"

He spoke to Chamberlain; but Chamberlain looked at him in silence, with a slightly dazed expression. Obviously he had not been listening. Léger replied, addressing himself to Masarik's back. Masarik swung his chair round until he could see Léger in profile.

"The reference is," said Léger, "to majorities calculated in accordance with the proposals already accepted by you." . . .

"This Commission," Mastny continued, "will also fix the conditions under which the plebiscite shall be conducted, taking as a basis the organization of the plebiscite in the Saar. It will, moreover, fix a date for the opening of the plebiscite, not being later than the end of November."

He stopped again and said to Chamberlain in a faintly ironic tone: "Will the Czechoslovak member of the Commission have an equal right of vote with the other members?"

"Of course," said Mr. Chamberlain benevolently.

A turgidity, sticky, like blood, tingled over Ivich's thighs and stomach and slipped into her blood, I'm not a girl you can force, then she yielded, shivers of ice and fire thrilled up into her chest, but her head remained serene and secure, and in her head she cried: "I hate you!" . . .

"Within the same period, the Czechoslovak Government will release the Sudeten German prisoners at present serving sentences of imprisonment for political offenses.

"Done at Munich, September 29th, 1938.

"That's all," he said.

He looked at the paper as though he had not finished it. Mr. Chamberlain yawned and began to drum on the table with his fingers.

"That's all," repeated Mastny.

It was all over, the Czechoslovakia of 1918 had ceased to exist. Masarik gazed at the white document, which Mastny then laid on the table; then he turned to Daladier and Léger and eyed them fixedly. Daladier was sitting hunched in his chair, his chin on his chest. He took a cigarette out of his pocket, looked at it for an instant, and then replaced it in the packet. Léger was rather flushed and looked impatient.

"Do you expect," said Masarik to Daladier, "a statement or a reply from my Government?"

Daladier did not reply. Léger bent his head and said rapidly:

"Monsieur Mussolini has to get back to Italy this evening; there is not much time."

Masarik was still looking at Daladier. He said: "Not even a reply? Am I to understand that we are *obliged* to accept?"

Daladier waved a hand wearily, and Léger, from behind him, answered: "What else can you do?"

She had turned her face to the wall and was crying silently, her shoulders quivered with sobbing.

"Why are you crying" he asked hesitantly.

"Because I hate you," she replied.

Masarik rose, Mastny also; and Mr. Chamberlain indulged in a prodigious yawn [pp. 430–36].

BECKETT

Beckett defies any philosophical pigeonholing, for the simple reason that he neither developed a specific philosophical system of his own nor identified himself with that of another. Unlike Kierkegaard or Sartre, he is above all a creative writer, and his philosophical preoccupations—though undeniable—have never been given theoretical expression. Yet his work abounds in references to a number of philosophers. His protagonists allude to them quite frequently—even if only to mock their jargon. He chose Descartes as the protagonist of his first published poem "Whoroscope."[1] His familiarity with Schopenhauer is evidenced by his discussion of the philosopher's conception of music, which may also attest to his knowledge of Nietzsche's *Birth of Tragedy.*[2] Geulincx is not only cited and mentioned by name in *Murphy* and *The End* but is also the source of the philosophical argument according to which Murphy lives and dies: Samuel I. Mintz perceptively stated that the doctrine of the seventeenth-century Belgian Occasionalist "as

1. See Ruby Cohn, *Beckett, the Comic Gamut* (New Brunswick, N.J., Rutgers University Press, 1962), pp. 10 ff.

2. Samuel Beckett, *Proust* (New York, Grove Press, 1931), pp. 70–72; henceforth cited in the text as *Pr.* Cf. *BT,* 99.

used in the novel . . . is modified in one important respect; otherwise it is clearly traceable to its source, and so carefully is it woven into the fabric of the book that *Murphy* is inexplicable except by reference to it."[3]

In an ingenious essay on the novel *Watt,* Jacqueline Hoefer has shown it to be fundamentally a debate with logical positivism, as engendered by Wittgenstein.[4] To me her argument remains convincing, even if John Fletcher—naming as his source Beckett himself—deflates her assumption that the work contains not only allusions to the philosopher but also to his proverbial "ladder."[5] The novel *Molloy,* with its Molloy-Moran dichotomy, suggested itself to me as a parallel to the Nietzschean concept of the Apollo-Dionysus dualism in art which is resolved in the preponderance of the Dionysiac.[6] In his masterly study of Beckett's work, Hugh Kenner called attention not only to the many traces of Cartesian, Geulincxian, Malebranchean, and Newtonian thought it contains, but also to its emulation of the very modes of Cartesian speculation.[7] Fletcher's careful analysis finds Beckett—whose tutor at Dublin's Trinity College had been A. A. Luce, the coeditor of Berkeley—to be anti-Berkeleyan, influenced by Hume, and owing something to "Leibnizian monadism and Geulincxian dualism."[8] And Richard N. Coe brilliantly supported and further developed the views of critics

3. Samuel I. Mintz, "Beckett's *Murphy:* A Cartesian Novel," *Perspective* (Autumn 1959), 156.

4. Jacqueline Hoefer, "Watt," *Perspective* (Autumn 1959), 166–82.

5. John Fletcher, *The Novels of Samuel Beckett* (New York, Barnes & Noble, 1964), p. 87.

6. Edith Kern, "Moran—Molly: The Hero as Author," *Perspective* (Autumn 1959), 183–93.

7. Hugh Kenner, *Samuel Beckett* (New York, Grove Press, 1961), p. 119.

8. Fletcher, *The Novels of Samuel Beckett,* p. 50.

who had been cognizant of Beckett's preoccupation with Pythagorean ideas.[9]

In addition to such links with specific philosophers, existential
themes and thoughts have been detected in Beckett's work.
Writing about *Happy Days* in 1962, I considered Winnie's
cheerful attention to the futile details of everyday existence as a
theatrical realization of Kierkegaard's concept of the "Knight of
Infinite Resignation."[10] The play's setting—Winnie alone under
a scorching sun, half buried in a mound of earth, and Willie invisible to her and with his back turned toward her—seemed to
me a concretization of the Heideggerian concept of *Geworfen-
heit,* that is, of man as "thrown" into the universe and into
desolate isolation. Winnie's desire to bear witness seems to represent an aspect that both Heidegger and Sarte have considered
as essentially human. Her need to be witnessed, while evoking
Berkeley, seems to correspond also to the Sartrean concept of
the Other whose Look confirms the Self's existence and at the
same time threatens it and encroaches upon its freedom with
objectifying judgments. In the same year, yet quite independently, Milton Rickels discussed the presence of existential
themes in Beckett's *The Unnamable.*[11] He spoke of the protagonist's loneliness as contrasted with the anonymous, dic-
tatorial mass of the "they," his quest for an authentic Self, and
his view of the Other as someone who limits his freedom to be
and become. A year later, Coe pointed out with great acumen
an even more essential relationship between Beckett and Sartrean
thought by maintaining that the *pour-soi,* the for-itself, "being

9. Richard N. Coe, *Beckett* (Edinburgh and London, Oliver & Boyd;
New York, Grove Press, 1964), pp. 48 ff., 89 ff.

10. Edith Kern, "Beckett's Knight of Infinite Resignation," *Yale
French Studies, 29* (1962), 49–56.

11. Milton Rickels, "Existential Themes in Beckett's *Unnamable,*"
Criticism, 4 (1962), 134–47.

negative . . . has all the attributes of the Beckettian 'Self,' " the more so because it is essentially without a subject.[12]

An awareness of Beckett's philosophical preoccupations can help us gain a better understanding of his fictional intentions and techniques. Of course, too eager a search for neatness of identification might turn us into the analogymongers whom Beckett detests and whom he accuses of wringing the neck of a certain system in order to stuff it into a contemporary pigeon-hole.[13] We should not forget that Beckett distanced himself from existentialism, that he found the language of Heidegger and Sartre too philosophical and any differentiation between Being and Existence irrelevant to himself. At the same time, we must not remain deaf to Kierkegaardian echoes in Beckett's very assertion that he is not a philosopher and can speak only of what is in front of him.[14] It was Kierkegaard who, as we have seen, condemned all system as something equivalent to death, who conceived of existence in terms of paradox and dialectics, and who, long before Beckett's *Unnamable*[15]—so clearly con-

12. Coe, *Beckett,* p. 75.

13. Beckett et al., *Our Exagmination Round His Factification For Incamination of Work in Progress,* p. 3.

14. Tom Driver, "Beckett by the Madeleine," *Columbia Forum,* 4 (1961), 21–25, 23.

15. Beckett's works will henceforth be cited in the text with the following abbreviations:

    E   *Endgame* (New York, Grove Press, 1958).
    F   *Film,* in *Eh Joe and Other Writings* (London, Faber & Faber, 1967).
    G   *Waiting For Godot* (New York, Grove Press, 1954).
    HD *Happy Days* (New York, Grove Press, 1961).
    HII *How It Is* (New York, Grove Press, 1964).
    IDI *Imagination Dead Imagine,* in *No's Knife* (London, Calder and Boyars, 1967).
    M *Murphy* (New York, Grove Press, 1957).

cerned with problems of thought and form—felt the need to remind himself that the "thing to avoid, I don't know why, is the spirit of system" *(U, 4)*. We have to realize above all that Beckett's work has been increasingly expressive of the fact that the individual is isolated, that his communication with Others is precariously dependent on the Look, that whatever exists comes to light through the individual, and that he therefore must be a witness, an author-hero.

Hard as he may try to deny this fact, Beckett must be considered a serious thinker because he restates the age-old questions concerning the What?, the Why?, the Whence?, Where?, and Whither? of man's existence. He proffers no answers, but his very manner of asking places him in the camp of the dualists with their division of body and mind, reality and unreality—a division that must affect the nature and form of fiction. John Fletcher aptly maintains that Beckett's work

> owes a great deal to philosophical dualism . . . which under one form or another is almost as old as civilization itself. The dualist sees the universe in terms of two quite different and incompatible entities, mind and matter. It is therefore evident that much Eastern philosophy and religion is dualist; so is Plato's thought and Plotinus'; Christianity is a dualist religion despite its past hostility to other and more extreme forms of the doctrine . . . Descartes's philosophy is of course radically dualistic, following up on medieval thought; after him Malebranche, Spinoza, Geulincx and

----

Ma *Malone Dies* (New York, Grove Press, 1956).
Mo *Molloy* (New York, Grove Press, 1955).
 P *Ping,* in *No's Knife.*
 T *Texts For Nothing,* in *No's Knife.*
 U *The Unnamable* (New York, Grove Press, 1958).
W *Watt* (New York, Grove Press, 1959).

> Leibniz perpetuate and modify the doctrine. It is still very
> much alive today, despite the efforts of behaviorists in
> psychology and philosophy to refute it.[16]

Beckettian and Sartrean thinking meet in this tradition of
dualism, both partaking of it in certain ways. To Beckett's
concept of the Self, the world of objects and the Other—indeed,
the individual himself—are as resistant as they are to the Sartrean pour-soi. Since even their own identity forever eludes
them, both Beckett's Self and Sartre's pour-soi are—like Heidegger's *Dasein*—impersonal in their very individuality. They are
consciousnesses without subjectivity.[17]

As Coe implies, Beckett's dialogues with Duthuit gain true
significance when seen in this light. In them, man, and the artist
in particular, emerges as facing a paradox in his endeavor to be
a witness to Being. As his intelligence differentiates and defines
the forms in which Being discloses itself, the essential characteristic of Being—becoming—is destroyed: life is turned into
death; man into an object; the Self into something from which
the Self has escaped. The whole universe, as a consequence,
assumes the aspect of Sartre's *huis-clos* where all is confined to
immobility, deprived of the possibility of change, and objectified.
Because of this paradox the artist is essentially doomed to
failure. It is in this existentialist sense that we can understand
the praise which Beckett has lavished on the Dutch painter,
Bram van Velde, as being "the first to admit that to be an artist
is to fail, as no other dare fail, that failure is his world and the
shrink from it desertion, art and craft, good housekeeping,
living."[18]

16. Fletcher, *The Novels of Samuel Beckett,* p. 229.

17. Coe, *Beckett,* pp. 4 ff.

18. Samuel Beckett and Georges Duthuit, "Three Dialogues," in
Martin Esslin, *Samuel Beckett: A Collection of Critical Essays* (Englewood Cliffs, N.J., Prentice-Hall, 1965), p. 21.

As if to avoid at all cost such solidification and reification, Beckett has created fictional worlds and protagonists of an increasingly fluid nature, lacking in well-defined human relationships, and deprived of the objects that ordinarily belong to human existence. Events are literally reduced to essentials and become "light commenting bodies, stillness motion" (W, 73). Already Murphy, Beckett's first fictional protagonist, who is not yet seen in the essential isolation of the author's subsequent fictional heroes, is happiest when he can withdraw from the world of ordinary relationships between people and things into that of his mind where the "real" world exists in the abstract and its pieces can be rearranged at will. He withdraws from the "real" world by tying himself to a rocking chair, and it is in his mind, while his body lapses, that he finds a variety of freedoms. Ultimately, his physical refuge becomes the Magdalen Mental Mercyseat; his earthly paradise: a padded cell. The mysterious figure of Mr. Knott, who is the ever-elusive and self-contained Nought of Watt, symbolically foreshadows, it seems to me, the pose which all of Beckett's protagonists are to assume sooner or later. Mr. Knott's only characteristic gesture, we learn from Watt, "consisted in the simultaneous obturation of the facial cavities, the thumbs in the mouth, the forefingers in the ears, the little fingers in the nostrils, the third fingers in the eyes, and the second fingers, free in a crisis to promote intellection, laid along the temples. And this was less a gesture than an attitude, sustained by Mr. Knott for long periods of time, without visible discomfort" (W, 212). As Beckett's protagonists gradually lose the use of their senses and the members of their bodies, they are like Mr. Knott immured in a world of their own and only use the second fingers as it were to promote intellection.

Yet they do not seem to consider life in their minds an impoverishment. Murphy, though he thinks of his mind as a body-tight sphere closed to the universe without, claims that "nothing ever had been, was or would be in the universe outside it but was already present as virtual, or actual, or virtual rising into actual, or actual falling into virtual, in the universe inside it" *(M,* 107). While no such claims are made by Beckett's later heroes, they seem to dwell in universes equally closed and having all the attributes of Murphy's mind. Like him, they seemingly enjoy in the first, the light zone, the liberty of rearranging mentally the physical world, there paralleled in the abstract: "here the kick that the physical Murphy received, the mental Murphy gave" *(M,* 111). Like him, they seem to avoid the second zone. For though it offers a choice of various forms of bliss, it requires, nevertheless, the tedium of choice. They finally seem to emulate Murphy by dwelling mainly in the mind's third zone, described by him as "a flux of forms, a perpetual coming together and falling asunder of forms . . . nothing but forms becoming and crumbling into fragments of a new becoming, without love or hate or any intelligible principle of change" *(M,* 112). In this zone there was "nothing but commotion and the pure forms of commotion." Murphy was not free, "but a mote in the dark of absolute freedom. He did not move, he was a point in the ceaseless unconditioned generation and passing away of line." He felt there "a missile without provenance or target, caught up in a tumult of non-Newtonian motion" *(M,* 112). While Beckett's characters thus move away from what Kierkegaard would have designated as the ethico-religious either/or of existence, they move more and more towards a view of Being as a becoming and towards the recognition that any witnessing and rendering of its flux must remain a vain attempt.

But if Beckett's later characters seem to live, like Murphy, in a dark "matrix of surds" and feel themselves "a point in the ceaseless unconditioned generation and passing away of line," they no longer induce such feelings by tying themselves to rocking chairs. Nor do they derive the same enjoyment from them.

Like Roquentin in his hour of revelation before the root of the chestnut tree, they are invaded rather by a sensation of absurdity and sadness. From Watt, who leaves Mr. Knott's premises, his logistic exercises brought to nought, to the Unnamable, who sits in solitude, to the nameless creatures in the mud of *How It Is,* they weep. Watt "stood there . . . and his tears fell, a slow minute rain, to the ground, which had recently been repaired . . . The humidity thus lent to the road surface must, he reckoned, have survived his departure by as long as two minutes at least, if not three" *(W,* 208). The Unnamable feels the "tears stream down" from his "unblinking eyes" and asks himself "What makes me weep so? From time to time. There is nothing saddening here" *(U,* 6). And as the man in the mud of *How It Is* turns his head toward his torturer, both have tears in their eyes. Such will-lessness as prevails in the third zone of Murphy's mind, especially if combined with suffering, was presented by Beckett in his *Proust* as the prerequisite to artistic creation, and consequently, most of his will-less protagonists are engaged in writing and deeply concerned with the ramifications of their art.

Since *Murphy* belongs to an early stage of Beckettian fiction, its protagonist, when not taking refuge in his mind, partakes of a traditional human world full of human certainties, uncertainties, and needs of a spiritual as well as a material nature. Murphy's world contains rocking chairs of undressed teak, guaranteed not to crack, warp, shrink, corrode, or creak at night; clocks; curtains; grasping landladies in perpetual need of money; selfish friends; and Celia, whose exact bodily measurements are recorded, to whom he is physically attracted, and for whom he feels something vaguely resembling love. But although Murphy is *en situation* in the sense that he has to make a fundamental decision (one cannot speak of Murphy's Being-in-the-world in any existential sense), his universe is not disclosed to us through his consciousness. We see him and his world rather through

the consciousness of an intermediary, an unidentified but omniscient and ubiquitous narrator, who is equally well instructed
concerning the motivations and reasonings of each character.
He knows why Murphy wants to sit at Neary's feet, and why
Neary is engaged in Pythagorean thought. He can instantaneously displace himself from the seclusion of Murphy's room
to the telephone booth where Celia is calling him. Though himself invisible, he observes "the fiery darts of the amorously disposed" that follow her, and can accompany her to the room of
her bedridden grandfather, Mr. Willoughby Kelly. He is aware
of the existential choice with which Murphy is faced, that of
choosing between body and mind: being with Celia and earning
a living in what he considers the "mercantile gehenna," or
deadening the senses of his body and living in the bliss of his
body-tight mind. The narrator-author knows that Murphy decides in favor of his mind, and maliciously arranges the "revenge"
of the world of matter in such a way that, through the malfunc-
tion of certain objects, it brings about the complete dissolution of
Murphy's body and mind: his combustion through gas (whose
etymon is "chaos").

When writing the novel, Beckett obviously ignored or defied
such technical questions as the point of view or the limits of individual consciousness. He could, therefore, entrust the story to an
author or narrator of such omniscient and ubiquitous qualities
and have him refer to the protagonist in the third person. Aided
by the narrator, the reader learns of Murphy's lonely bliss as well
as of Celia's mental and emotional reactions to Murphy: "She
felt, as she felt so often with Murphy, spattered with words that
went dead as soon as they sounded; each word obliterated, before
it had time to make sense, by the word that came next; so that
in the end she did not know what had been said. It was like difficult music heard for the first time" (M, 40). Yet, while this
reaction is Celia's, the manner in which it is presented and

analyzed must be ascribed to the narrator. He freely permits his judgments, moreover, to intrude into the story in the form of generalizations about life or even statements concerning his own way of narrating. "For what was all working for a living," he asks philosophically, "but a procuring and a pimping for the money-bags, one's lecherous tyrants the money-bags, so that they might breed" (M, 76). And he confides to us on another occasion that a certain phrase "is chosen with care, lest the filthy censors should lack an occasion to commit their filthy synecdoche" (M, 76). In a later novel, The Unnamable, the protagonist was to say of Murphy that it was clumsily done and that "you could see the ventriloquist" (U, 85).

But the novel Watt, written several years after Murphy, is informed by a different philosophical attitude and, consequently, has a different and more intricate formal structure. Again the story begins and ends with an omniscient and omnipresent author or narrator, who speaks of the hero and all other characters in the third person. Watt appears suddenly, alighting from a streetcar, while a threesome of townsfolk gathered by chance on a late evening on a public bench are engaged in conversation. The narrator refers to Watt by name, while to the threesome, Mr. Hackett and Mr. and Mrs. Nixon, he appears "motionless, a solitary figure . . . scarcely to be distinguished from the dim wall behind it" and might be "a man or a woman . . . a parcel, a carpet . . . a roll of tarpaulin, wrapped up in dark paper and tied about in the middle with a cord" (W, 16–17). Yet soon Mr. Nixon also recognizes and quickly accosts him, while his wife and friend remain seated. As he rejoins them he supplies them with totally nonsensical information concerning Watt, as someone who owes him money, whom he does not really know and yet seems to have known all his life, though he concedes there must have been a time when he did not know him (W, 18). In the discussion which follows the sudden appearance and disappearance of

Watt, all three observers indulge in hypotheses as to the reasons for his arrival and departure, and it is above all Mr. Hackett's tendency to develop arguments—as logical as they are hypothetical—that "explain" it all: "The thought of leaving town was most painful to him ... but the thought of not doing so no less so. So he sets off for the station, half hoping he may miss the train ... Too fearful to assume himself the onus of a decision ... he refers to the frigid machinery of a time-space relation" (W, 21). Mr. Hackett's reasoning resembles so perfectly those numerous hypotheses Watt himself is to indulge in throughout the novel that Mr. Nixon betrays uncanny insight when he insists that the two men remind him of one another.

Once they have served the narrator to identify Watt for the reader, if only in the vaguest and most contradictory terms, he abandons the Hackett-Nixon threesome and—remaining invisible—observes Watt as he enters the railroad station, inevitably collides with a porter who absurdly moves milkcans from one end of the platform to the other and back again, falls, rises, and sheepishly submits to a scolding. Certain that the travelers who have witnessed the sorry scene are content, the narrator digresses at length on Watt's manner of smiling, enters with him—still invisible—a compartment of the train, and overhears his conversation with his fellow traveler Mr. Spiro, the editor of *Crux*. Due to his omniscience, the narrator knows that Watt hears nothing of the lengthy disquisitions of Mr. Spiro, whom his friends call Dum (anagram of "mud"). For Watt, he tells us, hears his own voices, which are apparently as familiar to the narrator as Mr. Spiro's quotations. The narrator descends with Watt at his destination, which also happens to be that of Lady McCann, whom he describes to us as keeping a certain distance between herself and Watt, "though not a timorous woman as a rule, thanks to her traditions, catholic and military" (W, 31). Still seemingly guided by the narrator, we accompany Watt on his lonely, nightly road to Mr. Knott's house, share his experience of arriving, of scurrying from one closed door to another, and his final inexplicable admittance. Watt's arrival, his mysterious entering, his fascination with the dim fire in the kitchen range whose "ashes grey" turned "pale red, when he covered the lamp, with his hat" *(W,* 37)—all these experiences, which would seem to be exclusively Watt's own, are told, or so it seems, by the omniscient narrator. And it is the same narrator who, at the novel's end, relates Watt's departure from Mr. Knott's house, his return to the same small railroad station, his clownish misadventures in the waiting room, his request for a ticket to the "further end of the line," and his apparent vanishing into thin air.

Though it is not clear where the function of this objective, ubiquitous narrator ends, it does end somewhere, and the largest part of the novel is evidently not told but merely edited by him. Unheralded, another voice intrudes into the story. Somewhere, somehow Beckett seems to have felt that only the consciousness that had been face to face with Mr. Knott could know and speak of this experience. We find therefore that both Arsene and Watt tell of their sojourn in Mr. Knott's house in the first person. Arsene reports to Watt. Watt relates to Sam both Arsene's and his own account. Sam records both. Sam intrudes at first as an impersonal and unidentified voice, then speaks as an "I," and finally refers to himself as Sam—thereby challenging us to identify him with Beckett the way Proust's Marcel referred us back to his author without quite doing so. While Sam's appearance invites such identification, his sudden disappearance denies it. Somewhere, the objective narrator takes over again. Calling attention to lacunae and indicating illegible passages in the manuscript, he reveals himself as the editor of what were probably Sam's notebooks.

Sam's function as a listener and recorder gives plausibility to the manner in which Watt's intimately subjective experience came to be known. The fact that Sam actually enters into the story and is not merely an outside narrator also affords us glimpses of Watt that are far more intimate than those of the Hacketts, Nixons, and Lady McCanns. As Sam describes his friendship with Watt and their meetings in the garden of the institution where both are patients, Watt no longer remains the walking automaton or the hapless clown that he was when first presented. He now emerges as a human being capable of deep sadness and joy. Sam speaks of him with profound feeling:

> The kind of weather we liked was a high wind and a bright sun mixed. But whereas for Watt the important thing was the wind, the sun was the important thing for Sam. With the result that though the sun though bright were not so bright as it might have been, if the wind were high Watt did not audibly complain, and that I, when illuminated by rays of appropriate splendour, could forgive a wind which, while strong, might with advantage have been stronger . . . when on Sam the sun shone bright, then in a vacuum panted Watt, and when Watt like a leaf was tossed, then stumbled Sam in deepest night. But ah, when exceptionally the desired degrees of ventilation and radiance were united, in the little garden, then we were peers in peace, each in his own way, until the wind fell, the sun declined. [*W*, 153]

In a later meeting of the two, Watt even appears a tragic figure to Sam, one bearing the cross of all mankind. Both having been moved to different pavilions, Sam unexpectedly espies Watt one day in the garden adjoining his. Watt was advancing backward toward Sam, slowly, painfully swaying, and striking against trees, while catching his feet in the tangled underwood,

> until he lay against the fence, with his hands at arm's length grasping the wires. Then he turned with the intention very likely of going back the way he had come and I

saw his face and the rest of his front. His face was bloody, his hands also, and thorns were in his scalp. (His resemblance, at that moment, to the Christ believed by Bosch, then hanging in Trafalgar Square, was so striking, that I remarked it.) And at the same instant suddenly I felt as though I were standing before a great mirror, in which my garden was reflected, and my fence, and I, and the very birds tossing in the wind, so that I looked at my hands, and felt my face, and glossy skull, with an anxiety as real as unfounded. (For if anyone, at that time, could be truly said not to resemble the Christ supposed by Bosch, then hanging in Trafalgar Square, I flatter myself it was I.) Why, Watt, I cried, that is a nice state you have got yourself into, to be sure. Not it is, yes, replied Watt. [*W*, 159]

Asked by Watt to clean his face, Sam finds a way to rejoin him, wipe off his blood, and "anoint" him. Then "as one man," they pace up and down together.

Then I turned him round until he faced me. Then I placed his hands, on my shoulders . . . Then I placed my hands, on his shoulders . . . Then I took a single pace forward, with my left leg, and he a single pace back, with his right leg (he could scarcely do otherwise). Then I took a double pace forward with my right leg, and he of course with his left leg a double pace back. And so we paced together between the fences. I forwards, he backwards . . . And then turning, as one man, we paced back the way we had paced back the way we had come, I looking whither we were going, and he looking whence we were coming . . . To be together again, after so long, who love the sunny wind, the windy sun, in the sun, in the wind, that is perhaps something, perhaps something. [W, 163]

If we disregard the parenthetical statement in which Sam denies all resemblance with Christ and ironically destroys the bold image he was intent on creating—as is Beckett's wont so often—the narrator emerges here as Sam–Watt–Christ carrying the cross. The effect of the mirror identity is established not only visually but also vocally and linguistically as Watt replies in mirror language and "Yes, is it not?" becomes "Not it is, yes" (W, 159).

While "teller and told" thus almost merge and appear as one man, their unreliability as narrators is compounded, especially in view of the time elapsed between the events and their recording. Sam sees the problem with uncanny lucidity:

> For when Watt at last spoke of this time, it was a long time past, and of which his recollections were, in a sense, perhaps less clear than he would have wished, though too clear for his liking, in another. Add to this the notorious difficulty of recapturing, at will, modes of feeling peculiar to a certain time, and to a certain place, and perhaps also to a certain state of the health, when the time is past, and the place left, and the body struggling with quite a new situation. Add to this the obscurity of Watt's communication, the rapidity of his utterance and the eccentricities of his syntax, as elsewhere recorded. Add to this the material conditions in which these communications were made. Add to this the scant aptitude to receive of him to whom they were proposed. Add to this the scant aptitude to give of him to whom they were committed. And some idea will perhaps be obtained of the difficulties experienced in formulating, not only such matters as those here in question, but the entire body of Watt's experience, from the moment of his entering Mr. Knott's establishment to the moment of his leaving it. [W, 75]

To these deficiencies caused by the time lag and the imperfections of narrator and recorder is added an even graver aspect, one of a metaphysical nature: the elusiveness of truth. Objects and events show themselves to Watt in different ways at different times, and it becomes more and more difficult for Watt to distinguish "between what happened and what did not happen, between what was and what was not, in Mr. Knott's house" (W, 126). Indeed, several incidents related by Watt as separate and distinct might well have been in reality the same incident, Sam tells us (W, 78).

The language Watt uses is expressive of this elusiveness of existence. In analogy with the objects and events around him, it more and more defies categories and habitual form. As Sam tells us, it was in a voice so low and rapid as might be heard only in moments of delirium or during the service of a mass that Watt spoke "with scant regard for grammar, for syntax, for pronunciation, for enunciation, and very likely, if the truth were known, for spelling too . . . The labour of composition, the uncertainty as to how to proceed, or whether to proceed at all, inseparable from even our most happy improvisations, and from which neither the songs of birds, nor even the cries of quadrupeds are exempt, had here no part, apparently." He only articulated proper names with great deliberation. Otherwise, he "spoke as one speaking to dictation, or reciting, parrot-like, a text, by long repetition become familiar" (W, 156). We learn of the moving accents Watt found to speak of his encounter with Mr. Knott—and it is significant that Beckett felt the need to record this account in the first person, while Sam reports the rest in that third person which is actually a first-person point of view: "Of nought. To the source. To the teacher. To the temple. To him I brought. This emptied heart. These emptied hands. This mind ignoring. This body homeless. To love him my little reviled. My little rejected to have him. My little to learn him forgot. Abandoned my little to find him" (W, 166). Sam's function here is both that of scribe and that of Watt's witness. It is through his witnessing that we come to equate Watt's figure with Christ, with Sam himself, and perhaps all mankind.

The novel's formal structure, then, is a very intricate one. We are reminded of Kierkegaard's technique of placing one author inside another in the manner of a Chinese puzzle box. Did Beckett simply give a new twist to the "old trick of the novelist"? Did he simply invent intermediaries so as to remove from the person of the true author the intimacy of what is recorded, without totally destroying its plausibility? Did he wish, in a manner closely related to Kierkegaard's irony, to establish identity with himself and at the same time deny it? Needless to say, Beckett's technical problems are similar to Kierkegaard's—regardless of whether or not we classify the Irish author as an existentialist.

Beginning with *Watt,* Beckett's fiction, not unlike Kierkegaard's is expressive of the individual's essential isolation and the incommunicability of his most crucial experience. In *Murphy* Beckett still presented human relationships within a social framework. In *Watt* they assume a metaphysical scope, if we exclude the book's beginning and end. The inhabitants of Mr. Knott's household never speak to each other. If they speak at all, it is in the form of long monologues—Arsene's long parting speech, for instance, or Arthur's exhilarating account of the committee meeting, or Watt's report to Sam. Because of this monolithic quality, Watt's sojourn at Mr. Knott's establishment almost resembles Murphy's withdrawal into his mind: all that exists outside is paralleled within and can be arranged at will, since it is not bound to the laws of the outside world. Like Murphy, Watt at times experiences indolent bliss, and at other times feels himself a mote floating will-lessly in darkness, all contact with the outside world completely broken. But rational comprehension of what is either inside or outside is more and more denied to Watt.

How and by whom, then, can his experience be told except by Watt himself—and imperfectly at that? Only he can give evidence of the collapse of his former world of logic and purposefulness. Only he can be a witness to Mr. Knott's existence—though his testimony may well differ from that of others who also have been face to face with Mr. Knott. Erskine, Arsene, Walter, and Vincent, Sam feels certain, "might have told something of Mr. Knott. Then we would have had Erskine's Mr. Knott, and Arsene's Mr. Knott, and Walter's Mr. Knott, and Vincent's Mr. Knott, to compare with Watt's Mr. Knott." (*W*, 126). But what counts is not the nature of the testimony. It is that even Mr. Knott's self-sufficient elusiveness needs a witness "not that he might know, no, but that he might not cease" (*W*, 202–03). To Watt, Mr. Knott *is* because he is observed, in Berkeley's sense. But Watt also plays, in a way, the role of the Sartrean Other, confirming Mr. Knott's existence without ever fully grasping it because it shows itself to him under varying aspects.

In the universe of isolated existents with which the novel presents us, Mr. Knott is at the center, all his senses closed to the world. He is the Nought witnessed by a lone consciousness which in turn is witnessed. As Watt is a witness to Mr. Knott—and accidentally to Arsene, who himself had witnessed Mr. Knott's existence—so Sam is a witness to himself, to Watt, and indirectly to Arsene and Mr. Knott. Arsene's and Watt's stories would have been lost, had they not been recorded by Sam as they were told to him by Watt. Likewise, Sam's notebooks might have vanished, had they not been edited and provided with a beginning and an end by an unknown, unidentified author. Each witness, each narrator is not only immured in his own consciousness but is also presented as imperfect and unreliable by him who witnesses him. And to compound the uncertainties, we learn that "Watt told the beginning of his story, not first, but second, so not fourth, but third . . . he told its end. Two, one, four, three, that was the order in which Watt told his story." This at least is what the highly unreliable Sam imparts to us, adding ambiguously that "heroic quatrains are not otherwise elaborated" *(W,* 215). As is to be expected, the novel's formal structure reflects and, indeed, is expressive of the universe as Beckett evisions it: a Kierkegaardian universe peopled with isolated existents, unable to know each other, except as possibilities. As in Kierkegaard's work, manuscript is enclosed within manuscript, so in *Watt,* account is enclosed within account, the teller always being told. The old trick of the novelist is changed, however, in that Beckett does not use it to create a semblance of truth but rather to pile unreliable narrator upon unreliable narrator. His double and triple negatives add up to one important certainty, however: that of the elusiveness of Being and the failure to which any attempt at revealing it is doomed.

As he prepares to leave Mr. Knott's house, Arsene warns Watt, in his lengthy disquisition, of the loneliness he will encounter during his sojourn and also of the frustration he will experience at not being able to communicate what he has experienced. "And now," Arsene tells Watt, "for a little while along the way that lies between you and me Erskine will go by your side, to be your guide, and then for the rest you will travel alone, or with only shades to keep you company, and that I think you will find, if your experience at all resembles mine, the best part of the outing" *(W,* 63). In fact, loneliness hardly matters as communication becomes less and less possible and all

> partakes in no small measure of the nature of what has so happily been called the unutterable or ineffable, so that any attempt to utter or eff it is doomed to fail, doomed, doomed to fail. Why even I myself, strolling all alone in some hard earned suspension of labour in this charming garden, have tried and tried to formulate this delicious haw! and I may

add quite useless wisdom so dearly won, and with which I
am so to speak from the crown of my head to the soles of
my feet imbued. [*W*, 62]

Watt himself, as we have seen, comes to sense the unutterability
of his experiences and feels more and more helpless about
saddling them with "meaning and a formula," so that eventually
he can "neither think of them, nor speak of them, but only
suffer them" (*W*, 79).

Arsene's most crucial adventure of this kind foreshadows the
nature of those experiences Watt is to encounter, although *his*
carry with them greater immediacy and drama. All these adventures are, of course, of a subjective nature and yet transcend
subjectivity in any truly personal sense. In contrast to Watt,
Arsene is able to recount his experience with comparative coherence: "It was a Tuesday afternoon, in the month of October,
a beautiful October afternoon. I was sitting on the step, in the
yard, looking at the light on the wall. I was in the sun, and the
wall was in the sun. I was the sun, need I add, and the wall, and
the step, and the yard, and the time of year, and the time of day,
to mention only these" (*W*, 42). This mystical moment, which
seems to obliterate all distinction between subject and object,
evokes the Heideggerian concept of Dasein, of man as the here
and now of Being, differentiating its parts with the light of his
understanding without ever being separated from it, ever being
an outside observer. It is, it seems to me, because of this sensation of being both free intelligence and contingency that suddenly all is changed for Arsene, as if he had been transported to
some different yard. For he continues:

> And I have little doubt, that I was the only person living to
> discover [the change] . . . [Yet] to conclude from this that
> the incident was internal would, I think, be rash. For my—
> how shall I say?—my personal system was so distended at

the period of which I speak that the distinction of what was inside it and what was outside it was not at all easy to draw. Everything that happened happened inside it, and at the same time everything that happened happened outside it. I trust I make myself plain. I did not, need I add, see the thing happen, nor hear it, but I perceived it with a perception . . . sensuous. . . . What was changed was existence off the ladder. Do not come down the ladder, Ifor, I haf taken it away. This I am happy to inform you is the reversed metamorphosis. [*W*, 43, 44]

I find it hard to see Arsene's experience other than in the terms of the interpretation so ingeniously presented by Jacqueline Hoefer. The entire context seems to indicate that what happens to Arsene is a realization of the universe's being there (himself included) in its purposelessness and total disregard for the logic to which man wants to reduce it. The Wittgensteinian ladder—with its rungs of philosophical propositions that lead to the rarefied realm of pure logic and factual information—having been taken away, Arsene's realization resembles a fall, a collapse of all the fictitious structures that are built with pure facts. And lest we do not understand, Arsene does not fail to illustrate by means of the burlesque tale of Mr. Ash, the contempt in which he has come to hold mere factual information. Mr. Ash, disregarding discomfort and even suffering, is able to supply, with what he considers great accuracy, the factual information that it is precisely seventeen minutes past five—information totally unsolicited and immediately contradicted by Big Ben's striking six (*W*, 46).

For Arsene the Wittgensteinian metaphor has been reversed. Logical accuracy of expression is no longer possible. Instead of climbing the philosopher's ladder from darkness and complex questioning toward light and simple answers, he has fallen into the nonfactual depths of not-knowing, not-understanding and has thus encountered absurdity. "And what is this coming," he wonders, "that was not our coming and this being that is not our being and this going that will not be our going but the coming and being and going in purposelessness? And though in purposelessness I may seem now to go, yet I do not, any more than in purposelessness then I came, for I go now with my purpose as with it then I came, the only difference being this, that then it was living and now it is dead" (W, 58). To an analogy-monger like me, Arsene evokes Roquentin's experience of fundamental absurdity. The realization of the purposelessness and absurdity of the universe turns the certainties of Mr. Ash or a Self-Taught Man into inanities. It affects the value given to facts, their explanation, and their expression.

Watt's universe is to be shaken in a manner which parallels that of Arsene's experience. The validity of his logical infer-ences—hitherto unquestioned—is jolted severely by the inci-dent with the Galls, father and son piano tuners. Inexplicably and absurdly, they appear in Mr. Knott's household, engage in odd dialogue, and disappear as mysteriously as they came. The event (if it was an event) continues to unfold in Watt's head and soon ceases "to signify for Watt a piano tuned, an obscure family and professional relation, an exchange of judgments more or less intelligible." It dissolves for him into a "mere example of light commenting bodies, and stillness motion, and silence sound, and comment comment." Like Arsene at his mo-ment of revelation, Watt feels more and more certain that nothing has happened at all. But this "nothing" (we are after all in the house of Mr. Nought-Knott) makes him sense the fragility of all outer meanings so that he "who had not seen a symbol, nor executed an interpretation, since the age of four-teen or fifteen, and who had lived, miserably it is true, among face values all his adult life," comes to seek for another meaning of "*what* had passed in the image of *how* it had passed" (*W*, 73). Watt, who had spent his life pathetically explaining the *how*, now begins to live up to the promise suggested by his name and becomes the personification of a *what*. Yet, as he himself states, he is still less interested in what things really mean than in "what they might be induced to mean, with the help of a little patience, a little ingenuity" (*W*, 75).

This first doubt that enters his mind concerning the meaning of events has grave consequences, however. It prevents him henceforth from saying of anything in retrospect "that is what happened then," as he was wont to do "since the age of fourteen, or fifteen." Like Roquentin in *Nausea*, he loses all certainty in talking about the past. As in Sartre's novel, certainty prevails only among the "they": the Hacketts and the Lady McCanns. As he repeats to himself, moreover, that nothing has happened in Mr. Knott's house, he becomes aware of the fact that "the only way one can speak of nothing is to speak of it as though it were something, just as the only way one can speak of God is to speak of him as if he were a man" (*W*, 77). He also realizes that one gives something meaning in the very process of speaking of it. In speaking, he feels, he can evolve "from the meticulous phantoms that beset him, a hypothesis proper to disperse them." For to him, "to explain had always been to exorcize" (*W*, 78). Again we are reminded of Roquentin, who tried to dispel the unsettling experience of Bouville's fog, which engulfed and dehumanized the habitual forms and objects around him, by telling himself forcefully "this is a gaslight, this is a house." Explaining and naming are man's weapons to exorcize an otherwise demonic universe that is threatening in its purposelessness.

Sartre and Beckett evoke in this respect analogous situations and even use similar terms to describe them. Like the Roquentin of *Nausea*, Watt feels closing in on him a world that has lost its human meaning and can no longer be put into human categories or safely expressed in ordinary human language. Roquentin feels himself "in the midst of things, nameless things. Alone, without words, defenceless" (N, 169). Watt, "in the midst of things which, if they consented to be named, did so as it were with reluctance" (W, 81). Roquentin, seated on the streetcar, reassures himself: " 'It's a seat,' a little like an exorcism," but the word stays on his lips, "it refuses to go and put itself on the thing" so that he decides that this thing "called a seat . . . is not a seat. It could just as well be a dead donkey, tossed about in the water." For Roquentin things have become "divorced from their names." Watt, alone in Mr. Knott's kitchen, has an almost identical problem with a pot. The "pot remained a pot, Watt felt sure of that, for everyone but Watt. For Watt alone it was not a pot, any more" (W, 82). As the thing refuses to assume for him the name and identity others, the "they," have given it, as he himself no longer feels identical with the word "man," he tries "names on things, and on himself, almost as a woman hats." He tries to say of the pot, "it's a shield, a growing bolder, It is a raven," but to no avail. In Nausea only the salauds succeed in taming and concealing the absurdity of the world by means of language. In Watt it is Erskine whom the protagonist thinks capable of wrapping up "safe in words the kitchen space, the extraordinary newel-lamp, the stairs that were never the same and of which even the number of steps seemed to vary" (W, 83). Erskine's testimony might help Watt, or so he believes, to make "things appear, and himself appear, in their ancient guise, and content to be named, with the time-honoured names, and forgotten," that is, restored "to their comparative innocuousness" (W, 84). But Erskine, of course—and this is essential—does not communicate with Watt.

In his account to Sam, Watt presents himself as exceedingly reluctant to give up the succor of language. For some time he continued to believe that by merely speaking of his sojourn in Mr. Knott's house he could turn little by little "a disturbance into words," could make "a pillow of old words for a head." He therefore continued to express, if only in short and isolated phrases, what he assumed to have been happening. But he had to realize more and more that he could not penetrate the forces at play, or even perceive the forms that they "upheaved," or yet obtain the least useful information concerning himself, or Mr. Knott (*W*, 117). As has been shown earlier, the unspeakableness of his experience so overwhelms him at last that he can impart the most crucial moments of it only in the form of a language removed from that of everyday usage. Sam describes it as shunning grammar and logic, a language essentially inverted. At first "the inversion affected, not the order of the sentences, but that of the words only . . . the inversion was imperfect . . . elipse . . . frequent . . . euphony was a preoccupation . . . spontaneity was perhaps not absent . . . there was perhaps more than a reversal of discourse . . . the thought was perhaps inverted." Later Watt "began to invert, no longer the order of the words in the sentence, but that of the letters in the word" (*W*, 164–65). This is the language of suffering and madness, the language of one who has dared look, without averting his eyes, at the sun or the face of the godhead. (And it is interesting to realize that there is a suggestion that Mr. Knott resembles both: he is reported as sleeping in a round bed and changing his position every night as the sun does in relation to the earth.) But the literary critic must also recognize this language as the author's attempt to steer away from the logical language of the "they" and to arrive at another, expressive of that part of Being which eludes rationality. Heidegger had found such a language by startlingly juxtaposing words or by stripping them to their essentials in such a manner that they yielded meanings habit had made us forget. Kierkegaard had sought it in the objective correlative of the myth. Beckett, while also turning to myth at times, has been more and more developing a language which—though remaining amazingly lucid and poetical——undermines traditional pat-

terns and thereby reflects that failure he has come to consider
the sign of the true artist.

In the trilogy published after *Watt*,[19] Beckett further pursues
the problem of the elusiveness of Being, while shifting his emphasis to the teller, the witness. This means that the heroes of
the trilogy are, unlike Watt, not merely tellers told but also, more
essentially yet, *writers*. This is, of course, very much in keeping
with existential thinking. As I noted above, Heidegger thought
of poet and thinker as closest to Being and therefore most authentic among men. Similarly, Roquentin saw his salvation from
the absurdity of existence in writing, and in his autobiography
Sartre himself, not unlike the protagonist of *Nausea,* expressed
his need to continue writing, even if he no longer knew why. It
is perhaps more remarkable yet to realize that even some of the
characters of Beckett's plays also arrogate to themselves the right
to be authors. Many of them tell stories and, in the telling, look
at themselves and judge their art. In *Waiting For Godot,* Pozzo
assumes the stance of the improvising poet and actor. He bullies
Lucky, Vladimir, and Estragon into listening to him and then
declames dramatically about the evening sky and philosophizes
about life. His performance finished, he peevishly asks for their
criticism and humbly criticizes himself. Hamm in *Endgame* tells
stories from his past, interrupting himself with such exclama-
tions as "Nicely put, that." or "There's English for you. Ah well,"
or "A bit feeble, that." Winnie of *Happy Days,* "when all fails,"
tells her story of Mildred: "Beginning in the womb, where life
used to begin. Mildred has memories, she will have memories, of
the womb, before she dies, the mother's womb . . . The sun was
not well up when Milly rose . . . entered the nursery . . . Suddenly
a mouse—" and interrupts herself with "Gently, Winnie" *(HD,*

19. In deference to the author, who did not wish to publish it, I
shall not discuss Beckett's *Mercier et Camier.* I have been able to
peruse this typescript through the courtesy of Hugh Kenner.

54–55). But what remains comparatively brief in the theater, becomes elaborate and gains central importance in Beckett's novels.

The titular hero of Beckett's *Molloy* resembles Roquentin in that he is an author struggling with problems of literary creation. For no evident reason, writing has for him the same importance that it has for Roquentin. It is his only raison d'être. For the sake of writing he was rescued more dead than alive from a ditch into which he had fallen, helpless cripple that he had become. His rescue was miraculously achieved by those mysterious forces which usually come to the aid of heroes in despair. "Don't fret, Molloy," they had assured him, "we're coming" *(Mo,* 123). With their help he is kept alive so that he can fulfill his task as a writer, the only purpose for which he desires to live. Earlier experience —which deprived him of all human comfort and companionship, made his body wither, broke his will, and destroyed his conscious memory—served only to lead him to his present abode. Although he refers to it as his "mother's room," this asylum he has arrived at reminds us of Murphy's mind in its vacuity, its half-light, its will-lessness. In it writing is identical with existence and existence means writing.

The views on writing that Molloy expresses, as well as the style he uses while writing in his mother's room, have grown out of his experiences on the via dolorosa which led him there: "a veritable cavalry, with no limits to its stations" *(Mo,* 105). In describing the Molloy who has arrived in his mother's room, one is tempted to borrow the very statements which Beckett made in *Proust* with reference to Marcel become a writer: "He is almost exempt from the impurity of will. He deplores his lack of will until he understands that will, being utilitarian, a servant of intelligence and habit, is not a condition of the artistic experience. When the subject is exempt from will the object is exempt from causality (Time and Space taken together). And this human vegetation is purified in the transcendental aperception that can capture the Model, the Idea, the Thing in itself" *(Pr, 69)*. Not unlike Proust's Marcel, Molloy "understands the necessity of art" after "having emerged from the darkness of time and habit and passion and intelligence" *(Pr. 57)*. We must, therefore, look at the manner in which he arrived at his understanding—a task made difficult by the fact that Molloy is as unreliable a narrator as Watt (he even forgets his name) and that he is forced by his mysterious agent to rearrange his story: "It was he told me I'd begun all wrong, that I should have begun differently . . . Here it is. It gave me a lot of trouble. It was the beginning, do you understand? Whereas now it's nearly the end" *(Mo, 8)*.

If we combine this hint with several others in the story, we are not totally unprepared to find Molloy's tale—told by himself in a flashback—ending by about the middle of the book and followed by another, told in a similar manner by a character called Moran. Since Moran is not accounted for by the novel's title and is never referred to by Molloy, one is tempted to see in him an earlier phase of the latter—an assumption supported by much textual evidence. On the other hand, the very ambiguity of the novel's formal structure also induces us to see Molloy as a creation of Moran's. If, following Molloy's suggestion we assume that the novel's beginning is now its end, the entire story emerges as a Moran-Molloy trek towards authorship, a Künstlerroman, a writer's fusion of the Apollonian and the Dionysiac in Nietzschean terms, or his development from what Beckett called in his conversations with Duthuit "art and craft, good housekeeping, living" to the admission "that to be an artist is to fail."[20] To fail, in this sense, would be a realization of the artist's existential paradox, of the fact that the writer's pour-soi turns all it reveals into an en-soi. It would signify the elusiveness of Being, including that of the Self—a development that continues and is intensified in the second and third parts of the trilogy and in Beckett's

20. Beckett and Duthuit, "Three Dialogues," p. 21.

later work. Moran recalls Nietzsche's Apollonian in the rationality of his existence and quite readily fits the description "art and craft, good housekeping, living." While giving a clear and coherent account of the adventures that befell him in his task to find and rescue a certain Molloy, Moran outlines the existence he led before accepting the Molloy mission. He prides himself on having abhorred vagueness *(Mo,* 135), on having had a methodical mind *(Mo,* 134). His life was arranged by the clock. It was a life governed by reason, discipline, and above all, habit. Between assignments received from his distant "employer," Youdi, to search for "clients," he lived as an aesthete amidst his possessions: enjoying the scent of his lemon verbena and the dance pattern of his bees. To turn his son into a worthy member of his petty, well-ordered universe, he implanted upon his mind the principles of "sollst entbehren"—the very limitation Care imposed upon the genius of Goethe's Faust.

Since Moran writes his report in the first person, it is through his consciousness that his world is revealed to us. *Molloy* is Beckett's first novel to establish a definite point of view (or possibly two different ones, if Moran and Molloy are not seen as different stages of the same person) though one whose perspective changes as the viewer develops. The world that comes to light within the horizon of Moran's intelligence—to speak in Heideggerian terms—is comparable to that of Roquentin's *salauds:* describable, respectable, comprehensible, and full of clichés. Its lack of authenticity is perhaps most strikingly illustrated by Moran's visit to Father Ambrose. Having missed Mass because of the unexpected visit of one of Youdi's messengers, Moran feels the need to see Father Ambrose privately and ask to be served communion:

> Passing the church, something made me stop. I looked at
> the door, baroque, very fine. I found it hideous. I hastened

on to the presbytery. The Father is sleeping, said the servant . . . She showed me into the sitting-room, bare and bleak, dreadful. Father Ambrose came in, rubbing his eyes . . . I shall not describe our attitudes, characteristic his of him, mine of me. He offered me a cigar which I accepted with good grace and put in my pocket, between my fountain-pen and my propelling-pencil. He flattered himself, Father Ambrose, with being a man of the world and knowing its ways, he who never smoked...May I offer you a little glass of something? he said. I was in a quandary. [He wonders whether Father Ambrose might have guessed that he already consumed a beer before coming to him.] I came to ask you a favour, I said. Granted, he said. We observed each other. It's this, I said, Sunday for me without the Body and Blood is like—He raised his hand. Above all no profane comparisons, he said . . . you want communion. I bowed my head. It's a little unusual, he said . . . Not a word to a soul, he said, let it remain between us and—. He broke off, raising a finger, and his eyes, to the ceiling. Heavens, he said, what is that stain? I looked in turn at the ceiling. Damp, I said . . . There are times, he said, when one feels like weeping. He got up. I'll go and get my kit, he said. He called that his kit . . . He came back with a kind of portable pyx, opened it and dispatched me without an instant's hesitation. I rose and thanked him warmly. Pah! he said, it's nothing. Now we can talk.

I had nothing else to say to him. All I wanted was to return home as quickly as possible and stuff myself with stew. My soul appeased, I was ravenous . . . He informed me that Mrs. Clement, the chemist's wife . . . had fallen in her laboratory, from the top of the ladder . . . And I, not to be outdone, told him how worried I was about my hens, particularly my grey hen, which would neither brood nor lay and for the past month and more had done nothing but sit with her arse in the dust, from morning to night. Like Job, haha, he said. I too said haha. What a joy it is to laugh, from time to time, he said. Is it not? I said. It is peculiar to man, he said. So I have noticed, I said. A brief silence ensued. What do you feed her on? he said. Corn chiefly, I said. Cooked or raw? he said. Both, I said, I added that she ate nothing any more. Nothing! he cried. Next to nothing, I said . . .

This interview with Father Ambrose left me with a painful impression. He was still the same dear man, and yet not. I seemed to have surprised, on his face, a lack, how shall I say, a lack of nobility. The host, it is only fair to say, was lying heavy on my stomach. And as I made my way home I felt like one who, having swallowed a pain-killer, is first astonished, then indignant, on obtaining no relief. [*Mo*, 136–39]

But this world of clichés and trivialities is soon to lose its matter-of-factness for Moran. What makes him sensitive to the changes in Father Ambrose's face seems to be his own feeling of uncertainty that has prevailed ever since the messenger's visit to him. This Sunday, which marks the beginning of his Molloy mission, is also for him the beginning of the ever-increasing doubt and suffering that undermine the certitude he had so carefully fostered. "I found it painful at that period not to understand," he admits *(Mo,* 139). With his horror of vagueness and uncertainty he had hitherto—like Roquentin's salauds—excluded from his life all that is mysterious, incomprehensible, or irrational *(Mo,* 135).

But once he has accepted the assignment to search for Molloy, irrationality approaches and invades him everywhere, not only from the outside but also from within. He realizes with a feeling of horror that he has always "known" Molloy; that, though seemingly his opposite, Molloy is also a part of his innermost being. "Molloy, or Mollose, was no stranger to me," he reports (*Mo,* 152). Yet no one had ever spoken to him of Molloy, and it is as if he had "invented him." He explains his uncertainty about Molloy's name by the circumstance that he first heard it in his soul "where the acoustics are so bad." What he had heard "was a first syllable, Mol, very clear, followed almost at once by a second, very thick, as though gobbled by the first, and which might have been oy as it might have been ose, or one, or even oc" (*Mo,* 153–54). Moran admits that he knew about Molloy without ever knowing much about him and proceeds to describe this strangely chaotic being:

> He had very little room. His time too was limited. He hastened incessantly on, as if in despair, towards extremely close objectives. Now, a prisoner, he hurled himself at I know not what narrow confines, and now, hunted, he sought refuge near the centre . . . Even in open country he seemed to be crashing through jungle. He did not so much walk as charge. In spite of this he advanced but slowly. He swayed to and fro, like a bear.
>
> He rolled his head, uttering incomprehensible words.
>
> He was massive and hulking, to the point of misshapenness. And, without being black, of a dark colour.
>
> He was forever on the move. I had never seen him rest. Occasionally he stopped and glared furiously about him.
> [*Mo,* 154–55]

Molloy visits Moran at intervals, although such visits seem to him rather as a rising up within himself. Their effect, whether from without or within, is that Moran is "filled with panting," that he is "nothing but uproar, bulk, rage, suffocation, effort unceasing, frenzied and vain . . . just the opposite of myself" (*Mo,* 155). Again one is reminded of *Proust,* in which Marcel's development into a writer is seen above all as the painful process of stripping away the comforts of habit: "The old ego dies hard. Such as it was, a minister of dullness, it was also an agent of security. When it ceases to perform that second function, when it is opposed by a phenomenon that it cannot reduce to the condition of a comfortable and familiar concept, when, in a word, it betrays its trust as a screen to spare its victim the spectacle of reality, it disappears . . . with wailing and gnashing of teeth. The mortal microcosm cannot forgive the relative immortality of the macrocosm" *(Pr,* 10). For in the pursuit of Molloy, the fulfillment of the mission assigned to him, Moran rids himself in a similar way of habit.

As he sets out on his journey, change accompanied by suffering becomes the only constant in his life until he is turned into his opposite whom he pursues. All is departure from the comforts of his previous life and encounter with the unknown, the irrational. His very body deteriorates. Moran is aware of himself as being in the process of "crumbling, a frenzied collapsing of all that had always protected me from all that I was always condemned to be. Or it was like a kind of clawing toward a light and countenance I could not name, that I had once known and long denied" *(Mo,* 203). His trek in search of Molloy, whom he never attains, makes him more and more resemble Molloy, whom he has always known and denied, but who, as another aspect of himself, had lived within him. "And to tell the truth," he asserts toward the end of his account, "I not only knew who I was, but I had a sharper and clearer sense of my identity than ever before, in spite of the deep lesions and the wounds with which it was covered" *(Mo,* 233). The identity he feels is that of the writer. He believes he understands now the voice he always used to hear, the voice which now tells him to write his report. But it is a changed voice, one that "did not use the words that Moran had been taught when he was little and that he in his turn had taught to his little one" *(Mo,* 241).

Moran's quest does not seem to end upon his return to his house where once he had lived so securely and which now is crumbling. It is rather as if Molloy's journey is but a continuation of Moran's. One gains the impression that Molloy's desire to see his mother has symbolic significance. His relationship to her (he realizes at one point that he has always been on his way to her) has all the aspects of myth. She seems to represent to Molloy that center of Being to which the artist must aspire and which he cannot attain without dread and immense suffering. Goethe had his Faust descend to the great and terrible Mothers, the sources of all Being and Becoming, and Nietzsche equally saw in the artist's contact with them a trial essential to his growth. It is not surprising therefore that Molloy, upon arrival in his mother's room, is concerned with writing and finds a language and accents even more removed from the ordinary than the voice that spoke to Moran at the end of his trek. Molloy, in his mother's room, seems to experience that "brief eternity" of which Beckett speaks in reference to Proust's Marcel, that moment during which, exempt from will, he is "purified in the transcendental aperception that can capture the Model, the Idea, the Thing in itself" *(Pr,* 69).

Having arrived in his mother's room, Molloy experiences what Nietzsche might have considered a Dionysiac return to Being. Like Arsene of *Watt,* he is at one with Being, is its human here and now, and reveals it in the accents of the poet:

> And that night . . . was a night of listening, a night given to the faint soughing and sighing stirring at night in little pleasure gardens, the shy sabbath of leaves and petals and the air that eddies there as it does not in other places . . . And there was another noise, that of my life become the life of this garden as it rode the earth of deeps and wildernesses. Yes, there were times when I forgot not only who I was, but that I was, forgot to be. Then I was no longer that sealed

> jar to which I owed my being so well preserved, but a wall gave way and I filled with roots and tame stems for example, stakes long since dead and ready for burning, the recess of night and the imminence of dawn, and then the labour of the planet rolling eager into winter . . . Or of that winter I was the precarious calm, the thaw of the snows which make no difference and all the horrors of it all all over again. [*Mo*, 65]

In his mother's room Molloy thinks "almost without stopping," but he complains, at the same time, of his "lack of understanding not only what others said to me, but also what I said to them" *(Mo,* 67). His understanding "began to vibrate [only] on repeated solicitations or . . . at a lower frequency, or a higher, than that of ratiocination, if such a thing is conceivable, and such a thing is conceivable" *(Mo,* 66). The words he heard seemed to him "pure sounds, free of all meaning" and conversation was therefore "unspeakably painful" to him *(Mo,* 66). In his mother's room, he comes to the conclusion that "all that is false may more readily be reduced, to notions clear and distinct" than that which is true *(Mo,* 110). There he realizes—not unlike Roquentin—the inauthenticity of the writer who tries to recapture either past or present. He not only feels his own "sense of identity . . . wrapped in a namelessness often hard to penetrate," but all other things also make merry with his senses. "Yes, even then, when already all was fading, waves and particles, there could be no things but nameless things, no names but thingless names" *(Mo,* 41). What he knows of the past is merely contained in "icy words" and "icy meanings," "and the world dies too, foully named." And he sums it all up in the haunting phrase: "All I know is what the words know, and the dead things, and that makes a handsome little sum, with a beginning, a middle and an end as in the well-built phrase and the long sonata of the dead" *(Mo,* 41). He feels compelled, therefore, to justify his own writing of the past:

> And when I say I said, etc., all I mean is that I knew confusedly things were so, without knowing exactly what it was all about. And every time I say, I said this, or, I said that, or speak of a voice saying, far inside me, Molloy, and then a fine phrase more or less clear and simple, or find myself compelled to contribute to others intelligible words, or hear my own voice uttering to others more or less articulate sounds, I am merely complying with the convention that demands you either lie or hold your peace. For what really happened was quite different. [*Mo,* 118–19]

"Saying is inventing," he maintains not unlike Sartre's Roquentin. But he corrects himself immediately: "Wrong, very rightly wrong. You invent nothing" *(Mo,* 41). What he has written, he explains, he "might doubtless have expressed otherwise and better," had he gone to enough trouble. Moran, upon returning from his quest, had already become aware of that freedom of the writer to create *his* world, a world contrary to actuality. Having been freed from his past meticulousness and adherence to facts, he is enabled to end his report by stating boldly: "Then I went back into the house and wrote, It is midnight. The rain is beating on the windows. It was not midnight. It was not raining" *(Mo,* 241). Moran-become-Molloy continues his process toward an artistic freedom based on the elusiveness of Being and its truth. "Let me cry out then," he pleads, "it's said to be good for you" *(Mo,* 33). Yet as he cries out, he remains and becomes more and more the conscious artist rendering as best he can the immediacy of experience and realizing that "it is one of the features of this penance that I may not pass over what is over and straightway come to the heart of the matter. But that must again be unknow n to me which is no longer so and that again fondly believed which then I fondly believed, at my setting out. And if I occasionally break this rule, it is only over details of little importance. And in the main I observe it. And with such zeal that I am far more he who finds than he who tells what he has found" *(Mo,* 182).

If such technical scruples on the part of the writer contribute to the novel's complexity, it is still further increased because Molloy is not only Moran's opposite—the part of himself that he must pursue and assimilate and that forever eludes him—but also his artistic vision and creation. Moran dwells emphatically on his role as the author-creator of Molloy, suggesting, as we have seen, that the image of Molloy originated in his own mind and that, in fact, he "invented" him *(Mo,* 152). It is only in the light of this complex relationship that we can grasp Moran's ambiguous observation that "where Molloy could not be, nor Moran either for that matter, there Moran could bend over Molloy" *(Mo,* 152). It is only in the light of the author's concern for the creation of his fictional hero that Moran can ask himself why he did not invest his man "from the outset, with the air of a fabulous being, which something told me could not fail to help me later on" *(Mo,* 152). Everything, indeed, in Moran's preoccupation with Molloy points in the direction that his "Molloy mission" is an analogue to the artist's relationship to his creature:

> It is lying down, in the warmth, in the gloom, that I best pierce the outer turmoil's veil, discern my quarry, sense what course to follow, find peace in another's ludicrous distress. Far from the world, its clamours, frenzies, bitterness and dingy light, I pass judgment on it and on those, like me, who are plunged in it beyond recall, and on him who has need of me to be delivered, who cannot deliver myself. All is dark, but with that simple darkness that

follows like a balm upon the great dismemberings. From their places masses move, stark as laws. Masses of what? One does not ask. There somewhere man is too, vast conglomerate of all of nature's kingdoms, as lonely and as bound. And in that block the prey is lodged and thinks himself a being apart. Anyone would serve. But I am paid to seek. I arrive, he comes away. His life has been nothing but a waiting for this, to see himself preferred, to fancy himself damned, blessed, to fancy himself everyman, above all others. [*Mo,* 151]

Only in quiet and darkness can the writer discern his quarry and find the block where his prey is lodged and waiting for him. As soon as he leaves his lonely room, he feels himself drowning "in the spray of phenomena" *(Mo,* 151).

Lest the reader still fail to recognize that, in this sense, Molloy is Moran's creature, Beckett further underlines the relationship by having Moran recollect earlier "missions" and name among his charges the very protagonists of Beckett's earlier novels. "Oh the stories I could tell you, if I were easy," Moran exclaims: "What a rabble in my head, what a gallery of moribunds. Murphy, Watt, Yerk, Mercier and all the others. I would never have believed that—yes, I believe it willingly. Stories, stories. I have not been able to tell them. I shall not be able to tell this one" *(Mo,* 188). And in the spirit of the existential writer, he insists: "what I was doing I was doing neither for Molloy, who mattered nothing to me, nor for myself, of whom I despaired, but on behalf of a cause which, while having need of us to be accomplished, was in its essence anonymous, and would subsist, haunting the minds of men, when its miserable artisans should be no more" *(Mo,* 156–57). For Moran, writing is obviously, as it is for Heidegger and Sartre, a task that transcends the individual. Even before reaching the Molloy stage, Moran is thus

conscious of writing as a pensum, an assignment whose fulfillment implicates him in problems of a faithful rendering of
existence.

At the same time Moran (and through him Beckett) never
forgets the elusiveness of Being and even of the creatures of his
own imagination. Moran never succeeds in ascertaining the true
features of Molloy. "Between the Molloy I stalked within me
thus and the true Molloy, after whom I was so soon to be in
full cry, over hill and dale, the resemblance cannot have been
great," he feels. He even might have annexed to his private
Molloy, he fears, the elements described by the messenger
Gaber.

> The fact was there were three, no, four Molloys. He that
> inhabited me, my caricature of same, Gaber's and the man
> of flesh and blood somewhere awaiting me. To these I
> would add Youdi's were it not for Gaber's corpse fidelity
> to the letter of his messages. Bad reasoning. For could it be
> seriously supposed that Youdi had confided to Gaber all he
> knew, or thought he knew (all one to Youdi) about his
> protégé? Assuredly not. He had only revealed what he
> deemed of relevance for the prompt and proper execution
> of his orders. I will therefore add a fifth Molloy, that of
> Youdi. But would not this fifth Molloy necessarily coincide
> with the fourth, the real one as the saying is, him dogged
> by his shadow? I would have given a lot to know. [Mo, 157]

Moran, once the individualist, becomes in the course of his
trek more and more like Nietzsche's Dionysiac man who has
broken the principle of individuation. Both physically and
mentally, he approaches the essence of Molloy, the "mol" which
means softness. And as his body progressively decays, his sense
of identity also more and more vanishes. "I had forgotten who
I was (excusably)," he admits at one point in his report, "and

spoken of myself as I would have of another." It happens to him quite often "that I forget who I am and strut before my eyes, like a stranger. Then I see the sky different from what it is and the earth too takes on false colours. It looks like rest, it is not, I vanish happy in that alien light, which must have once been mine, I am willing to believe it, then the anguish of return, I won't say where, I can't, to absence perhaps" *(Mo,* 56). This seems but the poetic analogue of Sartre's disquisition on the transcendence of the ego:

> If the *I* becomes a transcendent it participates in all the vicissitudes of the world. It is no absolute; it has not created the universe . . . and solipsism becomes unthinkable from the moment that the *I* no longer has a privileged status. Instead of expressing itself in effect as "I alone exist as absolute," it must assert that "absolute consciousness alone exists as absolute," which is obviously a truism. My *I,* in effect, *is no more certain for consciousness than the I of other men.* It is only more intimate.[21]

It seems to represent likewise the Sartrean pour-soi in futile quest of a Self that becomes a stranger, an en-soi, an object as soon as it is seen by an intelligence which classifies and judges it. Molloy's Self is quite similar to the Sartrean in that it remains forever unattainable to him. But Molloy's situation also evokes for us that of the Nietzschean poet who merges with the god of art, becomes Dionysiac and, in the act of creation, can look at himself and understand the essence of art.

Molloy is the writer of a report of which he himself is both author and protagonist. He is also the critic concerned with the most crucial problems of his art. And as he sounds the very

21. Jean-Paul Sartre, *The Transcendance of the Ego: An Existential Theory of Consciousness,* trans. Forrest Williams and Robert Kirkpatrick (New York, Farrar, Straus & Cudahy, 1960), pp. 105–06.

depths of it, as he tries to find its essence, he has to realize that his art must be failure. But what is interesting is that Molloy, in spite of his growing conviction that failure is intrinsic to his undertaking, must go on writing. Like the existential man of Heidegger or Sartre, he considers it his task to be a witness to Being, to be a writer: "Not to want to say, not to know what you want to say, not to be able to say what you think you want to say, and never stop saying, or hardly ever, that is the thing to keep in mind, even in the heat of composition" *(Mo, 36)*. "Whatever I do," Molloy realizes, "that is to say whatever I say, it will always as it were be the same thing" *(Mo, 61)*. *Doing* and *saying* are as identical to him as *dire* and *agir* are to Sartre. This dedication to writing; this obsession of the author-hero to reveal his via dolorosa, the stages of his passion of creation and through them the essence of art, become more intense yet in the second and third part of Beckett's trilogy.

Malone, the protagonist of the novel entitled *Malone Dies,* spends his days and nights in a bed that seems to be in the very room where Molloy arrived and gave account of his adventures. "This room seems to be mine," he states. "Perhaps I came in for the room on the death of whoever was in it before me. I enquire no further in any case. It is not a room in a hospital, or in a madhouse, I can feel that" *(Ma, 57)*. Sometimes the gray incandescence of the place makes him feel that he is inside a head *(Ma, 47)*. At other times, he thinks of himself in the room as a fetus in the womb, the only window serving as his umbilicus *(Ma, 49–51)*. All this is reminiscent again of Murphy's withdrawal into his mind. Not unlike Murphy in this state of withdrawal from the world or Molloy in his mother's room, Malone is hardly aware of his limbs. Even of his head he cannot be altogether certain and wonders whether his skull is a vacuum *(Ma, 47)*. He describes himself as speechless and shapeless. Although he remembers having walked all his life, he now does not even crawl any longer. His senses are trained full on himself *(Ma, 9)*. He is *immured*. If he did not feel himself dying, he could well believe himself dead *(Ma, 6)*.

Malone's contact with objects outside his bed is reduced to those he can reach with a long stick. But he has in his immediate possession a pencil and a notebook. Inevitably, the little pencil he has sharpened at both ends is dwindling so that he dreads the day "when nothing will remain but a fragment too tiny to hold" *(Ma, 48)*. It is fortunate therefore that he is secure in the knowledge of having another pencil somewhere in his bed, "another pencil, made in France, a long cylinder hardly broached, in the bed with me, somewhere I think. So I have nothing to worry about, on this score. And yet I do worry" *(Ma, 49)*. Malone's days are filled with the telling of stories: with writing. He hears inside him a children's choir reminding him of Easter week and the Resurrection *(Ma, 33)*. His gradual bodily decomposition means for him a symbolic rebirth, as it did for Molloy. As in the great myths of birth, death, and rebirth, womb and tomb seem to be one and the same thing. And the book ends on a variation of this theme, as the dying Malone writes: "I am being given, if I may venture the expression, birth to into death, such is my impression" *(Ma, 114)*. Writing is his life, he realizes: "This exercise-book is my life, this big child's exercise-book, it has taken me a long time to resign myself to that" *(Ma, 105)*. With his "distant" hand he counts the pages that remain and concludes that "they will do." They will do for him, that is, to tell his stories. Malone is that much farther advanced upon the road started by Moran and continued by Molloy. He has not merely lost the use of his limbs to the extent where, as he assures us, his body has become completely impotent. He is so exclusively concerned with writing that the only noise he hears is that of his little finger gliding before his pencil across the page *(Ma, 32)*.

It is in this room and this state of complete isolation and insulation that Malone comes to realize his destiny. He is a writer: "I now knew what I had to do, I whose every move has always been a groping, and whose motionlessness too was a kind of groping" *(Ma,* 50). It is true that the triumphant note of this realization is dampened immediately afterwards by the statement, "And here again naturally I was utterly deceived, I mean in imagining I had grasped at last the true nature of my absurd tribulations, but not so utterly as to feel the need to reproach myself with it now" *(Ma,* 50). Strangely enough Malone himself is aware of his inclination to irony. He admits with amazing lucidity, "But my notes have a curious tendency, as I realize at last, to annihilate all they purport to record" *(Ma,* 88). Yet his double irony seems at times to reinforce doubly what he ostensibly denies. This is particularly striking when one finds him repeating in many different ways how much he considers it to be "in the natural order of things" that he must write, must fill his exercise-book with what concerns him: "All that pertains to me must be written there, including my inability to grasp what order is meant. For I have never seen any sign of any, inside me or outside me" *(Ma,* 35). He feels forced to write almost against his own will: "At first I did not write, but I had to resign myself to it in the end. It is in order to know where I have got to, where he has got to. At first I did not write, I just said the thing. Then I forgot what I had said." He is imbued, moreover, with a feeling of urgency about it all: "I have no time to pick my words" *(Ma,* 32).

The situation in which Malone finds himself would seem to permit only of solipsism. He is completely isolated and even insulated from the world. He is, indeed, as much withdrawn from ordinary life as was Murphy when he withdrew into his mind. But for Beckett, as we have seen, the *I* has become as impersonal as for Sartrean consciousness. Malone's consciousness is impersonal in this manner. It is without subjectivity. His own *I* has become to him a *me,* an object in the Sartrean sense of the word, opaque and impenetrable, though more intimate than the *I* of others. It is because of this that Malone can say, "And yet I write about myself with the same pencil and in the same exercise-book as about him. It is because it is no longer I, I must have said so long ago, but another whose life is just beginning" *(Ma,* 32). His own *I* has become to him an Other. He may subsequently refer to himself as Malone: "I mean the business of Malone (since that is what I am called now)" *(Ma,* 48). He is as it were witness to the workings of his own mind. "During all this time," he writes, upon having recovered his exercise-book which he had lost, "so fertile in incidents and mishaps, in my head I suppose all was streaming and emptying away as through a sluice, to my great joy, until finally nothing remained, either of Malone or of the other. And what is more I was able to follow without difficulty the various phases of this deliverance" *(Ma,* 50).

As the *I* becomes a *me,* however, it becomes ultimately as unattainable as any other human reality. For it can never be fixed and defined without being thereby deprived of its freedom, that is, of life. Although Malone—like any other human—partakes of his *I* to a certain degree, he can never become fully identical with it. The result is paradox and ambiguity: the artistic achievement becomes the very failure of which Beckett speaks in his dialogues with Duthuit. Malone restates it in his own way and with reference to his inability to know himself: "Decidedly this evening I shall say nothing that is not calculated to leave me in doubt as to my real intentions" *(Ma,* 32). Beckett has grasped like Sartre, that the writer disclosing the Truth of Being can disclose it only in its ambiguity, as something which all disclosure must falsify since it *is* not, but is perpetually becoming. But Beckett has gone beyond Sartre in the fictional realization of this view.

Yet as the *I* becomes a *me* and thereby just another of the many possibilities wherein "the unchanging seeks relief from its formlessness" *(Ma,* 21), it can easily be replaced by any other human reality. "Live and cause to live," Malone tells himself. "I began again to try to live, cause to live, be another, in myself, in another. How false all this is. No time now to explain. I begin again. But . . . no longer in order to succeed, but in order to fail" *(Ma,* 19). In the paradoxical world of such artistic endeavor, it can never become clear whether the Other is the Self become a *me* or an Other altogether, living in the outside world and remembered by Malone or created by him. "My concern is not with me," Malone reminds himself, "but with another, far beneath me and whom I try to envy, of whose crass adventures I can now tell at last, I don't know how." And he thrusts us into utter ambiguity, though we can only agree with him, when he adds: "Of myself I could never tell, any more than live or tell of others" *(Ma,* 19). Beckett was later to give concrete pictorial expression to this ambiguity. In his film entitled *Film* and presented in 1964, the protagonist is split asunder into Eye (E) and Object (O) with E pursuing in vain the O who cannot stand E's scrutiny, until they finally realize that the "pursuing perceiver is not extraneous, but self" *(F,* 31).

Sapo and Macmann, the protagonists of the stories Malone proceeds to tell, are considered by him to be his "creatures" and made in his image: "I shall try to make a little creature," he decides, "to hold in my arms, a little creature in my image, no matter what I say" *(Ma,* 52). He imagines his creature Sapo, his homunculus, as despairing of "ever knowing what manner being he was, and how he was going to live, and lived vanquished, blindly, in a mad world, in the midst of strangers" *(Ma,* 16). Not satisfied, however, with having created Sapo and Macmann, he also lays claim to Murphy, Mercier, Molloy, Moran, and even Malone, referring to himself in the third person, and reassures us that they will die when he dies *(Ma, 63)*. He too, then, arrogates to himself Beckett's heroes and suggests his identity with the novelist. It is as if Malone (or Beckett), like the Sapo he created, tried to find himself and succeeded "in being another," while fearing that "if this continues it is myself I shall lose and the thousand ways that lead there" *(Ma, 17)*. This consciousness, which tries to find its Self as if it were that of an Other, ultimately becomes a "many." Once he has found his characters, he "slips into" them *(Ma, 52)*. Or, at will, he may kill them. But when he dies, they will all have to die with him. And yet he can imagine that "perhaps we'll all come back, reunited, done with parting, done with prying on one another," as he hears them "clamouring after me down the corridors, stumbling through the rubble, beseeching me to take them with me" *(Ma, 63)*. For their story is in fact his own story: "I have only to open my mouth for it to testify to the old story, my old story" *(Ma, 63)*.

The Sapos and Macmanns are then, like the Murphys, Morans, Molloys, and Malones the "possibles" of the narrator now called Malone. And although Malone's material world is reduced to a minimum, it is through these "creatures" and their stories that an entire universe enters the room of the dying man. In telling their stories, he appropriately assumes the role of the omniscient author and refers to them in the third person. It is Malone's voice that is heard throughout, his consciousness that discloses the world of Sapo:

> Sapo remained alone, by the window, the bowl of goat's milk on the table before him, forgotten. It was summer . . . And Sapo, his face turned towards an earth so resplendent that it hurt his eyes, felt at his back and all about him the unconquerable dark, and it licked the light on his face . . . Then he heard more clearly the sounds of those at work, the

> daughter calling to her goats, the father cursing his mule.
> But silence was in the heart of the dark, the silence of dust
> and the things that would never stir, if left alone. [*Ma*, 27]

The world Malone reveals to us is one in which there is little
communication between people, as he himself knows by interpreting their behavior. "They had no conversation properly
speaking. They made use of the spoken word in much the same
way as the guard of a train makes use of his flags, or of his lan-
tern" (*Ma*, 11). He tells of Sapo that "he went, often unnoticed,
in spite of his strange walk, his halts and sudden starts" (*Ma*, 29).
We learn from the narrator that the Lamberts, at whose house
Sapo was staying, "did not try to detain him or even call good-
bye, unresentful at his leaving them in a way that seemed so
lacking in friendliness, for they knew he meant no harm" (*Ma*,
29). In this almost speechless world, "all raised their heads and
watched him as he went, then looked at one another, before
stooping to the earth again" (*Ma*, 30).

In the Sapo universe men and women are as silent and bur-
dened with inexplicable tasks as characters in a fairy tale. Mrs.
Lambert sorts lentils "so that soon there were two heaps on the
table, one big heap getting smaller and one small heap getting
bigger. But suddenly with a furious gesture she swept the two
together, annihilating thus in less than a second the work of two
or three minutes . . . She could have gone on sorting her lentils
all night and never achieved her purpose, which was to free them
from all admixture" (*Ma*, 39). Edmund, the son of the family,
and the father are engaged in conversation without ever listening to each other: "There they sat, the table between them, in
the gloom, one speaking, the other listening, and far removed
the one from what he said, the other from what he heard, and far
from each other" (*Ma*, 38). The mother's relation to husband and
son is similar: "Edmund and his mother passed each other by in

silence . . . Before her husband too she rapidly passed, without a glance, and in his attitude there was nothing to suggest that he had seen her either" *(Ma,* 38). Her own life is futile gesture and suffering: "Often she stood up and moved about the room, or out and round the ruinous old house. . . . Night seemed less night in the kitchen pervaded with the everyday tribulations, day less dead. It helped her, when things were bad, to cling with her fingers to the worn table at which her family would soon be united, waiting for her to serve them, and to feel about her, ready for use, the lifelong pots and pans" *(Ma,* 42). The objects about the Lamberts assume their place according to strange laws of their own: "She lit the lamp where it stood at its usual place on the chimney-piece, beside the alarm-clock flanked in its turn by the crucifix hanging from a nail. The clock, being the lowest of the three had to remain in the middle, and the lamp and crucifix could not change places because of the nail from which the latter was hung" *(Ma,* 39).

Sapo, whose name in the context of the book might suggest homo sapiens, is given a different name by about the middle of the novel. "For Sapo—," Malone begins to say, but he continues, "no, I can't call him that any more, and I even wonder how I was able to stomach such a name till now. So then for, let me see, for Macmann, that's not much better but there is no time to lose" *(Ma,* 55). The different name is not so different after all; for Macmann, meaning "son of man," is as impersonal as homo sapiens. Both refer to man in a sense that surpasses the individual and is metaphysical. It is somewhat later in the novel, however, that we are given, rather obliquely, the reason for the change. Macmann is described there as being rather "of the earth earthy and ill-fitted for reason" *(Ma,* 70), thus the opposite of homo sapiens. Of Macmann, Malone tells us that "he was no more than human, than the son and grandson and greatgrandson of humans," and that "his link with the species was through his ascendants only" *(Ma,* 68). He also suggests that to Macmann the hour has come "when nothing more can happen and nobody more can come and all is ended but the waiting that knows itself in vain" *(Ma,* 68). It is as if Macmann belonged to those who are waiting for Godot, knowing that his waiting is in vain. At the same time he is shown as assuming the position of one crucified, like one of the sinners referred to in *Godot.* Surprised by a downpour as he crosses an open field, he lies down on the ground, his arms outstretched, and, looking up at the dark streaming mass of sky and air, lets the rain pelt down on his palms *(Ma,* 69). Macmann is thus man in general, submitting to the suffering which comes to him from above, and the woman he encounters is Moll (a name whose Latin etymon is *mulier,* "woman").

As these generic names indicate, the individual is stripped in this novel of almost all that is accidental, and reduced to what is essential. Life becomes stylized gesture, as we have seen in the description of Mrs. Lambert. The institution where Macmann lived is described in such terms. Looked at from the summit called the Rock, its buildings loomed large in spite of the remoteness "and all was astir with little dots or flecks forever appearing and disappearing, in reality the keepers coming and going, perhaps mingled with I was going to say with the prisoners! For seen from this distance the striped cloak had no stripes, nor indeed any great resemblance to a cloak at all. So that one could only say, when the first shock of surprise was past, Those are men and women, you know, people, without being able to specify further" *(Ma,* 108). This essentializing technique, traces of which are to be found even in *Molloy* and which Beckett has brought to a climax in *The Unnamable* and *How It Is,* is beautifully symbolized in Malone's experience with his stick. It is only after having lost it that, in his mind, he painfully ascends to "an understanding of the Stick, shorn of all its accidents" *(Ma,* 82).

It is interesting to juxtapose the view of a city, as it emerges for Macmann in such an essentializing manner, with the more accidental approaches of Kierkegaard's "Seducer" and Sartre's *Nausea* at which we looked earlier:

> The tugs, their black funnels striped with red, tow to their moorings the last barges, freighted with empty barrels. The water cradles already the distant fires of the sunset, orange, rose and green, quenches them in its ruffles and then in trembling pools spreads them bright again. His [Macmann's] back is turned to the river, but perhaps it appears to him in the dreadful cries of the gulls that evening assembles, in paroxysms of hunger, round the outflow of the sewers, opposite the Bellevue Hotel . . . But his face is towards the people that throng the streets at this hour, their long day ended and the whole long evening before them. The doors open and spew them out, each door its contingent. For an instant they cluster in a daze, huddled on the sidewalk or in the gutter, then set off singly on their appointed ways . . . And God help him who longs, for once, in his recovered freedom, to walk a little way with a fellow-creature, no matter which, unless of course by a merciful chance he stumble on one in the same plight. Then they take a few paces happily side by side, then part . . . At this hour then erotic craving accounts for the majority of couples. But these are few compared to the solitaries pressing forward through the throng, obstructing the access to places of amusement, bowed over the parapets, propped against vacant walls. But soon they come to the appointed place, at home, or at some other home, or abroad, as the saying is, in a public place, or in a doorway in view of possible rain. And the first to arrive have seldom long to wait, for all hasten towards one another, knowing how short the time in which to say all the things that lie heavy on the heart and con-

science and do all the things they have to do together, things one cannot do alone. So there they are for a few hours in safety ... And if as suggested it is dusk, then another phenomenon to be observed is the number of windows and shop-windows that light up an instant, almost after the fashion of the setting sun, though all depends on the season. But for Macmann, thank God he's still there, for Macmann it is a true spring evening ... Or it is perhaps an evening in autumn. [*Ma,* 56–58]

The narrator here does not record vivid impressions as did the Seducer. He is even further removed from the inhabitants of the city than Roquentin. As in Murphy's head, reality has become a flux of forms, and Malone, the narrator, a "mote in its absolute freedom." All is stripped for inaction. The world, like Macmann, is waiting. Yet there are in this description touches of irony and even humor not unlike those in Roquentin's rendering of Sunday in Bouville.

Malone—whether narrator or author—clearly tells his stories from the vantage point Molloy had reached before him. He feels that "the noises of the world, so various in themselves and which I used to be so clever at distinguishing from one another, had been dinning at me for so long, always the same old noises, as gradually to have merged into a single noise, so that all I heard was one vast continuous buzzing. The volume of sound perceived remained no doubt the same, I had simply lost the faculty of decomposing it" *(Ma,* 31–32).[22] He has separated himself from the "they" of the world, and the axioms of the Saposcats [Sapo's parents] establishing, for instance, the "criminal absurdity of a garden without roses and with its paths and lawns uncared for," have become foreign to him *(Ma,* 10). From his viewpoint, time cannot be measured in the manner in which the "they" measure

22. See p. 237 below.

it. "They taught me the names of the days and I marvelled at their being so few and flourished my little fists, crying out for more, and how to tell the time, and what are two or three days, more or less, in the long run, a joke" *(Ma,* 60). When he was younger he, too, used to count. "That passed the time, I was time, I devoured the world. Not now, any more. A man changes. As he gets on" *(Ma,* 26). As the division of time becomes immaterial, so does the succession of local phenomena *(Ma,* 61). Thus his stories not only are shorn of the accidental, as we have seen, but his manner of telling them changes accordingly: "My fingers too write in other latitudes and the air that breathes through my pages and turns them without my knowing, when I doze off, so that the subject falls far from the verb and the object lands somewhere in the void, is not the air of this second-last abode" *(Ma,* 61).

In this atmosphere all that identifies an individual in the eyes of the "they" becomes absurd. As Malone thinks of his imminent death, he trusts that he will be buried with a minimum of ceremony and that his vital statistics will read simply: "Here lies Malone at last, with the dates to give a faint idea of the time he took to be excused and then to distinguish him from his namesakes, numerous in the island . . . Here lies a ne'er-do-well, six feet under hell" *(Ma,* 101). He is bemused by the odd desire of man "to know who people are and what they do for a living and what they want with you." But this bemusement does not keep him from wanting to ask his mysterious visitor—apparently death—these very questions. He is, in fact, planning to present him with a long questionnaire: "1. Who are you? 2. What do you do, for a living? 3. Are you looking for something in particular? What else? 4. Why are you so cross? 5. Have I offended you? 6. Do you know anything about me?" *(Ma,* 102) and so on, twenty-one questions in all, which under the circumstances are even more absurd and farcical than they would normally be.

When Malone is dealt a blow on his head by the unknown visitor, this blow coincides strangely enough with the beating of Macmann by the new guard Lemuel. Before being knocked out, Malone has a clear view of this visitor, the only human being who enters his room in the course of the novel. Malone's description of this clownlike character, this person who may well have been an undertaker, or someone in disguise, suggests an identity with Lemuel:

> Black suit of antiquated cut, or perhaps come back into fashion, black tie, snow-white shirt, heavily starched clown's cuffs almost entirely covering the hands, oily black hair, a long, dismal, glabrous, floury face, sombre, lacklustre eyes, medium height and build, block-hat pressed delicately to stomach with fingertips, then without warning in a gesture of extraordinary suddenness and precision slapped on skull. A folding-rule, together with a fin of white handkerchief, emerged from the breast pocket. I took him at first for the undertaker's man, annoyed at having called prematurely . . . His umbrella, have I mentioned his umbrella, the tightest rolled I ever saw? Shifting it every few minutes from one hand to the other he leaned his weight upon it, standing beside the bed. Then it bent . . . In spite of the ease with which he wore his black and manipulated his umbrella and his consummate mastery of the block-hat, I had for a time the impression he was disguised, but from what if I may say so, and as what? [*Ma*, 99–102]

Fortifying the impression that he is disguised is the fact that the curious outfit is completed by brown boots, still caked with mud like those of Lemuel. Both the visitor and Lemuel have sprung from the same tragicomic imagination, but their relationship seems yet more intricate, as a glance at the novel's formal structure reveals.

The story is apparently told on two levels. On the one there is Malone dying and busying himself with his reminiscences, his stories, inventing, writing, while he feels that "it is the present I must establish" *(Ma, 6)*. It is on this level, or rather within this framework, that the clown-figure of death appears to him. On the other level are the stories into which Malone delves and which he tells in the past and in the third person. Only at the moment of death do the two levels fuse, past and present meet, and Malone dies simultaneously with his hero, Sapo-Macmann. It is at that moment also that Lemuel is in charge of Macmann, Lemuel who may well be he who, in disguise, kills Malone. Who is this Lemuel who so strangely unites the two levels of existence? He makes his appearance in the novel, when Malone decides to get rid of Moll. "Moll," Malone tells us, "I'm going to kill her" *(Ma, 94)*. It is Lemuel who soon afterwards takes her place, briefly mentioning her death and murmuring—or is it Malone who does so?—"There is one out of the way at least" *(Ma, 95)*. At the end of the novel, Lemuel's role blends amazingly with that of the writer: "Lemuel is in charge, he raises his hatchet on which the blood will never dry, but not to hit anyone, he will not hit anyone any more, he will not touch anyone any more, either with it, or with it or with it or with or—or with it or with his hammer or with his stick or with his fist or in thought or in dream I mean never he will never—or with his pencil or with his stick or" *(Ma,* 119). If we realize that "Lemuel" is the Hebrew form of "Samuel," Lemuel—like the Sam of *Watt*—challenges us tongue-in-cheek to identify him with Beckett. In this light Lemuel's murders appear rather an author's ridding himself of the characters he has created. They are an author's way of ending a story that has no natural end. For Malone's death seems but the fictional continuation of the long trek towards spiritualization and essentialization begun by Beckett's first author-hero, Moran. The trek is resumed again in *The Unnamable,* and it is there that we find an even stronger insistence on man's inescapable need to witness and write and to witness the writing—even if such wit-nesssing must be failure.

In *The Unnamable* human consciousness is still further cleansed of a definite "I" and has truly become unnamable, except in the most general metaphysical terms. The Sapos, Macmanns, and Molls of *Malone Dies,* still less defined, become Mahoods (mankind) and, metaphorically, Worms. While human consciousness proves yet more isolated and insulated than Kierkegaardian subjectivity, and bodily existence becomes irrelevant to the extent that it remains unproven, the Unnamable is closer still than Malone to the impersonal intelligence of the Sartrean pour-soi or the Heideggerian Dasein. At the same time, however, he remains bound to time and place. A language has been transmitted to him by the "they," words that seem to him even less appropriate to express truth than those of Heidegger's *man,* Sartre's *salauds,* or Beckett's previous protagonists. While for him the word may assume the magic power of disclosing and even creating reality, as it did for Roquentin and for Sartre himself, it is also seen as mere sound and nothingness.

Quite appropriately, therefore, the novel begins with the questions "Where now? Who now? When now?" Even the "I" telling the story admits "I, say I. Unbelieving," and realizes "I seem to speak, it is not I, about me, it is not about me" *(U, 3)*. Yet this "I," which is not an "I" and seems to speak about itself without really speaking about itself, has a dim identity it describes to us. "I do not move and never shall again . . . of the great traveler I had been, on my hands and knees in the later stages, then crawling on my belly or rolling on the ground, only the trunk remains (in sorry trim), surmounted by the head . . . this is the part of myself the description of which I have best assimilated and retained. Stuck like a sheaf of flowers in a deep jar, its neck flush with my mouth, on the side of a quiet street near the shambles,

I am at rest at least" *(U,* 54–55). He feels himself, perhaps legitimately, entitled to "suppose that one-armed one-legged wayfarer of a moment ago and the wedge-headed trunk in which I am now marooned are simply two phases of the same carnal envelope, the soul being notoriously immune from deterioration and dismemberment" *(U,* 59, 60). He even likes to think that he occupies the center of the universe, his universe: "The best is to think of myself as fixed and at the centre, of this place, whatever its shape and extent may be" *(U,* 9). "I like to think I occupy the centre, but nothing is less certain" *(U,* 8).

The Unnamable considers himself so totally alone that he thinks himself on an island: "The island, I'm on the island, I've never left the island. God help me. I was under the impression I spent my life in spirals round the earth. Wrong . . . The island that's all the earth I know" *(U,* 54). Since he not only seems to record his story but also to create it (he is constantly concerned with problems of writing), he decides to surround himself with characters: "I shall have company. In the beginning. A few puppets. Then I'll scatter them, to the winds, if I can" *(U,* 4). Since things are barely present in his life and he deplores their absence, he wishes for them *(U,* 151), while deliberating, from the point of view of the writer, what he should do with them if he had them at his disposal: "And things, what is the correct attitude to adopt towards things? And, to begin with, are they necessary? . . . But I have few illusions, things are to be expected . . . If a thing turns up, for some reason or another, take it into consideration" *(U,* 4).

Though he does not move, though he exists in utter isolation, as a writer the Unnamable is not alone. Round about him are whirling all his former "I's," all the previous protagonists of Beckett's novels: "They are all here, at least from Murphy on, I believe we are all here" *(U,* 6). He thinks of the Murphys, Molloys, and Malones as his "forbears" *(U,* 7). Thus the unnamable is permitted to claim both kinship with and authorship of Beckett's own fictional characters. He fully usurps Beckett's own place and even reports the collision and sudden disappearance of two "oblong shapes" whom he assumes to have been Mercier-Camier, the two protagonists of Beckett's unpublished novel. While the Unnamable sees these creatures whirl about him, he also realizes that they are figments of his imagination and "have never been, only I and this black void have ever been . . . Nothing then but me, of which I know nothing, except that I have never uttered, and this black, of which I know nothing either, except that it is black, and empty" (U, 21). He enlisted these characters, he explains, as "sufferers of my pains," thinking that he could thus "witness it" as if it were not his own (U, 21). But he comes to realize that they never suffered *his* pains. Like other Beckett characters before him, the Unnamable both claims and disclaims identity with and authorship of all. "Mahood," he muses. "Before him there were others, taking themselves for me, it must be a sinecure handed down from generation to generation, to judge by their family air" (U, 37). It does occur to him to ponder, "What if we were one and the same after all, as he affirms and I deny?" (U, 37). But he reassures himself in the end, "I am neither, I needn't say, Murphy, nor Watt, nor Mercier, nor—no, I can't even bring myself to name them, nor any of the others whose very names I forget, who told me I was they, who I must have tried to be, under duress, or through fear, or to avoid acknowledging me" (U, 53). Or are all these characters "more likely the same foul brute all the time, amusing himself pretending to be a many, varying his register, his tone, his accent and his drivel"? (U 89). In that case, he asks himself, "What am I doing in Mahood's story, and in Worm's, or rather what are they doing in mine?" After all, he has never stirred; "all I've said, said I've done, said I've been. It's they who said it, I've said nothing" (U, 125- 27). What he realizes more and more is that it is all a question of identities and that all these characters have perhaps "reference to a single existence, the confusion of identities being merely apparent and due to my inaptitude to assume any" *(U,* 59). Even so, others presume that he has an ego all his own "and can speak of it as they of theirs" *(U,* 81). The characters the Unnamable creates are, then, but his "possibles," and their identity, their human reality as well as his own "eludes direct knowledge to the degree that it *makes itself,"* as Sartre has stated.

The Unnamable's Self becomes to him an Other at the very moment that he begins to contemplate it. It is so changeable that it may take on the form of a Murphy, a Moran, a Molloy, or Malone, and even Mahood or Worm. Its experiences, even its suffering, become those of an Other, as soon as they are being looked at and identified. Pain, Sartre has said, becomes that of an Other when it is recounted. As a consequence the pronoun "I" is no longer appropriate: "I say I, knowing it's not I" *(U,* 165). No wonder the Unnamable resolves: "I shall not say I again, ever again, it's too farcical. I shall put in its place, whenever I hear it, the third person, if I think of it. Anything to please them. It will make no difference" *(U,* 94). The problem concerns him both as a writer and a philosopher: "Enough of this cursed first person . . . I'll get out of my depth if I'm not careful. But what then is the subject? Mahood? No, not yet. Worm? Even less. Bah, any old pronoun will do, provided one sees through it. Matter of habit" *(U,* 77). Do his characters have the right to speak in the first person? "He feels me in him, then he says I, as if I were he, or in another, let us be just, then he says Murphy, or Molloy, I forget, as if I were Malone . . . it's the fault of the pronouns, there is no name for me, no pronoun for me" *(U,* 163–64). The impression we are left with is similar to that created by Kierkegaard's author-editors, except that Kierkegaard's problem was that of making a fictional world possible, whereas Beckett is concerned with existence, which forever eludes him. "Our concern is with someone, or our concern is with something, now we're getting it, someone or something that is not there, or that is not anywhere, or that is there, here" *(U,* 164).

It is only if seen by an Other that the Unnamable is given a name and substance. He tells us that Basil (are we to think of a basilisk and the fatal fixation of its look?), "without opening his mouth, fastening on me his eyes like cinders with all their seeing . . . changed me a little more each time into what he wanted me to be. Is he still glaring at me from the shadows? Is he still usurping my name, the one they foisted on me, up there in their world?" *(U,* 13). Worm, who somewhere in the novel is identified with Mahood (both, of course, being the Unnamable) exists only by virtue of Others:

> Worm, to say he does not know what he is, where he is, what is happening, is to underestimate him. What he does not know is that there is anything to know. His senses tell him nothing, nothing about himself, nothing about the rest, and this distinction is beyond him. Feeling nothing, knowing nothing, he exists nevertheless, but not for himself, for others, others conceive him and say, Worm is, since we conceive him, as if there could be no being but being conceived, if only by the beer. Others. One alone, then others. [*U,* 82]

It is the Sartrean Look, then, that lends existence and at the same time turns beings into what it wants them to be, petrifies them. Quite in keeping with this allegory of the novel, the weeping Unnamable looking at his ever-elusive Self and the fixating onlooker Basil are ultimately both Mahood. "Decidedly," the Unnamable muses, "Basil is becoming important, I'll call him Mahood instead, I prefer that, I'm queer. It was he told me stories about me, lived in my stead, issued forth from me, came back to me, entered back into me, heaped stories upon my head. I don't know how it was done" *(U, 29)*. Basil's relationship to the Unnamable thus resembles that of the existentialist writer to his fictional creatures. The Unnamable is always both "the teller and the told" *(U, 30)*. He is forever aware of a crowd of onlookers who expect him to tell their stories, which are also his stories, and he does so in a voice he thinks is not his: "It is not mine, I have none, I have no voice and must speak, that is all I know, its round that I must revolve, of that I must speak, with this voice that is not mine, but can only be mine, since there is no one but me, or if there are others, to whom it might belong, they have never come near me" *(U, 26)*. The Unnamable is consciousness without subjectivity, consciousness existing barely by virtue of its being seen by others and yet forever doubting their existence and his own. He is merely the vessel through which passes the voice of Being; he is Dasein's here and now, a clearing in the impenetrable forest of Being, the nothingness of intelligence.

In accordance with what both Heidegger and Sartre would consider the essence of man, this unnamable and unnamed representative of mankind must, nevertheless be a witness to Being, must write. He feels himself, in fact, "condemned to talk" *(U, 114)*: "I spoke, I must have spoken of a lesson, it was a pensum I should have said, I confused pensum with lesson," the Unnamable realizes. "Yes, I have a pensum to discharge, before I can be free, free to dribble, free to speak no more . . . Strange task, which consists in speaking of oneself" *(U, 30–31)*. What he regrets is that there are no things to talk about: "They took away things when they departed, they took away nature, there was never anyone, anyone but me, anything but me, talking to me of me, impossible to stop, impossible to go on, but I must go on, I'll go on" *(U, 151)*. But as he realizes that he must keep talking regardless, he also is aware that the language at his disposal is inadequate. Unlike Watt, he does not attempt to invent a new one, unless his breathless style, unencumbered by punctuation, is to be considered as such. He thinks of himself as "Two holes and me in the middle, slightly choked. Or a single one, entrance and exit, where the words swarm and jostle like ants, hasty, indifferent, bringing nothing, taking nothing away, too light to leave a mark" *(U,* 94). For these words, these meaningless words are the language of the "they." "Keep on talking, that's what they're paid for, not for results . . . The dulling effect of habit, how do they deal with that?" *(U,* 111). The Unnamable resigns himself to the fact that he has "no words but the words of others," "no language but theirs" *(U,* 36), and he decides, "Perhaps I'll say it, even with their language, for me alone, so as not to have not lived in vain, and so as to go silent, if that is what confers the right to silence" *(U,* 52).

At the same time, the Unnamable believes, like the Sartre of *Words* and *Saint Genet,* in the power of the word. This is borne out, indirectly, by the fact that, in spite of the utter futility of his existence and in spite of its meaninglessness, he is compelled to be a writer and one who is deeply concerned with the problems of his art. But it is also expressed more directly and even literally: the Unnamable, through the power of the word, becomes a creator. "I'll shut myself up," he decides in the manner of a writer drunk with the power of manipulating his heroes and their destiny,

> it won't be I, quick, I'll make a place, it won't be mine, it doesn't matter, I don't feel any place for me, perhaps that will come, I'll make it mine, I'll put myself in it, I'll put someone in it, I'll find someone in it, I'll put myself in him, I'll say he's I, perhaps he'll keep me, perhaps the place will keep us, me inside the other, the place all round us, it will be over, all over, I won't have to try and move any more, I'll close my eyes, all I have to do is talk, that will be easy. [*U,* 159]

We are reminded of Sartre's reminiscence of how, as a budding writer, he created his protagonists in his own image but gave them different bodies and gestures, thus enjoying the ambiguity of their being him without his quite being them. Like these creatures of Sartre's imagination, the Unnamable thinks of himself as being nothing but words: "words among words, or silence in the midst of silence" (U, 142). Even memories exist for him— as they did for Sartre's Roquentin—only in the form of words. When he remembers Worm, the name is all he retains. When he thinks of Mahood, he remembers having talked about him: "the same words recur and they are your memories." And it is with words that he invents:

> It is I invented him [Mahood], him and so many others, and the places where they passed, the places where they stayed in order to speak, since I had to speak, without speaking of me, I couldn't speak of me . . . I invented my memories . . . not one is of me. It is they asked me to speak of them, they wanted to know what they were, how they lived, that suited me, I thought that would suit me, since I had nothing to say and had to say something, I thought I was free to say any old thing, so long as I didn't go silent. [U, 152–53]

The novel's formal structure is expressive of the author-hero's need to invent, to construct with words heroes who, in their turn, tell stories. It all begins with the Unnamable speaking in the first person, telling the stories of Mahood. But he tells them as if Mahood were speaking. "Still Mahood speaking," he reminds us every so often. Yet, as he speaks in the first person, he also obliquely suggests that he himself is Mahood: "Never once have I stopped" (U, 45). By the middle of the book he assures us, however, that he now has left Mahood's world: "the street, the chophouse, the slaughter, the statue and, through the railings, the sky like a slate-pencil. I shall never hear again the lowing of the cattle, nor the clinking of the forks and glasses, nor the angry voices of the butchers, nor the litany of the dishes and the prices. There will never be another woman wanting me in vain to live, my shadow at evening will not darken the ground. The stories of Mahood are ended" *(U,* 80). It is at this point that the voice of Worm begins. Again, however, we are given to understand that the Unnamable and Worm are one and the same person: "I'm Worm, no, if I were Worm I wouldn't know it, I wouldn't say it, I wouldn't say anything. I'd be Worm" *(U,* 83). Quite in keeping with the title of the novel, the Unnamable is both Mahood, that is an intelligent being, and Worm, that is a being without intelligence, and yet is neither. Only Others can define him: "Since I couldn't be Mahood, as I might have been, I must be Worm as I cannot be . . . I am ready to be whatever they want" *(U,* 84).

Among these author-heroes, a definite development can be noticed from Moran to Molloy and from there, via Malone, to the Unnamable. This development seems to confirm the hypothesis I stated above: that Moran is an earlier stage of Molloy. Seen in this manner, each change of name in the trilogy would correspond to a stage in the hero's development. It is as if Beckett had resumed the medieval tradition in which Ywain becomes the Knight of the Lion. Or, more likely still, as if he had let himself be inspired by Cervantes, whose nobleman of uncertain name becomes Don Quixote and later the Knight of the Sad Countenance. Cervantes creates as much doubt as to whether the Don was called Quixana, Quixada, Quisana, or Quixote as Beckett creates with regard to the name of Molloy, Malone, or the Unnamable. Both change of name and uncertainty of name are essential to the works of these authors. If, in the case of Cervantes, they seem to be prompted by a baroque uncertainty concerning the nature of reality, they seem to reflect, with regard to Beckett, his view of the perpetual becoming and elusiveness of

Being. This is most strongly expressed through namelessness. And it is perhaps not irrelevant to remember here that the God of the Israelites did not wish to be named or rendered pictorially, revealing himself to Moses as "I-am-becoming."[23]

This namelessness, which yet remains a first-person consciousness, also prevails in Beckett's *Texts For Nothing*. Thus the narrator of the eleventh *Text* sighs: "It's still the same old road I'm trudging, up yes and down no, towards one yet to be named" *(T,* 127). And in the spirit of Sartre, the "I" of the fourth *Text* realizes that "It's the same old stranger as ever, for whom alone accusative I exist, in the pit of my inexistence, of his, of ours, there's a simple answer" *(T,* 91), and grumbles "If at least he would dignify me with the third person, like his other figments, not he, he'll be satisfied with nothing less than me, for his me" *(T,* 92). The nameless "I" of *Texts* is, in conformity with existential thinking, aware of his task to witness: "I'm the clerk, I'm the scribe, at the hearings of what cause I know not." It knows itself "to be judge and party, witness and advocate, and he, attentive, indifferent, who sits and notes" *(T,* 95). The "they" have taught it all it knows "about things above, and all I'm said to know about me, they want to create me, they want to make me" *(T,* 99). The "I" concludes therefore that there is no reason to talk about oneself when there is X to talk about, "that paradigm of human kind" *(T,* 108). Like the Molloys and Malones who preceded the nameless "I" of *Texts,* it both seeks identification with its author and denies such identification. "And who is this speaking in me," the "I" asks, "and who's this disowning me?" *(T,* 134). "And who is this clot who doesn't know where to go, who can't stop, who takes himself for me and for whom I take myself?" *(T,* 129).

In his trilogy, Beckett placed author within author in an al-

23. Erich Fromm, *The Art of Loving* (New York, Bantam Books, 1963), p. 58.

most Kierkegaardian manner and, like Sartre, had his first-person consciousnesses look at themselves as if they were a "me" not an "I." Because of this he could save his fictional world from solipsism. Because of this he could also have his author-heroes look at themselves in the manner of Nietzsche's Dionysiac artist and understand the essence of their art. Under the impact of the Other's Look, his fictional creatures assumed form and identity. But, as he came to see Being more and more as Becoming, his author-heroes became less and less defined and definable. The range of names Beckett has given his fictional creatures reflects his road towards a namelessness that ultimately defies even the "I." He has run the gamut from the seemingly traditional Murphy, Watt, Moran, Molloy, and Malone (although even these names have symbolic overtones) to such generic designations of man as Sapo, Macmann, Mahood, down to the metaphoric reference to man as Worm. With the Unnamable, he finally arrived at using an adjectival noun that might refer both to someone and something that has no name and cannot be named. But while in *The Unnamable* and in *Texts For Nothing* it is still a nameless "I" which arrogates to itself the role of the author-hero, it is in *How It Is* that the question of Who has almost completely given way to a How. The novel's narrator has fully become the X, "the paradigm of human kind" towards which the "I" of *Texts* points. In the work's title the "It" (as does the "ce" in the French original) refers neither to beings nor objects but rather to something by its very nature unknown and unidentifiable, while the worm-like narrator of the story arbitrarily confers upon himself and others the names of Pim and Bom, which seem but the onomatopaeic renderings of sound in back-and-forth movement.

But although subjectivity seems to have shrunk here to a minimum ("I quote on is it me is it me" [*HII*, 16]), *How It Is* is still told by a first-person consciousness: "how it was I quote before Pim . . . I say it as I hear it." As this consciousness thinks of itself, of its "life in the light" (the expression seems to be used as if this were life before death or, at any rate, life in the real world) it sees itself as "un quidam quelconque" (in the French original) or "some creature or other" *(HII, 9,* in Beckett's less effective translation). "The fingers deceived the mouth resigned," it is a consciousness that no longer has any preferences, no longer searches, "not even for a language meet for me meet for here no more searching" *(HII,* 17). This consciousness, like the Heideggerian *Da* [of Dasein] and the Sartrean pour-soi, is filled consecutively with the varying forms and aspects under which Being or existence, including its own, shows itself: "et moi suite ininterrompue d'altérations définitives." (In the English translation Beckett has unfortunately omitted this passage.) It represents what he has designated in *Film* as the "Search of non-being in flight from extraneous perception breaking down in escapability of self-perception" *(F,* 31). Nothing remains certain or can even gain certainty within the horizon of such perpetual change except consciousness itself: "alone in the mud yes the dark yes sure yes panting yes someone hears me no no one hears me no murmuring sometimes yet when the panting stops yes not at other times no in the mud yes to the mud yes my voice yes mine yes not another's no mine alone yes sure yes when the panting stops yes on and off yes a few words yes a few scraps yes that no one hears no but less and less no answer LESS AND LESS yes" *(HII,* 146). Such a consciousness must remain nameless, even if it desperately clamors for a name: "and what's my name no answer WHAT'S MY NAME screams good" *(HII,* 146).

What comes to light through this nameless consciousness is itself as a creature crawling through the mud. As it crawls— its movements are reduced to the barest essentials of those of mouth, bowels, legs, and arms—it encounters another being

in the mud, whom it both tortures and loves. It, in turn, will
be found by another who will love and torture it. Pim, or Bom,
or whatever name may be conferred upon each creature (it is
always the torturer who names his victim and himself after it),
the victim and the victimized are but links in a chain, a series
of innumerable couples, forever meeting and abandoning each
other: "unwitting that each always leaves the same always goes
towards the same always loses the same always goes towards
him who leaves him always leaves him who goes towards him
our justice . . . millions millions there are millions of us and
there are three I place myself at my point of view Bem is Bom
Bom Bem let us say Bom it's preferable Bom then me and Pim
me in the middle" *(HII,* 114). Important in this procession of
nameless creatures, whose designations merely indicate their
temporary location, is the sack. The narrating consciousness, as
learned as Beckett himself, realizes "sack old word first to come
one syllable k at the end seek no other all would vanish a sack
that will do the word the thing it's a possible thing" and knows
that "that thing could possibly be so many things" *(HII,* 66,
105). All basic human organs seem to have the form of a sack.
The sack is the narrator's source of food, into it he seems to dip
for his memories, and he seems to pass it on—as if it were that
ancient light of knowledge—to those who come after him:
"leaving then without a sack I had a sack I had found it on my
way there is that difficulty overcome we leave our sacks to those
who do not need them we take their sacks from those who
soon will need them we leave without a sack we find one on our
way we can continue on our way" *(HII,* 111).

But the nameless creature in the mud of *How It Is* is also a
creating consciousness. He not only sees luminous images that
belong to life in the light but, to a large extent, creates those
he encounters: "my part who but for me he would never Pim
we're talking of Pim never be but for me anything but a dumb

limp lump flat for ever in the mud but I'll quicken him you wait and see" (HII, 52). Pim assumes whatever attitude he has been given by his creator: "he stays whatever way he's put" (HII, 59). It is the narrating, creating consciousness who has given him his name: "no more than I by his own account or my imagination he had no name any more than I so I gave him one the name Pim for more commodity more convenience it's off again in the past . . . when this has sunk in I let him know that I too Pim my name Pim there he has more difficulty a moment of confusion irritation it's understandable it's a noble name" (HII, 60). In this manner they feel "less anonymous somehow or other less obscure" (HII, 60). And it is Beckett's irony seeping through this first-person consciousness when Pim assures us that in all these names, whether Bem, Bim, Bom, or Pim, it is the labial *m* that counts, since it readies the lips for kissing. (In Beckett's previous works this *m* occurs at the beginning rather than the end of names, as has been frequently observed.) Like Sartre in *Roads to Freedom* and Kierkegaard before him, the nameless author-hero of *How It Is* is willing to surrender all subjectivity: "see how I can efface myself behind my creature" (HII, 52). At the same time, by assuring us that his name is that of his creature and that he is actually telling *his* story, he creates the same ambiguity between the identity of author and hero which Kierkegaard and Sartre created. Like Kierkegaard, he makes his creature sing and tell of his life, although the manner in which this is done is one of utmost sadistic cruelty.

The consciousness of the Other is even less accessible to these mud crawlers than to the author-heroes of other existential writers. In spite of their brief intimacy, Pim/Pim and Bom/Bom remain strangers. In spite of weeping and singing together, in spite of crying out their pain and listening to the Other's for a little while, they leave like strangers, after having been like two strangers united "in the interest of torment" (HII, 121). "It's no I'm sorry," the narrator admits, "no one here knows anyone either personally or otherwise it's the no that turns up I murmur it . . . and no again I'm sorry again no one here knows himself it's the place without knowledge whence no doubt its peerlessness" *(HII,* 123). Still, realizing that he does not know either the Other or himself, he keeps a record and a record is kept of him: "all that not Pim I who murmur all that a voice mine alone and that bending over me noting down one word every three two words" *(HII,* 87). Mysteriously enough, Pim has a "little private book these secret things little book all my own the heart's outpourings day by day it's forbidden one big book and everything there Krim imagines I am drawing what then places faces loved forgotten" *(HII,* 84). It is Krim then, ultimately, who is the witness and notes down everything in his large book: "Kram who listens Krim who notes or Kram alone one is enough Kram alone witness and scribe his lamps their light upon me Kram with me bending over me" *(HII,* 133).

It appears then that *How It Is,* paradoxical though it may seem, is in its own tortured way also a Künstlerroman. Its narrator is an author-hero but one who, because of the evasiveness of his own being, has neither name nor specific features. Although he remains an individual and never becomes Everyman, he is simply one link in a long chain of creatures whose functions are singularly stylized and essentialized. It remains ambiguous whether he encounters or creates Others in his own image. But witnessing them, he names them and thereby renders them existent. As the title indicates, the author-hero of *How It Is* has effaced himself behind his creature to such a extent that the traditional Who of the Künstlerroman has become a mere How of existence.

Fritz Mauthner, the Austrian thinker who, at the turn of the century busied himself with the critique of language, rightly linked the elusiveness of the "I" with an assault upon language.

If the "I"-consciousness, if individuality, is seen to be but deception, then the very ground whereon we stand trembles and our last hope for even a trace of world knowledge collapses . . . The subject disappears behind an object and we no longer detect any difference between the philosophic endeavor of eons of humanity and the dream existence of an amoeba. Even the concept of individuality has become verbal abstraction without representational content . . . Then there is nothing but words in the "I."[24]

Mauthner's scepticism with regard to language and the individual belongs to a tradition that seems to have had its origin in Nietzsche and its culmination in Wittgenstein. "When Nietzsche discovered the 'death of God,'" Erich Heller observed in his brilliant study of Wittgenstein and Nietzsche, "the universe of meanings collapsed—everything, that is, that was founded upon the transcendent faith, or was leaning against it, or was intertwined with it: in fact, *everything,* as Nietzsche believed; and henceforward everything was in need of re-evaluation." Heller has shown to what extent the two philosophers are united in their doubt as to whether language is "the adequate expression for all realities" and in their judgment that "the grammatical and syntactical order of language, its subjects, predicates, objects, causal and conditional connections" are but "'the petrified fallacies of reason' which continued to exercise their 'seductive spell' upon our intelligence."[25] Fritz Mauthner, who was intimately familiar with the thought of Nietzsche and who, in turn, has had a seminal influence on many modern writers, including Hoffmansthal, Morgenstern, and the Surrealists, not only arrived at similar conclusions but even went beyond the skepticism of Nietzsche. He realized that "we can learn with

24. Quoted in Alfred Liede, *Dichtung als Spiel,* 1 (Berlin, Walter de Gruyter, 1963), p. 262. The translation is mine.

25. Heller, *The Artist's Journey into the Interior,* pp. 216, 218.

the help of language only what the so-called things *are for man;*
we lack the linguistic means to designate what things might
perhaps be in themselves."[26] In a manner of which Wittgenstein's *Tractatus* seems to be reminiscent, Mauthner declared
that

> he who, filled with the vanity of words and with hunger
> and love for them, sets out to write a book in the language
> of yesterday, today, or tomorrow, or in the established lan-
> guage of an era, cannot save language. Whoever wishes to
> climb the ladder of language critique—which now is the
> most urgent preoccupation of man—must with each step
> destroy the language that is behind, before, and within
> him. He must break every rung of the ladder as he steps
> upon it. Whoever follows must build his own rung only
> to break it in his turn.[27]

It is quite in keeping with this spirit of Mauthner that the
language of Beckett's *How It Is* is at some remove from traditional linguistic patterns. Compared to it, the language of *Watt*
seems but a consciously playful inversion. In *How It is* language
is seriously challenged: Beckett totally defies punctuation, omits
all conjunctions, has a minimum of verbal structures, and yet
succeeds in conveying meaning. Later, in *Ping,* he was to bring
such linguistic experimentation to a climax. As the work's title
implies, language here is further essentialized and has come to
be that "single noise" and the "vast continuous buzzing" into
which language started to merge for Malone so that it became
increasingly difficult for him to decompose it *(Ma,* 45).[28] *Ping*

26. "Fritz Mauthner," in Raymond Schmidt, *Philosophie der Gegenwart in Selbstdarstellungen,* Bd. 3 (Leipzig, F. Meiner Verlag, 1928)
p. 136. The translation is mine.

27. Fritz Mauthner, *Beiträge zu einer Kritik der Sprache* (Stuttgart,
Cotta, 1901), p. 3.

28. See p. 218 above.

no longer has a clearly defined narrator and, in fact, dispenses with all personal pronouns. The word *ping* frequently represents a mere sound, and in the French version is rendered as *hop,* an ejaculation. Yet at other times it seems to have the function of a noun or even a name, as David Lodge has well observed. In this work Beckett dispenses with all conjugated verbs. Whatever verb forms occur are participles with adjectival meaning. As Lodge noted, there is "a drastic reduction of such aids to communication as punctuation . . . conjunctions, articles, prepositions, and subordinations." In proportion to the work's brevity, an unusual number of words are repeated to an unusual extent in various combination, so that Lodge felt justified in speaking of a "permutation of language." But what is remarkable is that Beckett's word groupings are governed by a sort of syntax that in a rudimentary way "does control the possible range of meaning."[29] While *Ping* reflects the isolation of man in acoustical and linguistic terms and Beckett's *Imagination Dead, Imagine* does so visually by placing together within one circle two human beings who cannot possibly see each other, both confirm at the same time that language and imagery and writing will and cannot but remain essential to man. "The critique of language," Morgenstern wrote as early as 1907, "is in its final analysis but a social game. There is no word which would have meaning outside the realm of language. He who wants to sit outside of language finds no chair. He cannot even say: Now I know at least that knowledge is impossible. 'Knowledge' is as much a chip in the game as 'is,' 'impossible,' 'language,' and 'outside.' "[30]

This is the paradox that has permeated Beckett's entire work, has made it an affirmation and a negation of individuality,

29. David Lodge, "Some Ping Understood," *Encounter, 30* (February 1968), 88–89, 86, 89.

30. Quoted in Liede, *Dichtung als Spiel, 1,* p. 334. The translation is mine.

and has made it seminal in the modern flowering of the Künstlerroman, while it has at the same time undermined the genre. Although the protagonists of all of Beckett's novels published after *Murphy* are narrators or writers, they have become more and more anonymous and uncertain in their very subjectivity. While in Sartre's concept of the elusiveness of human reality there is the intrinsic conviction that man must assume the responsibility of giving himself an essence, Beckett contents himself with accepting the elusiveness of Being. He has progressively stripped of subjectivity all existential affirmation of the importance of the individual as a responsible existent and a witness to Being, and has replaced such subjectivity by a vision of man as an anonymous link in a meaningless and repetitive chain of suffering mankind. Since the fluid becoming of Being would be destroyed by any artisan capturing it in a static moment and giving it order, the artist rendering it in language or any other medium cannot help but realize that the essence of his art must be failure. But in spite of such views, it is equally in keeping with the paradox of the Beckettian world that the author has more fervently than any other contemporary writer been in search of new fictional forms and linguistic patterns expressive of his metaphysical insights. One can confidently say of him what he has said of Proust, namely, that he has made "no attempt to dissociate form from content" and that "the one is a concretion of the other, the revelation of a world" *(Pr, 67)*.

Epilogue

To existentialist writers, with their basic conception of the individual's isolation and his incapability of understanding the Other, the author-hero creating other author-heroes has proved a crucial device to lend perspective to an otherwise solipsistic world. Sartre, who considers human consciousness as revealing the universe and the subject as "me" within it, found the author-hero quite naturally conforming to his image of man, while at the same time capable of understanding the essence of an art that could salvage man from absurdity. To Beckett he became "the teller and the told" who, author within author, could reveal existence from the vantage point of the first person. But both a desire to conceal any author-hero identification—so natural to existential thinking—and a conviction that the individual has many shadows, many possibles, led existential writers to sub-stitute a third person for the first-person consciousness of the author-hero and even several consciousnesses for that of the author. As the conviction of the absurdity of existence grew, an abandonment of logic and chronology in storytelling grew con-comitantly. To give expression to the paradox of existence, dialectical juxtaposition of diverse views was indulged in. The existential concept of the elusiveness of Being and the perpetual becoming of human reality have increasingly emptied the subject of its subjectivity, and Alain Robbe-Grillet has rightly noticed the development toward a less anthropomorphic literature.[1] While Sartre's metaphysic of the Look has made it possible for him to establish interrelationships within fictional worlds where each individual is isolated, the same concept combined with Berkeley's *esse est percipi* has led Beckett and some other contemporary novelists to a concern with the mere thereness of things that remain as impervious to human interpretation as the reality of the Other. An existential quest for the authenticity of language beneath everyday chatter has resulted in the fictional rendering of the language of the "they" in all its absurdity, but also to a rediscovery of its ancient wealth (Heidegger), its mysterious meaningfulness in myth (Kierkegaard), and an exploration of its possibilities to render the elusiveness of Being (Beckett). Language has come to be employed in rendering an eternal present, rather than a past or a future.

But in the course of such developments, the author-hero has come to efface himself behind his work to such an extent that Sartre has spoken of the modern novel as reflecting over itself, and Olivier de Magny has referred to it as in "search for itself" and "in negation of itself."[2] As author-heroes, engaged in a quest of the essence of their art and the revelation of an elusive human reality, become more and more "unreliable," they invite us to accept Nietzsche's realization that the truth about man is that he must live without truth. But even if it seems to be the novel itself, without the help of a clearly defined narrator, that confronts us with the paradox of existence; if things merely

1. Alain Robbe-Grillet, *For A New Novel: Essays on Fiction*, trans. Richard Howard (New York, Grove Press, 1965), p. 29.

2. Quoted in Vivian Mercier, "Arrival of the Anti-Novel," *Commonweal*, (May 8, 1959) 149–50.

seem "to be there," as Robbe-Grillet has claimed, and people are only voices, as Nathalie Sarraute seems to imply; if universes are revealed to us through a *regard,* a Look, detached from a logical, ordering, and analytic mind, the novelists' consciousnesses still remain behind, above, and beyond these works. It is they who select the objects, the voices, the events and make them surge up within the consciousnesses of their fictional creatures. These consciousnesses can only be their own "possibles," for they can only fall within the limits of their own temporal and local horizons, their own *Da,* the here and now of Being which they represent. What masks the fundamental identity between the existential teller and the told are the ironic techniques that are utilized. They range in these novels from an array of "manuscripts discovered" by fictitious editors within editors to unreliable author or narrator heaped upon unreliable author or narrator, and to objective correlatives found in myths as well as a seemingly world-wide orchestration of consciousnesses.

Selected Bibliography

Audry, Colette. *Sartre et la Réalité humaine*. Paris, Editions Seghers, 1966.

Beauvoir, Simone de. *The Blood of Others*. Translated by Roger Senhouse and Yvonne Moyse. New York, Knopf, 1948.
Original: *Le Sang des Autres*. Paris, Gallimard, 1945.

———— *The Ethics of Ambiguity*. Translated by B. Frechtman. New York, Philosophical Library, 1948.
Original: *Pour une Morale de l'Ambiguité*. Paris, Gallimard, 1947.

———— *The Force of Circumstance*. Translated by Richard Howard. New York, Putnam, 1965.
Original: *La Force des Choses*. Paris, Gallimard, 1963.

———— "Literature and Metaphysics," *Art in Action*. New York, Twice a Year Press, tenth anniversary issue, 1948. Pp. 86–93.
Original: "Littérature et Métaphysique." *Les Temps Modernes* (1946): 1153–63.

———— *The Prime of Life*. Translated by Peter Green. Cleveland and New York, The World Publishing Company, 1962.
Original: *La Force de l'Age*. Paris, Gallimard, 1960.

Beckett, Samuel. "Dante . . . Bruno. Vico . . . Joyce." In Beckett et al., *Our Exagmination Round His Factification for Incamination of Work in Progress*. London, Faber & Faber, 1961. First published in 1929.

————— "The End." Translated by R. Seaver with author. *Evergreen Review* (1960) vol. 4, no. 15, pp. 22–41. First published in Summer 1954.

Original: "La Fin." *Nouvelles et Textes pour rien.* Paris, Editions de Minuit, 1955.

————— *Endgame.* Translated by author. New York, Grove Press, 1958.

Original: *Fin de partie* with *Actes sans paroles.* Paris, Editions de Minuit, 1957.

————— *Film.* In *Eh Joe and Other Writings.* London, Faber & Faber, 1967.

————— *Happy Days.* New York, Grove Press, 1961.

————— *How It Is.* Translated by author. New York, Grove Press, 1964.

Original: *Comment c'est.* Paris, Editions de Minuit, 1961.

————— *Imagination Dead Imagine.* Translated by author. In *No's Knife.* London, Calder & Boyars, 1967.

Original: *Imagination morte imaginez.* In *Têtes-mortes.* Paris, Editions de Minuit, 1967.

————— *Malone Dies.* Translated by author. New York, Grove Press, 1956.

Original: *Malone meurt.* Paris, Editions de Minuit, 1951.

————— *Molloy.* Translated by Patrick Bowles with author. New York, Grove Press, 1955.

Original: *Molloy.* Paris, Editions de Minuit, 1951.

————— *Murphy.* London, Routledge, 1938. Reprinted New York, Grove Press, 1957.

————— *Ping.* Translated by author. In *No's Knife.* London, Calder & Boyars, 1967.

Original: *Ping.* Paris, Editions de Minuit, 1966. Reprinted in *Têtes mortes.* Paris, Editions de Minuit, 1967.

————— *Play.* London, Faber & Faber, 1964.

————— *Proust.* London, Chatto & Windus, 1931. Reprinted New York, Grove Press, 1957.

————— *Texts For Nothing.* Translated by Richard Seaver with author. In *No's Knife.* London, Calder & Boyars, 1967.

Original: *Nouvelles et Textes pour rien.* Paris, Editions de Minuit, 1955.
———— *The Unnamable.* Translated by author. New York, Grove Press, 1958.
Original: *L'Innommable.* Paris, Editions de Minuit, 1953.
———— *Waiting for Godot.* Translated by author. New York, Grove Press, 1954.
Original: *En attendant Godot.* Paris, Editions de Minuit, 1952.
———— *Watt.* Paris, Olympia Press, 1953. Reprinted New York, Grove Press, 1959.
Beckett, Samuel, and Duthuit, Georges. "Three Dialogues." In *Samuel Beckett: A Collection of Critical Essays,* edited by Martin Esslin. Englewood Cliffs, N.J., Prentice-Hall, 1965. Reprinted from *Transition forty-nine* (1949), no. 5.
Bensimon, Marc "D'un Mythe à l'autre: Essai sur *Les Mots* de Jean-Paul Sartre." *Revue des Sciences Humaines* (1965): 415–30.
Booth, Wayne C. *The Rhetoric of Fiction.* Chicago, University of Chicago Press, 1961.
Brombert, Victor, ed. *The Hero in Literature.* Greenwich, Conn., Fawcett Publications, 1969.
———— " Sartre et la Biographie impossible." *Cahiers de l'Association Internationale des Études françaises* 19 (1967): 155–66.
Burdach, K. "Faust und die Sorge." *Deutsche Vierteljahrschrift für Literaturwissenschaft und Geistesgeschichte 1* (1923).
Camus, Albert. *The Myth of Sisyphus.* Translated by Justin O'Brien. New York, Random House, Vintage Books, 1955.
Original: *Le Mythe de Sisyphe.* Paris, Gallimard, 1942.
Cassirer, Ernst. *Language and Myth.* Translated by S. K. Langer. Dover, Dover Publications, 1946.
Champigny, Robert. *Stages on Sartre's Way 1938–52.* Bloomington, Indiana University Press, 1959.
Chapsal, Madeleine. *Les Écrivains en présence.* Paris, Julliard, 1960.
Coe, Richard N. *Beckett.* Edinburgh and London, Oliver & Boyd; New York, Grove Press, 1964.

Cohn, Ruby. *Beckett, the Comic Gamut.* New Brunswick, N.J., Rutgers University Press, 1962.

Cruttwell, Patrick. "Makers and Persons." *Hudson Review* 12 (Winter 1959–60): 487–507.

Dieckmann, Herbert. "Diderot's Conception of Genius." *Journal of the History of Ideas 2* (1941): 151–82.

Dort, Bernard. "A la Recherche du Roman." *Cahiers du Sud 42* (1955).

Driver, Tom. "Beckett by the Madeleine." *Columbia Forum 4* (1961): 21–25.

Edel, Leon. *The Modern Psychological Novel.* New York, Grove Press, 1955.

Esslin, Martin, ed. *Samuel Beckett: A Collection of Critical Essays.* Englewood Cliffs, N.J., Prentice-Hall, 1965.

Fernandez, Ramón. "The Method of Balzac." In *Messages,* Translated by Montgomery Belgion. New York, Harcourt, Brace, 1927.

Original: "La Méthode de Balzac." In *Messages.* Paris, Gallimard, 1926.

Flaubert, Gustave. *Madame Bovary.* New York, W. J. Black, 1904.

Fletcher, John. *The Novels of Samuel Beckett.* New York, Barnes & Noble, 1964.

Freedman, Ralph. *The Lyrical Novel.* Princeton, N. J., Princeton University Press, 1963.

Fromm, Erich. *The Art of Loving.* New York, Bantam Books, 1963.

Gide, André. *The Counterfeiters.* Translated by J. O'Brien. New York, Knopf, 1959.

Original: *Les Faux-monnayeurs.* Paris, Gallimard, 1926.

Gill, Brendan. "The Current Cinema." *The New Yorker* (June 1963).

Gobeil, Madeleine. "Playboy Interview: Jean-Paul Sartre." *Playboy Magazine 12* (1965).

Goethe, Wolfgang. *Faust II.* Vol. 2. Edited and translated by Bayard Taylor. Boston, Houghton Mifflin, 1898.

Gracq, Julien. *André Breton ou l'Âme d'un mouvement.* Paris, Fontaine, 1958.

Grimsley, Ronald. *Søren Kierkegaard and French Literature: Eight*

Comparative Studies. Cardiff, University of Wales Press, 1966.

Heidegger, Martin. *Being and Time.* Translated by John Macquarrie and Edward Robinson. London, SCM Press, 1962.

Original: *Sein und Zeit. Tübingen, Neomarius Verlag,* 1927.

————— "Letter on Humanism." Translated by E. Lohner. In *Philosophy of the Twentieth Century 3,* edited by W. Barrett and H. D. Aiken. New York, Random House, 1962.

Original: *Über den "Humanismus": Brief an Jean Beaufret, Paris.* Together with *Platons Lehre von der Wahrheit.* Bern, Francke Verlag, 1947.

Heller, Erich. *The Artist's Journey into the Interior.* New York, Random House, 1965.

Hindus, Milton. *A Reader's Guide to Marcel Proust.* New York, Farrar, Straus & Cudahy, 1962.

Hoefer, Jacqueline. "Watt." *Perspective* (Autumn 1959): 166–82.

Howe, Susanne. *Wilhelm Meister and His English Kinsmen.* New York, Columbia University Press, 1930.

Huertas-Jourda, José. *The Existentialism of Miguel de Unamuno.* University of Florida Monographs (Humanities), no. 13 (1963).

Hytier, Jean. *André Gide.* Garden City, N.Y., Doubleday, 1962.

Joyce, James. *A Portrait of the Artist as a Young Man.* New York, The Viking Press, 1960.

Kahn, Hans Peter. "Either/Or or Both/And: A Modern Interpretation of the Aesthetic Education Described by Kierkegaard and Schiller." M.A. thesis, New York University, 1951–52.

Kenner, Hugh. *Samuel Beckett.* New York, Grove Press, 1961.

Kern, Edith. "Beckett's Knight of Infinite Resignation." *Yale French Studies* 29 (1962).

————— "The Modern Hero: Phoenix or Ashes?" *Comparative Literature* 10 (Fall 1958): 325–34. Reprinted in Victoi Brombert, ed., *The Hero in Literature,* pp. 266–77. Greenwich, Conn. Fawcett Publications, 1969.

————— "Moran—Molloy: The Hero as Author." *Perspective* (Autumn 1959): 183–92.

————, ed. *Sartre: A Collection of Critical Essays.* Twentieth-Century Views. Englewood Cliffs, N.J., Prentice-Hall, 1962.

Kierkegaard, Søren. *The Concept of Irony.* Translated by Lee M. Capel. New York, Harper & Row, 1965.

———— *Concluding Unscientific Postscript.* Translated by David F. Swenson and Walter Lowrie. Princeton, Princeton University Press, 1941.

———— *Either/Or.* 2 vols. Translated by D. F. and L. M. Swenson. Garden City, N.Y., Doubleday, Anchor Books, 1959.

———— *Fear and Trembling.* Translated by Walter Lowrie. Garden City, N.Y., Doubleday, Anchor Books, 1954.

———— *The Journals of Søren Kierkegaard: A Selection.* Edited and translated by Alexander Dru. London, Oxford University Press, 1938.

———— "The Present Age: A Literary Review." In *A Kierkegaard Anthology,* edited by R. Bretall. New York, The Modern Library, 1946.

———— *The Sickness Unto Death.* Together with *Fear and Trembling.* Translated by Walter Lowrie. Garden City, N.Y., Doubleday, Anchor Books, 1954.

———— *Stages on Life's Way.* Translated by Walter Lowrie. Princeton, Princeton University Press, 1940.

Original: *Samlede Vaerker.* Copenhagen, 1901–06.

Lang, Renée. *Gide et la Pensée allemande.* Paris, L.U.F. Egloff, 1949.

Liede, Alfred. *Dichtung und Spiel.* Berlin, Walter de Gruyter, 1963.

Lodge, David. "Some Ping Understood." *Encounter* 30 (February 1968).

Lowrie, Walter. *Kierkegaard 1813–1855.* London, Oxford University Press, 1938.

Magny, Claude-Edmonde. *Histoire du Roman français depuis 1918.* Paris, Éditions du Seuil, 1950.

———— *Les Sandales d'Empédocle.* Switzerland, Boudry, Éditions de la Baconnière, 1945. Partly translated as "The Duplicity of of Being" by J. O. Morgan. In Edith Kern, *Sartre: A Collection of Critical Essays.* Twentieth Century Views. Englewood Cliffs, N.J., Prentice-Hall, 1962.

March, Harold. *The Worlds of Marcel Proust.* Philadelphia, University of Pennsylvania Press, 1948.

Mauthner, Fritz. *Beiträge zu einer Kritik der Sprache.* Stuttgart, Cotta, 1901.

———— "Fritz Mauthner." In Raymond Schmidt, *Philosophie der Gegenwart in Selbstdarstellungen,* Bd. 3. Leipzig, F. Meiner Verlag, 1928.

Mercier, Vivian. "Arrival of the Anti-Novel." *Commonweal* (May 8, 1959): 146–51.

Merleau-Ponty. *Sense and Non-Sense.* Translated by Hubert L. Dreyfus. Evanston, Ill., Northwestern University Press, 1964.

Original: *Sens et non-sens.* Paris, Nagel, 1948.

Mintz, Samuel. "Beckett's Murphy: A Cartesian Novel." *Perspective* (Autumn 1959): 156–65.

Nietzsche, Friedrich F. *The Birth of Tragedy.* Translated by Francis Golffing. Garden City, N.Y., Doubleday, Anchor Books, 1956.

———— Original: *Die Geburt der Tragödie.* Reprinted Stuttgart, Alfred Kröner Verlag, 1945.

Peyre, Henri. *French Novelists of Today.* New York, Oxford University Press, Galaxy Books, 1967.

Proust, Marcel. *Contre Sainte-Beuve.* Paris, Gallimard, 1954.

———— "A propos du 'style' de Flaubert." *Chroniques,* Paris, Gallimard, 1927.

———— *Remembrance of Things Past.* Vol. 2. Translated F. A. Blossom. New York, Random House, 1932.

Original: *A la Recherche du Temps perdu.* 3 vols. Paris, Gallimard, Bibliothèque de la Pléiade, 1964.

Rickels, Milton. "Existential Themes in Beckett's *Unnamable.*" *Criticism* 4 (1962): 134–47.

Rilke, Rainer Maria. *The Notebooks of Malte Laurids Brigge.* Translated by H. Norton. New York, Putnam, 1958.

Robbe-Grillet, Alain. *For a New Novel: Essays on Fiction.* Translated by Richard Howard. New York, Grove Press, 1965.

Sartre, Jean-Paul. *Being and Nothingness.* Translated by Hazel

Barnes. New York, Philosophical Library, 1956.

Original: *L'Etre et le Néant, essai d'ontologie phénoménologique.* Paris, Gallimard, 1943.

———— "Camus' *The Outsider.*" *Literary and Philosophical Essays,* Translated by Annette Michelson. New York, The Crowell-Collier Publishing Company, Collier Books, 1962.

Original: "Explication de l'Etranger." In *Situations I.* Paris, Gallimard, 1947.

———— *Existentialism Is a Humanism.* Translated by Bernard Frechtman. New York, Philosophical Library, 1947.

Original: *L'Existentialisme est un humanisme.* Paris, Nagel, 1946.

———— "Forgers of Myth, the Young Playwrights of France." *Theatre Arts 30* (1946): 324–35.

———— "Une Idée fondamentale de Husserl." *Situations I.* Paris, Gallimard, 1947.

———— *Intimacy and Other Stories.* Translated by Lloyd Alexander. New York, New Directions, 1948.

Original: *Le Mur.* Paris, Gallimard, 1939.

———— "François Mauriac and Freedom." In *Literary and Philosophical Essays,* translated by Annette Michelson. New York, The Crowell-Collier Publishing Company, Collier Books, 1962.

Original: "M. François Mauriac et la Liberté." In *Situations I* (Paris, Gallimard, 1947).

———— *Nausea.* Translated by Lloyd Alexander. New York, New Directions, 1959.

Original: *La Nausée.* Paris, Gallimard, 1938.

———— *The Problem of Method.* Translated by Hazel Barnes. London, Methuen, 1963.

Original: "Question de la Méthode." *Critique de la Raison dialectique.* Paris, Gallimard, 1960.

———— *The Psychology of Imagination.* Translated by Bernard Frechtman. New York, Philosophical Library, 1948.

Original: *L'Imaginaire, psychologie phénoménologique de l'imagination.* Paris, Gallimard, 1940.

——— *The Roads to Freedom.*
Original: *Les Chemins de la Liberté.*
1. *The Age of Reason.* Translated by Eric Sutton. New York, Knopf, 1947; London, Hamilton, 1947.
Original: *L'Age de raison.* Paris, Gallimard, 1945.
2. *The Reprieve.* Translated by Eric Sutton. New York, Knopf, 1947; London, Hamilton, 1947.
Original: *Le Sursis.* Paris, Gallimard, 1945.
3. *Iron in the Soul.* Translated by Gerard Hopkins. London, Hamilton, 1950; New York, Knopf, 1951 *(Troubled Sleep).*
Original: *La Mort dans l'âme.* Paris, Gallimard, 1949.
4. "Drôle d'amitié." *Les Temps Modernes* (1949): 769–806, 1009–1039.
——— "On the *Sound and the Fury:* Time in the Work of Faulkner." In *Literary and Philosophical Essays,* translated by Annette Michelson. New York, The Crowell-Collier Publishing Company, Collier Books, 1962.
Original: "Le Bruit et la Fureur: la temporalité chez Faulkner" (1939). In *Situations I.* Paris, Gallimard, 1947.
——— *The Transcendence of the Ego: An Existential Theory of Consciousness.* Translated by Forrest Williams and Robert Kirkpatrick. New York, Farrar, Straus, & Cudahy, 1960. Previously translated in 1957.
Original: *"La Transcendance de l'Égo, esquisse d'une description* phénoménologique." *Recherches Philosophiques* 6 (1936): 85–123.
——— *What Is Literature?* Translated by Bernard Frechtman. New York, Washington Square Press, 1966.
Original: "Quest-ce que la littérature?" In *Situations II.* Paris, Gallimard, 1948.
——— *The Words.* Translated by Bernard Frechtman. New York, George Braziller, 1964.
Original: *Les Mots.* Paris, Gallimard, 1963.
Schlegel, Friedrich. *Lucinde* in *Deutsche Litteratur.* Ser. 17, vol. 4. Edited by Paul Kluckhohn. Leipzig, Philipp Reclam, 1931.

Schlegel, Friedrich und Novalis. *Biographie einer Romantiker-freundschaft in ihren Briefen.* Edited by Max Preitz. Darmstadt, Gentner Verlag, 1957.

Schmidt, Raymond. "Fritz Mauthner." In *Philosophie der Gegenwart in Selbstdarstellungen.* Bd. 3. Leipzig, F. Meiner Verlag, 1928.

Starobinski, Jean. "Racine et la poétique du regard." *Nouvelle Nouvelle Revue Française* 5 (1957): 246–63.

Strauss, Walter A. *Proust and Literature, the Novelist as Critic.* Cambridge, Harvard University Press, 1957.

Wahl, Jean. *A Short History of Existentialism.* Translated by F. Williams and S. Marin. New York, Philosophical Library, 1949.
Original: *Petite Histoire de l'Existentialisme.* Paris, Editions du Club Maintenant, 1947.

Walzel, Oskar. *German Romanticism.* Translated by A. E. Lussky. New York and London, Putnam, 1932.

Wellek, René. *The Romantic Age.* In his *A History of Modern Criticism.* Vol. 2. New Haven, Yale University Press, 1955.

Woolf, Virginia. *To the Lighthouse.* New York, Harcourt, Brace, 1927.

Index

(Extended discussions are indicated by italic page numbers.)

Index

Index

Index